THE
ICE HOCKEY
ANNUAL

2005-06

30th edition

THE
ICE HOCKEY
ANNUAL

EDITED AND COMPILED BY STEWART ROBERTS

First published in Great Britain by
Stewart Roberts
The Old Town Hall
142 Albion Street
Southwick
Brighton BN42 4AX

Cover Design by **Channel Graphic Communication**

British Library Cataloguing-in-Publication Data.
A catalogue record for this book is available from the British Library.

The Ice Hockey Annual 2005-06

ISBN 0-9536410-6-6

The Ice Hockey Annual's official website is at www.graphyle.com/IHA.

Past editions of The Ice Hockey Annual are archived in the Hockey Hall of Fame,
London Life Resource Centre, Toronto, Canada.

Printed in Great Britain by **L & S Printing Co Ltd**
Hazelwood Close, Hazelwood Trading Estate, Worthing, West Sussex BN14 8NP

CONTENTS

COVER - **Ashley Tait** celebrates Coventry Blaze winning the Elite League Playoff championship. Captain Tait scored the winning goal in overtime for Blaze, completing their Grand Slam of league, Playoffs and Challenge Cup. Tait also skippered Britain in the World Championships.

Photo: Dave Page

ACKNOWLEDGEMENTS

We know time flies, but 30 years? Yes, this publication has been running longer than any league than has ever operated in the UK. Who said that's not difficult? Shame on you.

A minority sport, ice hockey often seems to be on the verge of disaster, but remember, as long as there are ice rinks and fans there will always be ice hockey. And *The Ice Hockey Annual*? We'll be doing this at least until the new Brighton Arena opens. So there will be plenty more yet.

Down to the business in hand - showing our gratitude to the many people who have contributed to the *Annual*. Impossible to mention you all by name, so if yours doesn't appear below, please accept that this message is dedicated to you.

This book would have been impossible without our reporters, photographers, statisticians and advertisers.

Thanks go to all our reporters whose by-lines appear above their stories, but we must make special mention of the sport's handful of dedicated photographers, **Tony Boot**, **Roger Cook**, **Diane Davey**, **Dave Page** and **Bob Swann** who took time to send us generous quantities of photos from their collections.

We're also grateful to all the clubs who sent their team photos. These go a long way towards making the *Annual* a collector's item.

Along with the reports and photos are the players' statistics. The loss of **Gordon Wade**, the sport's longest serving and most dedicated stats-man, came as a bit of a blow here, but **Malcolm Preen** has been invaluable in compiling figures for just about every league below the Elite and the British National. You can find Malcolm's stats during the season at http://homepage.ntlworld.com/malcolm.preen/brit ish.html.

Our thanks also go to **Andy French** and **Simon Potter** for their help in producing the stats for those latter two leagues.

We ought to find room for **Sir Tim Berners-Lee**, the founder of the worldwide web, and *www.thehockeyforum.com*, the excellent UK chat-room, which Sir Tim would surely have also created if he'd had time and been a hockey fan.

While we hasten to point out that much of the information in the *Annual* appears nowhere else, we would find our job much more difficult without the limitless resources of the internet.

From the smallest UK club to the world governing body, these days just about every organisation has its own website (all the clubs' sites are listed at the back of the *Annual* in our unique Club Directory). Only our senior leagues have yet to find the balance between believing the internet is the most important medium of all (the Elite) and failing to have an informative website (the English Premier). Maybe next season...

We always leave our advertisers to last, and always apologise for doing so. Well, we must have some traditions after 30 years.

We're delighted to have **Bauer-Nike**, one of the world's largest manufacturers of equipment, thanks to their sole UK distributors, **Wheels** of Stockport.

National opticians' chain, **Specsavers**, is back with us as is **Zamboni**, the world famous ice cleaning machine, whose sole UK importer is **Airport & Road Equipment Ltd**.

Igloo will give you a keen price on skating and ice hockey equipment; its proprietor, **Kevin Barker**, also imports a wide range of North American hockey books and magazines through **Barkers Worldwide Publications**.

Britain's only ice hockey publication, apart from the *Annual*, is **Powerplay**, available weekly during the season at rinks or by mail order.

Skate Attack's shop in north London has one of the largest stocks of skating related goods in the country, and you can find more hockey goodies on the web at *www.crazykennys.com*.

For NHL fans: **Sports Travel Tours** arranges trips to games every season; you can buy a variety of licensed products on the internet from **Trans Atlantic Sports**; and you can watch games live on TV during the season on **NASN**, the North American Sports Network.

For youngsters who prefer the European style of hockey, you could do no better than attend the **Anglo-Czech Hockey School** and maybe you will win a trophy purchased from **D&P Trophies**, suppliers to the English IHA.

Andrew Weltch of **Weltch Media** is a Cardiff Devils' fan but his services are available to anyone, of course, regardless of club loyalty.

Finally, thanks go to our printers, **L&S Printing** of Worthing, and especially to **Paul Welch** who took the original manuscript, did some complicated things on his computer and, hey presto, *Annual* number 30.

And, of course, to you, dear reader, for buying this book. We hope you have all 30 now!

SR

EDITORIAL

Stewart Roberts

What the Annual believes

This is more of a Dark Age for ice hockey than a Golden Era.

But I don't want to be negative on the *Annual's* 30th birthday, so perhaps the best thing I can do is suggest some positive ways in which the sport can lift itself out of the hole it has dug.

For me, these are the priorities. They won't be easy to implement but, hey, nothing that's really worth doing is easy.

☐ Think big. This will only remain a minority sport if it continues to think small.

☐ A strong and independent national governing body. Now we know why the sport's in a hole! All leagues must sign agreements accepting the governing body's authority. And whoever decided it was a smart idea to have only representatives from our various bodies as directors of Ice Hockey UK needs a good kicking. It's obvious they would squabble. Of course, they must be on the governing body but there needs to be some knowledgeable independent folk as well, especially the chairman.

☐ A national senior men's team in the elite group of the World Championships. GB did well last time with a promising bunch of youngsters. We must build on this by adding three or four dedicated imports with British ancestry.

Only a well performing national team will bring public funds into the sport as well as favourable publicity. Just think of the Ashes!

☐ A major sponsor and a national TV contract. The whole sport can benefit from these. Remember *Heineken* and BBC Grandstand. We know *Sky Sports* are willing to televise games, and the sport attracts over 20,000 fans a week to live games, great exposure for some companies.

☐ Employ three or four people in a proper office, not just a couple of back bedroom volunteers.

☐ Accept that our top league can only afford to be semi-pro. It should be obvious by now that there aren't enough fans to support pro hockey without propping up weak teams with funds that would be better spent on improving the game.

☐ Club sides should be built around the best home-grown players with Europeans and North Americans in support, not the other way round. Then our national team will start to benefit.

☐ No goon hockey. It's the last refuge of those without faith in the game, and incapable or unwilling to promote it honestly.

☐ Start taking the sport seriously. It's too good to mess with.

Taggart's Premier League

If the Elite League with their teams stuffed with work permit holders and goons doesn't tick many of these boxes, at least I get a warm feeling about the English Premier League.

A league with a strict limit of three imports - sorry non-British trained players - on the ice at any one time, and no work permit players.

Moreover, it's a league which has stood the test of time having been created in the Eighties and lasted in much the same format until today.

Though their boss, **Ken Taggart**, is an American living in Colorado, he's a strong character who has proved able to keep the teams in line for many years.

However, my ideal league has a new challenge facing it this season - the addition of some former BNL teams who have been used to high levels of spending and at least twice as many foreign players.

The league has no wage cap and no intention of applying one in what, Ken insists, is a development league. This is a term used to ward off those who, usually for their own selfish interests, threaten to 'get the law on you' simply for running a league whose prime aim is to promote home-grown players.

I wish 'Taggs' the best of luck in keeping his league intact. I believe it's the future of this sport.

Enjoy your hockey and tell your friends,
Stewart Roberts
August 2005   stewice@aol.com

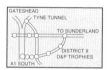

HONOURS & AWARDS

HONOURS ROLL-CALL 2004-05

ELITE LEAGUE
Playoff Champions
COVENTRY BLAZE
Elite League
COVENTRY BLAZE
The Challenge Cup
COVENTRY BLAZE

BRITISH NATIONAL LEAGUE
Playoff Champions
DUNDEE STARS
British National League
BRACKNELL BEES
Winter Cup
BRACKNELL BEES

ENGLISH LEAGUES
Premier League Playoff Champions
MILTON KEYNES LIGHTNING
Premier League
MILTON KEYNES LIGHTNING
Premier Cup
ROMFORD RAIDERS
National League Playoff Champions
SHEFFIELD SCIMITARS
National League North
SHEFFIELD SCIMITARS
National League South
INVICTA DYNAMOS

SCOTTISH NATIONAL LEAGUE
DUNDEE STARS
Scottish Div One Cup
PAISLEY PIRATES

WOMEN'S LEAGUE
SUNDERLAND SCORPIONS

Top League Points Scorers
Elite League
TONY HAND, Belfast
British National League
PETER CAMPBELL, Bracknell
English Premier League
ANDREW POWER, Romford

Best Goaltending Percentages
Elite League
SYLVAIN DAIGLE, London
British National League
STEVIE LYLE, Bracknell
English Premier League
CHRIS DOUGLAS, Romford

NEAL MARTIN, Coventry Blaze

BRITISH ICE HOCKEY WRITERS' ASSOCIATION AWARDS

ALL-STAR TEAMS

ELITE LEAGUE
First Team
Goal   JODY LEHMAN, Coventry
Defence   NEAL MARTIN, Coventry
            DOUG SCHUELLER, Coventry
Forwards   ADAM CALDER, Coventry
            TONY HAND, Belfast
            VEZIO SACRATINI, Cardiff
Second Team
Goal   MARTIN KLEMPA, Belfast
Defence   WADE BELAK, Coventry
            CALLE CARLSSON, Nottingham
Forwards   GEORGE AWADA, Belfast
            JON CULLEN, Cardiff
            ASHLEY TAIT, Coventry

BRITISH NATIONAL LEAGUE
Goal   STEVIE LYLE, Bracknell
Defence   PAUL DIXON, Guildford
            DANNY MEYERS, Bracknell,
Forwards   DINO BAUBA, Edinburgh
            PETER CAMPBELL, Bracknell
            LUKAS SMITAL, Bracknell

BRITISH AWARDS

Best British Defenceman (Alan Weeks Trophy)
DANNY MEYERS, Bracknell
Best British Netminder (BIHWA Trophy)
STEVIE LYLE, Cardiff
Best British Forward (BIHWA Trophy)
TONY HAND, Belfast
Best Young British Player (Vic Batchelder
Memorial Award/*Bauer-Nike*)
MARK RICHARDSON, Bracknell
Top British Scorer (*Ice Hockey Annual* Trophy)
TONY HAND, Belfast

MIKE ELLIS, Bracknell Bees

BRITISH ICE HOCKEY WRITERS' ASSOCIATION AWARDS, contd.

PLAYER OF THE YEAR

Elite League	tie - TONY HAND, Belfast
	NEAL MARTIN, Coventry
Brit Nat League	LUKAS SMITAL, Bracknell

TONY HAND MBE, Britain's most talented playmaker, topped the league scoring table with 68 points (49 assists), the ninth time in the last 13 seasons that he has achieved this feat. For the fourth year in a row, he combined playing with coaching. Indeed, he was a contender for Coach of the Year as he steered his Belfast Giants to runners-up place in his first Elite League campaign. He was also voted the Best British Forward.

The Edinburgh-born forward turned pro at the age of 14 and was the first British born and trained player to be drafted by the NHL. This was his 24th season in senior hockey.

Defenceman **NEAL MARTIN** was a key reason for Coventry Blaze's domination of the Elite League. The 28-year-old Canadian, who previously played in the UK with the Superleague's London Knights, has experience in the USA and Europe.

He was recruited by coach **Paul Thompson** who was impressed with his effectiveness in an offensive or defensive role. Neal was also voted the league's most valuable player in a fans' poll.

LUKAS SMITAL, 30, joined Bees from the American minor leagues and proved to be the ultimate team player. A right-winger, he usually played on a line with fellow Czech, **Martin Masa**, and British teenager **Mark Richardson**. He set up 53 goals in 55 league and cup games as well as scoring 36 times himself.

COACH OF THE YEAR

Elite League	PAUL THOMPSON, Coventry
Brit Nat League	MIKE ELLIS, Bracknell

Winning the Grand Slam of league, playoffs and Challenge Cup at the sport's top level were the crowning achievements for **PAUL THOMPSON**, an Englishman with a unique record.

Starting with an Autumn Trophy with Solihull Barons in 1994-95, 'Thommo', as he's universally known, has coached winning teams at all senior levels in the UK.

Moreover, all his sides have been in the same ownership as the Barons became Solihull Blaze before moving to Coventry in 2000. The Elite League was his second league title with Coventry and his tenth trophy in eleven seasons.

In only his second season as a head coach, **MIKE ELLIS** assembled a team that won the British National League by 13 points, as well as capturing the Winter Cup.

The 31-year-old British-Canadian from Burlington, Ontario combined playing with coaching as Bees won their first trophies since their Superleague title in 1999-2000.

After five years as a player and latterly as assistant coach with neighbouring club Basingstoke Bison, Mike took Bees to fourth place in 2003-04, their first BNL season. His first British side was Romford Raiders in 1994-95.

BRITISH AWARDS

Best Defenceman **DANNY MEYERS**, Bracknell
Born in Ascot, Berks, not far from the Bracknell ice rink, the 22-year-old was in his second year with the Bees, being one of coach Mike Ellis's first recruits. One of the finest home-grown players of his generation, he played in the World Championships for GB alongside his coach.

Best Goalie **STEVIE LYLE**, Bracknell
One of the most gifted native players to lace on the big pads, Stevie was one of the reasons that Bees allowed only 76 goals in 36 league games, a sparkling average of 2.11 goals per game.

Welshman Stevie, 25, turned pro at the age of 14 and played many years with his local team, Cardiff Devils, before joining Bees from Guildford Flames at the start of the season.

Best under-21 **MARK RICHARDSON**, Bracknell
Another Mike Ellis protégé who joined Bees in their first British National League season. Only 18, but six feet tall, Mark scored nearly a point a game during the current campaign with 46 (20 goals) in 53 league and cup outings. After captaining the Great Britain under-20 team at Sheffield, he went on to make his debut for the senior national team in Hungary.

ALL-STARS

Above, left: Bracknell Bees' **PETER CAMPBELL**, the BNL's top scorer; *right*: Belfast Giants' player-coach, **TONY HAND**, the Elite League's top scorer. *Below, left*: Coventry Blaze's NHL hard man, **WADE BELAK**; *right*: Bracknell Bees' **DANNY MEYERS**, the Best British Defenceman.

Photos: Diane Davey, Bob Swann

QUOTES OF THE YEAR

Headlines of the Year

'Steve's ditched the Gorillas for missus'
Over a January story in the Scottish Sun *about former Fife Flyers' netminder,* **Steve Briere,** *wanting to return to Scotland from his North American team, Amarillo Gorillas, to be with his fianceé and their baby.*
'I'm nut guilty'. *Over a piece in the* Daily Star *about Hull's* **Jeff Glowa** *being accused of head-butting Fife's* **Greg Kuznik.**

Taggart

"I told them this a development league, we don't need to see your business plan, and there's no wage cap. I ain't got the time to check on you to see if you're cheating." **Ken Taggart,** *the chairman of the English Ice Hockey Association, to the BNL teams wanting to join the EPL.*

Nice one

'Anyone got the Hull netminder's phone no?'
'0800 2-1 2-1 2-1'.
Exchange on the internet after the BNL's Stingrays famously defeated Sheffield Steelers, the Elite League's reigning champs.

Voice in the wilderness

"Signing these players goes against what the Elite League stands for - the growth of British talent in the game. [It] is like going back to the days of Superleague and clubs could find themselves having financial problems if they spend beyond their means." **John Elliott,** *Belfast Giants' general manager, on his fellow clubs' enthusiasm for locked-out NHL players.*

You know it makes sense

"If you want to finish high in the BNL table you have to win games against the Elite League teams." **Rick Strachan,** *coach of the BNL's Hull Stingrays, after his team's third defeat of an Elite League side in the Crossover Games.*

Neil in Black mood

"...we can't even beat Bracknell at home. I am shocked. We have 11 league games left and not one single further point dropped this season will be acceptable." **Neil Black,** *chairman of the Elite League's Nottingham Panthers, after his team were beaten 2-1 after overtime by the BNL's Bracknell Bees in a Crossover Game at the National Ice Centre on 30 January. Despite further defeats and threats, coach* **Paul Adey** *wasn't sacked until June.*

Winning friends

"Our situation is frustrated by ice rink management who have demonstrated a level of incompetence, intransigence, and general lack of interest in our programme that would astonish even the most hardened sceptics." **Roger Black,** *owner of London Racers, airing his views of the Lee Valley management.*

Six of the best

"Don't expect that every game!" **David Longstaff,** *after scoring six goals for Newcastle Vipers against Edinburgh Capitals in Vipers' first home game of the season.*

Where's yer guide dog, ref?

"If I was as bad at my job as the referee was at his, I would have been sacked nine-and-a-half years ago." **Paul Thompson,** *coach of the Elite League's Coventry Blaze, angry after their 1-0 defeat at the BNL's Dundee Stars in a Crossover Game on 6 February.*
"We didn't get anything because we had **Michael Hicks** disallowing goals again and the calls he made and didn't make were baffling. He disallowed a goal that nobody else in the arena saw and he is influencing what are very important games." **Tony Hand,** *player-coach of Belfast Giants after they lost 2-1 in Coventry.*
"There are so few officials that these guys can do nothing wrong and are answerable to no one. It's just the arrogance of them. They try to wind up players and coaches and we can do nothing about it. Their jobs are safe." **Paul Adey,** *Nottingham Panthers' coach, after his team were shutout 3-0 by Sheffield Steelers. As far as we heard, none of these (losing) coaches was punished for bringing the game into disrepute.*

'Proved I can play in Elite' - Hand

"I enjoyed my time in Belfast and proved to myself I can compete in the Elite League at the age of 37. I feel I have two more years as a player and want to enjoy every minute of that time." **Tony Hand,** *the country's best player, on re-joining Edinburgh Capitals, the newest member of the Elite League.*

With grateful acknowledgements to Powerplay, Daily Star, The Times, Bracknell News, Belfast Evening Telegraph and Sunday Life, Coventry Evening Telegraph, Fife Free Press, Hull Daily Mail, The Journal (Newcastle), Nottingham Evening Post, The Star (Sheffield), Scottish Sun, *various websites and match programmes.*

PEOPLE IN THE NEWS

FAREWELLS
Paul Adey - the greatest Panther

Paul **Adey**'s long association with Nottingham Panthers, which stretched back 17 years, came to an end when he was sacked as coach on 7 June 2005.

It was the second time in six years that the team's all-time highest scorer and most loyal servant - Panthers were his only British club - had left in unhappy circumstances.

Owner **Neil Black** had first let Adey go in the summer of 1999 when the forward joined Milan after failing to agree terms with Panthers.

This time, Mr Black was understandably concerned that Panthers had again missed out on a major trophy. Nottingham, though plagued with injuries all season, reached the playoff final, but this was not enough for the success-hungry owner who twice warned Adey publicly that his job was on the line.

In his eyes, probably the blackest mark against Adey was that since he took over the coaching reins in the 2002-03 season (he shared the duties in 2001-02 with **Alex Dampier**), Panthers had only one Challenge Cup to their name while their great rivals up the road in Sheffield had carried off five honours.

Neil Black told the Nottingham *Evening Post*: "It was a very difficult decision [but] it was an amicable parting. We are not closing the door on Paul and, in the future, there may be a possibility that he returns."

Before he flew back to Canada, a 'disappointed' Adey staunchly defended his record: "I helped to turn Panthers around and took them to six successive semi-finals. [Coaching Panthers] is a tough job as the new guy will discover."

Surprisingly, the new guy turned out to be former Sheffield and Nottingham coach, **Mike Blaisdell**, who knows exactly how tough the job

is. He, like Adey, fell out with Mr Black in 1999-2000. But that's another story.

Paul Adey, 41, a former GB international, joined Panthers as a player in season 1988-89 and, as their top scorer, he led them to their finest hour of the modern era, the *Heineken* British Championships at Wembley Arena.

His first departure, on the eve of the 1999-2000 campaign, came as a result of severe belt tightening due to the high-spending Superleague and the delay in opening the new National Ice Centre. He was said to be heartbroken by the club's decision.

He enjoyed more success as a player than as a coach, winning four (*Benson & Hedges*) Autumn Cups. In his eleven seasons in the black-and-gold he tallied 801 goals and 1,547 points in 626 games. As a coach, he won 109, lost 71 (11 in OT), and tied 25 games for a winning percentage of 61.95 in 2002-05.

The club honoured him by raising his no. 22 shirt to the rafters of the NIC. On their website, Panthers said: 'He is and will always be one of the all-time great Nottingham Panthers.'

Charlie Colon - Jets' goalie

Goalie, coach, director of hockey, rink manager - New Yorker **Charlie Colon** has done them all since coming to Britain in 1983-84 to play with Richmond Flyers.

His colourful British career came to an end 22 years later on 8 June 2005 at a party for the Basingstoke Bison fans in the rink's Visions Bar.

Bison coach, **Mark Bernard**, said on the club's website: "Charlie is a great friend who has helped me ever since I landed in the UK back in 1996. He was tremendous this past season as he always had time to listen and help me out with whatever problem I might have had."

Most of Charlie's playing career was spent with **Gary Stefan**'s Slough Jets whom he joined in their inaugural season of 1986-87. He tended Jets' goal for 12 seasons, becoming a big fan favourite, and only hung 'em up when he took over the coaching in 1998-99. During that time, Jets twice won the old British League, Div One and captured a *Benson & Hedges* Plate.

His first season as coach was probably his finest one as Jets won the British National League title. In that palmy year, they were funded by Slough Borough Council and had **Gary** and **Joe Stefan** up front (Joe helped out Charlie with the coaching), BNL player of the

JOHN NIKE OBE - 'WORTH £40 MILLION'

John Nike OBE, who sold the Bracknell Bees ice hockey club and the Thames Valley Tigers basketball team at the end of the season, entered the *Sunday Times* Rich List in 2005.

Mr Nike and his family own Nike Land Securities in Bracknell which has net assets worth £36.3 million. According to the paper, the family have 'other wealth' which makes the 68-year-old accountant and entrepreneur worth a total of £40 million and ranks him the 950th richest man in Britain.

year **Perry Pappas**, and **Richard Gallace** replacing Charlie in goal.

When the council withdrew their funding from the team, Charlie moved down to the road to Jets' rivals in Basingstoke and linked up with player-coach **Rick Strachan**. Bison finished third in the BNL but the next year they climbed to second, this time with **Mike Ellis** as Charlie's number two. On being appointed director of ice hockey and rink manager of Planet Ice Basingstoke in 2002-03, he handed over the coaching reins to **Steve Moria**.

Matt Coté - shot-stopper extraordinary

GB international defenceman, **Matt Coté**, 39, who was renowned for his fearless shot-blocking, retired from the sport at the end of season 2004-05 after 15 years in Britain.

He first came here in 1990 and joined Bracknell Bees in their third year. An all-round player, he managed 34 goals and 77 points in 38 games on the blueline in Division One of the old British League.

Throughout his ten seasons with the Bees, a spell that included four Superleague campaigns, he was a big favourite with the fans for the way he threw himself in front of the opposition's shots. His disregard for his own safety only seriously backfired once when, early in the 1994-95 season, he took a **Kevin Conway** slapshot to the head from close range. Though described at the time as 'potentially career-ending', it did little to change his style.

After winning the Superleague title with Bees in 1999-2000, he moved down the road to the Planet Ice rink at Basingstoke and played three seasons with the Bison, helping them to the runners-up spot in the British National League in 2000-01. A quiet, intense player, he ended his career playing two seasons with the English Premier League's Raiders in Ryde on the Isle of Wight, another Planet Ice rink.

Matt, who was born in Vancouver, gained his British citizenship and played 29 games for Britain in three World Championships and two Olympic qualifiers, competing in the elite A Pool in 1994.

Simon Kirkham - 18 years a stripey

Referee **Simon Kirkham** retired at the end of the season after 18 years as a match official. The Elite League's Belfast Giants presented him with farewell gifts of a bottle of whiskey and a signed Giants' shirt in front of their fans at the Odyssey arena.

Born in Arnold, Nottingham, Simon admitted he always fancied being a Panther, writes *Mick Holland*. He made it to the second team, the Trojans, when he was 16 but that was as far as he got. Then, skating one day at the old Ice Stadium, he bumped into the chief referee, **Nico Toemen**, who persuaded him to take up refereeing.

"I don't have any regrets, it's been a great 18 years," he said. During that time, he has officiated all over Europe. "I must have ref'ed over a thousand games at all levels, including eight or nine World Championships.

"The thing is, as I got older I didn't intend going down the slippery slope and wanted to get out at the highest level."

Naturally, he has a legion of stories to tell. Like the time he got the BBC in a huff when he used the f-word during a televised *Benson and Hedges* semi-final in Cardiff against Panthers.

"They were showing the games live on Grandstand," he explained, "and thought it would be a good idea for me to wear a mike. I wasn't keen on it. They warned me not to swear or get too near the players in a heated moment.

"Well, when Panthers had a player penalised and also injured, I insisted they put someone else in the penalty box while the player was treated. **Steve Carpenter** complained and I shouted at him: 'It's not my fault, I don't write the effing rules'... and was heard by millions sitting at home watching on television. At least they took the microphone off me then."

Kirkham started as a linesman and graduated to a referee. Linesmen's duties include separating fighting players and this was where he found a few tips from his policeman father came in handy.

"My dad taught me how to hold people and Whitley's **Bobby Brown** was playing the big I am during a scuffle, so I put him in an arm-lock. I warned him not to move otherwise he would get hurt. But he kept on struggling and regretted it. I had no trouble with him again and we still laugh about it when we bump into each other."

His biggest regret has been seeing the gradual demise of the British players, although that has improved recently with the Elite League openly encouraging local skaters.

He said: "In the *Heineken* League days, before the Superleague came about in 1996, you had local players busting a gut for their local team. It was more crash-bang hockey and less skilful with just three imports, but it was very entertaining."

Kirkham says he will continue to help and encourage anyone who is keen to take up the whistle. "If people go into ref'ing believing it's easy money they'd better think again," he added. "I've had a few holidays and seen a few different countries but it's hard work, dedication and mainly the love of the game that has kept me going all this time."

With thanks to the Nottingham Evening Post *for their permission to use extracts from Mick's article.*

BRITS OVERSEAS
'Murph' loves Sweden

GB's player of the tournament in the 2005 World Championships, Scotsman **Stephen Murphy**, 23, appears to have fallen in love with Swedish ice hockey.

After a dislocated shoulder wrecked most of his 2003-04 season with Bracknell Bees, the former Dundee and Fife keeper was hopeful of returning north of the border with the Flyers. But when contract negotiations fell through he joined Bracke Polar Bears, a low budget team in the Swedish third tier.

"When I got the chance to play for Bracke, I took it straight away," he said, "even though it wasn't the league I wanted to be in and I would be earning less money than in the UK. I knew it would give me the exposure that I wouldn't get here."

He was right. His talent was soon spotted and after Christmas he accepted an offer to move up to the second tier Allsvenskan league with Björklöven Green Devils. "They play in a town called Umea and attract up to 6,000 fans a game," he said. "All the teams had at least one NHLer which made it a high standard."

The GB fans who didn't know where he'd been playing were pleasantly surprised by his superb play in the Hungary World Championships. He started every game.

In the summer of 2005, Stephen signed a one-year deal with one of Björklöven's rivals, IFK Arboga, a team he played against in the 2005 playoffs.

Shields in *Slapshot*

GB international forward, **Colin Shields**, played minor pro hockey for three ECHL teams in season 2004-05. In April he was selected to play for the senior national men's team for the fifth time. (See *World Championships*.)

Glaswegian Colin, who turned 25 in January 2005, was the second British-born and trained player after **Tony Hand** to be drafted by an NHL team when he was chosen by Philadelphia Flyers in 2000. After three seasons in NCAA with the University of Maine, Flyers decided not to take up their rights to him and he attended Los Angeles Kings' NHL rookie camp in July 2004.

Colin was hoping to link up with an American Hockey League team but, with the NHL player lock-out looming, he was first offered a 15-day trial with Cleveland Barons of the ECHL. This is the parent club of the junior team for whom he turned out in 1998-2000 and led the league in points in his second year.

NICO TOEMEN IS BELGIUM'S CHIEF REF.

Brussels, Belgium - There was a shake-up in the Belgian Referee Commission after **Frans Van Ackeleyen** resigned as referee-in-chief last week.

Appointed to replace Van Ackeleyen by the Royal Belgian Ice Hockey Federation (RBIHF) is **Nico Toemen**, an experienced official whose career included 22 IIHF Championships and the 1980 Winter Olympic Games.

For the past two seasons Toemen supervised officials for the RBIHF and before that he served as the referee-in-chief and technical director in Great Britain.

from www.hockeyrefs.com, 10 October 2004

STEVE McKENNA, Nottingham Panthers

He played in a pre-season exhibition game for Barons but failed to make the final cut partly because Barons have a large pool of players to choose from. Instead, he signed for the San Diego Gulls in the same league and appeared in 34 games for the California-based team, scoring three goals and 14 points.

In February, he was contacted by Maine's assistant coach, **Matt Thomas**, who had been appointed head coach of the league's Atlantic City Broadwalk Bullies.

"Shields will bring an element of speed on the right side and will be an exciting player for our fans to watch," said Thomas in a press release.

Colin played in the *Slapshot* rink in Johnstown, Pennsylvania in his first game for the Bullies and, thanks to increased ice-time from the coach, scored five goals and ten points in his first ten games. But after 19 games and 18 points, he was on the move again.

This time he went in a trade to the Greenville Grrrowl where he tallied three assists in nine games. When their parent NHL team sent down two of their drafted junior players in March, the Grrrowl released Colin to play in Hungary.

"This was my first year as a pro and with the NHL lock-out it was hard to get a job," Colin told the Newcastle *Journal*. "I got around a little bit but no one seemed to be sticking with teams for long. In August 2005, Colin was traded by the Grrrowl to the Alaska Aces, again in the ECHL.

NHLers in the UK

Due to the NHL's lockout of its players throughout the whole of season 2004-05, British clubs were able for the first time to sign players who would otherwise have been in the world's top league. All bar one of the 12 NHLers who skated over here had been notable more for their time in the sin-bin than for their wizardry with the puck. However, they were willing to play for just living expenses.

One player, Washington Capital forward, **Roman Tvrdon**, signed before the lockout was officially declared. He played nine games for Nottingham Panthers before being injured. Two other players stayed for only a handful of games.

The signing of players in Europe generally - exactly 300 came over - caused controversy on both sides of the water.

Many were incensed that highly paid players - the world's best - refused to take million-dollar-plus cheques off their own league but were happy to come to Europe. There they played for comparative peanuts, took jobs off local players - just to keep in trim - and then returned to the NHL without caring about their previous team.

Details of the NHL's UK dozen follow with the date they signed. Their scoring statistics with their UK clubs are on our team pages:

ROB DAVISON

5 Oct, **Cardiff Devils** - defenceman, 24, played 70 NHL games in two years, all with San Jose Sharks, scoring six points and taking 114 penalty minutes. He earned US$450,000 with Sharks in season 2003-04.

SCOTT NICHOL

25 Oct, **London Racers** - the centreman's last NHL team was Chicago Blackhawks. Aged 30, he played 208 games over five seasons, scoring 45 points and having 415 penalty minutes. Although he returned to the States during December and January due to a 'family crisis', he was Racers' third highest scorer.

STEVE MCKENNA

26 Oct, **Nottingham Panthers** - the tallest player to come over was the 6ft, 8in Pittsburgh Penguins' winger, 31, who played 373 NHL games over eight seasons, scoring 32 points and taking 824 penalty minutes. A popular player in

> 'A solid goalie, he can play well after sitting on the bench for long periods.' *Description on nhl.com of goalie Jamie McLennan who played for Guildford Flames.*

Nottingham where he scored 21 points and spent only 28 minutes in the cooler.

ERIC CAIRNS
1 Nov, London Racers - Racers signed their second NHLer when coach **Dennis Maxwell** persuaded his friend to join. The New York Islanders' 6ft, 6in defenceman, 30, scored eight points and spent 189 minutes in the sin-bin in 72 games. In all, he played eight seasons in the Show with 40 points and 1,053 penalty minutes.

Cairns was a controversial figure in Lee Valley from the start when he replaced another 'good friend' of Maxwell's, GB international **Brent Pope**, to the end when he was suspended for striking a referee. (See *Review of the Year*).

DEREK BEKAR
7 Nov, Dundee Stars - the first player to join a BNL club, he quit after only three games, saying he had received a 'better offer' from Springfield Falcons of the AHL. He had signed for Stars for the full season. The 29-year-old centreman had played only 11 NHL games, latterly with New York Islanders.

WADE BELAK
8 Nov, Coventry Blaze - another giant defender with a bin full of penalty minutes, Belak, 28 and 6ft, 5in. played the last four of his ten NHL seasons with Toronto Maple Leafs who paid him US$850,000 in 2003-04. In 275 games, he scored 22 points and racked up 811 minutes.

BRENDAN WITT
21 Dec, Bracknell Bees - Bees were the second BNL club to pick up an NHLer, but the Washington Capitals' defenceman, 29, who earned $1.75 million in 2003-04, played only three games here before rushing back to Florida where his house had been engulfed by fire.

He played 568 NHL games over nine seasons, all with Caps, scoring 72 points and spending 894 minutes in the box. He was reported to have joined Bees only after Belfast's coach **Tony Hand** declined to sign him as he didn't want any locked out players on the Giants.

CHRIS MCALLISTER
6 Jan, Newcastle Vipers - they breed 'em big in the NHL! The Colorado/Rangers' mammoth defenceman, 29, was 6ft 7in. He appeared in 301 NHL games over seven seasons, scoring 21 points, collecting 634 penalty minutes and earning $650,000 in 2003-04. Sponsored by a Newcastle firm, his signing was announced by Vipers as a notice of the club's pending liquidation appeared in the local papers.

DAVID OLIVER

7 Jan, Guildford Flames - a veteran of 230 NHL games, the 33-year-old winger was the only one who had more points than penalty minutes. He scored 98 points and had 84 minutes over eight seasons. In the UK, he was the highest scoring NHLer with 29 points (12 goals) in 31 games.

IAN MORAN
25 Jan, Nottingham Panthers - Panthers' second locked out NHLer was a 6ft Boston Bruins' defenceman, 32, with 476 games, 69 points and 311 minutes in the big league. Earned $700,000 with Bruins in 2003-04.

NICK BOYNTON
26 Jan, Nottingham Panthers - an NHL All-Star in season 2003-04 earning $1.55 million, he was a former team-mate of Moran with the Bruins. Aged 25 the 6ft 2in defenceman was the second highest paid NHLer to come here. His career totals: 245 games, 72 points and 304 minutes.

JAMIE McLENNAN
17 Feb, Guildford Flames - the signing of the only NHL goalie, Flames' second locked out player, was controversial as it was announced after the deadline. The club insisted the Calgary Flame had actually signed earlier and was 'just in time for the playoffs'. Only 23, he shared duties with Flames' **Miroslav Bielik**. His save average of 2.10 with Flames bettered his NHL record of 2.62 in 228 games. Paid $650,000 in 2003-04.

A number of other NHLers were rumoured to be coming over but they never put pen to paper.

Sheffield Steelers were linked to three of them - Columbus winger, **JODY SHELLEY**, who pulled out after suffering a torn groin, St Louis Blues centreman, **RYAN JOHNSON**, whose phantom signing for Steelers appeared mysteriously on hockeydb.com, and Buffalo centreman, **ADAM MAIR**, who was also offered to the BNL's Edinburgh Capitals.

Basingstoke Bison chased Detroit Redwings' Stanley Cup winner, **KIRK MALTBY**, as they already had his brother, **Shawn Maltby**, under contract. But Bison couldn't find anyone willing to cover Kirk's £12,000 insurance premium. He generously signed autographs for Bison's fans in the rink bar during a game in February.

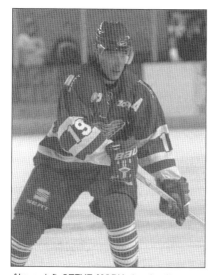 

Above, left: **STEVE MORIA**, London Racers, is the first player named to the University of Alaska Sports Hall of Fame; *right*: **DANNY MARSHALL**, captain of Romford Raiders, raises the English Premier Cup; *below, left*: **ANDRE PAYETTE**, Coventry Blaze, was the Elite League's dirtiest player; *right*: **NICK POOLE**, player-coach and top scorer with the EPL's double winning Milton Keynes Lightning.   *Photos*: Roger Cook, Diane Davey, Dave Page, Bob Swann

Two other big fish got away. *Newcastle Vipers'* co-coach **Rob Wilson** failed to hook his old team-mate **TIE DOMI** out of Toronto Maple Leafs' pool, and even his best friends were dubious of **Roger Black's** tall tale of landing Florida Panthers' highly thought of goalie, **ROBERTO LUONGO**, for *London Racers.* "We're always seeking to improve our team," he told the *Toronto Sun.* Aren't we all, Rog.

UNIVERSITY OF ALASKA HALL OF FAME
Steve Moria inducted

British ice hockey great, **Steve Moria**, is the first ever inductee into the University of Alaska's Sports Hall of Fame.

GB international Moria, who was London Racers' points leader in season 2004-05, was a scoring machine during his three years with the university's hockey team, the Nanooks.

He led the squad in goals, assists and points in each of his three seasons, 1982-85, with a total of 108 goals and 163 assists for 271 points in 86 games. Named to the All-American team, in his last season he tallied a NCAA single-season record of 109 points in 34 games. This was later broken, but Mo's legend lives on in Alaska where the team's MVP trophy is named after the Racers' forward.

Moria grew up in Vancouver, British Columbia, played competitive hockey throughout his youth and was eventually offered a scholarship by Nanooks' coach, **Ric Schafer**. After leaving university, he signed a contract with the NHL's New York Rangers in 1986 and was assigned to their American Hockey League team, New Haven (Connecticut) Nighthawks. After a couple of seasons in the 'A', 'Mo' crossed the Atlantic to join **John Lawless's** Cardiff Devils in 1988.

This year the University of Alaska decided to open a Sports Hall of Fame. Moria's number 19 shirt, which no one has worn since, was officially retired by the club at a ceremony in July 2005 at the Big Dipper Ice Arena's Hall of Fame Gallery. *Editor's note* - The popular and prolific 'Mo' is a certainty for the British Ice Hockey Writers' Hall of Fame. We're just waiting for the evergreen forward to retire!

Reports by Randy Zarnke, a director of the Fairbanks Hockey Hall of Fame, and Bob Eley, sports editor of the Fairbanks Daily News-Miner. Website:

http://www.gonanooks.com/artman/publish/pdfs/ hockeyMediaGuide/NanookHockeyRecords.pdf

FIRST FEMALE REF.
Joy Tottman

Joy Tottman became the first female to referee a senior game in Britain (and possibly the world) on 23 October 2004.

Joy, 21, an Oxford graduate in politics, philosophy and economics, wore the armbands for the Milton Keynes-Guildford [Winter Cup] game in the British National League.

Her unusual career began 11 years ago, when she decided to follow in the steps of her father, Dave, a long-time referee. By 1999, she had reached the professional leagues as a linesman.

Joy has already been successful on the international scene, progressing to the Women's World Championships and has high hopes of being at the next Olympics.

She has also played the game, being named best player in the 2003 women's Varsity Match between Oxford and Cambridge universities.

"As a referee, you're only as good as your last game," Tottman said. "That means I'm feeling pretty good at the moment, but you can never tell what's going to happen next."

Such as, for example, full-scale fisticuffs. At 5ft 7in (1.70m), Tottman is not physically imposing, but she insists that her size is not a disadvantage when tempers flare.

"Players in the professional leagues are very fit and strong and if they really want to fight, there probably aren't many men who could separate them," she said. "Women can be quite violent, as well.

"Basically, there's a procedure to follow. You let them throw a few punches, get tired and move in. There's a way to clamp arms, that kind of thing. You try and keep a level head, even when it seems like World War Three is breaking out. Coming out of it with an unscathed reputation can be difficult."

There were no brawls on Tottman's debut, just praise for the way she controlled the game. "She was vocal with the players and assertive. She did a good job," said **Stan Marple**, the Guildford Flames' coach.

■ Goalie **Barbara Zemann** made history in October 2004 by becoming first woman to be allowed to play in Austria's men's league. The 33-year-old played for SK Feuerwehr's third team and follows in footsteps of **Manon Rheaume**, a Canadian who in 1992 became the first female to play in the NHL, representing Tampa Bay Lightning in a pre-season exhibition game.

NEW RINKS NEWS

It was in 2003 that the last new ice rink opened in the UK: the superb, twin-pad iceSheffield complex next to the Hallam FM Arena.

The only serious contenders to open in the next 12 months are in **Cardiff** and **Manchester**. Coincidentally (?), both are planned to house Elite League teams, and both are temporary rinks pending the opening of permanent ones.

If permission is granted for these unusual buildings, it will be a first for the sport.

Arenas at **Bristol**, **Croydon** and **Southampton** are at various stages of planning (see last year's Annual) and there are preliminary plans for buildings in **Coleraine**, **Durham**, **Leeds** and **Liverpool**. But **Brighton** and **London** will probably be the first arenas to open.

ALTRINCHAM (MANCHESTER)

Losing two ice facilities in the Manchester area at the same time was traumatic for Altrincham Aces and Manchester Storm/Phoenix fans alike.

The man who refused to accept the situation is **Neil Morris**, whose Phoenix team used to play out of the 17,000-seat Manchester arena before he reluctantly decided at the end of season 2003-04 that he could no longer afford it.

In July 2005 after months of negotiations, he agreed a deal with the Trafford Borough Council. This called for a new rink at Oakfield Road in Altrincham, not far from where the old building closed in March 2003 after 40-odd years.

The new venue, known as Station Location, is to be developed by David McLean Nikal and will be operated by Planet Ice who already run several English rinks. As well as an Olympic-sized ice pad and seating for 3,000, the building will have facilities for the first extreme sports centre in the UK with an ice wall, surf wave and caving area.

This will not be ready for four or five years but Mr Morris, who has retained his seat on the board of the Elite League, is champing at the bit to get Phoenix back on the ice. So he has applied for permission to erect a 'semi-permanent' rink on the site, ahead of the permanent one.

According to their press release in July 2005, Phoenix have been advised by the council that 'plans are proceeding to full planning status'. The club hopes this means Phoenix will be able to play in the league again in season 2006-07.

Website: *www.manchester2002-uk.com/ sports/others/icehockey.html*

CARDIFF

With Devils being kicked out of the Wales National Ice Rink at the end of the coming season to make way for a superstore, **Bob Phillips**, the team owner, is working closely with the local council on plans for a new home for the Elite League team.

According to Mr Phillips, Devils will be getting two homes: the long promised arena in Cardiff Bay "in three years' time", and a temporary rink on the car park next to Glamorgan Cricket Club's indoor school at Sophia Gardens.

But the planning application for the latter, which was due to be considered in September, met with angry protests from local residents who wanted to preserve 'the green lungs of Cardiff'.

Cardiff Bay development website: *www.cardiff.gov.uk/sportsvillage/ sports_village_page2.htm#*

BRIGHTON AND HOVE

Since the Brighton International Arena consortium was given leave in 2003 to submit a planning application for a £50 million multi-purpose arena on a site next to Brighton Marina, negotiations have continued with developers, financiers and the local authority.

The arena is designed on similar lines to the National Ice Centre in Nottingham and would be home to the Brighton Tigers ice hockey team which last played in the city 40 years ago.

The consortium were expecting to be ready to submit their application this autumn. The project has the firm backing of the local authority which is keen to have a major venue for sports, concerts, conferences and exhibitions in the growing city.

Website: *www.brightonarena.com*

LONDON

THE O2 - Anschutz Entertainment, who used to own London Arena and Superleague's London Knights, are carrying out a massive refurbishment of the **MILLENNIUM DOME** which, in a £6 million a year deal, has been renamed *The O2*.

Sales director, **Brian Jokat**, Knights' former chief executive, told the Docklands newspaper, *The Wharf*, that the landmark building will have an ice pad when it re-opens - scheduled for April 2007 - and "We may do exclusive European championships or NHL exhibition games."

Website: *http://info.aegworldwide.co.uk*

RINK ATTENDANCES

OVERALL PICTURE	2004-05 TOTAL	ATTENDANCE GAMES	AVERAGE	2003-04 AVERAGE	*AVE. DIFF. ON 2003-04
ELITE LEAGUE					
*League	308,501	126	2,448	2,291	up 7%
Challenge Cup Finals	14,617	6	2,436	4,102	diff. teams
Playoffs	48,613	24	2,025	2,887	down 30%
Playoff Finals	24,900	4	6,225	6,629	down 6%
TOTALS	**396,631**	**160**	**2,479**	**2,418**	**up 2.5%**
BRITISH NATIONAL LEAGUE					
*League	98,455	84	1,172	1,077	up 9%
Playoffs	42,683	38	1,123	1,334	down 16%
Winter Cup	78,801	144	547	1,484	.inc. 2 EPL
TOTALS	**219,939**	**266**	**827**	**1,203**	**down 31%**
CROSSOVER GAMES					
Elite League	98,235	49	2,005	-	)
British National League	59,860	49	1,222	-	)new comp.
TOTALS	**158,095**	**98**	**1,613**	-	)
TOTALS	**774,665**	**524**	**1,478**	-	
ENGLISH LEAGUE					
Premier Division	71,705	144	498	555	down 10%
Playoffs	18,306	27	678	677	no diff.
TOTALS	**90,011**	**171**	**526**	**576**	**down 9%**
GRAND TOTALS	**864,676**	**695**	**1,244**	**1,508**	**down 17.5%**

* Crossover Games shown separately.

THE TOP LEAGUE* CROWD-PULLERS			2004-05 LEAGUE	ATTENDANCE Total	Average+	2003-04 Average	Notes/ Changes
1	(2)	Nottingham Panthers	Elite	77,287	4,294	3,863	up 11%
2	(1)	Sheffield Steelers	Elite	65,170	3,620	3,911	down 7%
3	(3)	Belfast Giants	Elite	62,922	3,496	3,350	up 4%
4	(4)	Coventry Blaze	Elite	42,919	2,384	2,165	up 10%
5	(6)	Cardiff Devils	Elite	33,102	1,839	1,614	up 14%
6	(11)	Dundee Stars	BNL	18,370	1,531	1,066	up 44%
7	(10)	Bracknell Bees	BNL	17,892	1,491	1,130	up 32%
8	(7)	Guildford Flames	BNL	16,800	1,400	1,477	down 5%
9	(8)	Fife Flyers	BNL	16,544	1,379	1,446	down 5%
10	(9)	Newcastle Vipers	BNL	15,119	1,260	1,386	down 9%
11	(12)	Milton Keynes Kings	EPL	16,784	1,049	1,073	down 2%

List includes teams that averaged at least 1,000 fans at league games (excluding playoffs).
Last season's position in brackets.
* excluding Crossover Games.
+ Home games - Elite League teams each played 18; British National League (BNL) teams each played 12 and the EPL's Milton Keynes Kings played 16.
Figures are based wherever possible on information sent out by the teams. Otherwise, the Annual uses its own sources.

No playoffs, please, we're British

British fans like league ice hockey. Both the Elite and the British National put on crowds last season and six leading clubs increased their gates for league games.

But playoffs? No thanks. Especially not if the teams stick up their prices (London Racers put theirs up from £12 to £16 in the post-season) and play so many mid-week games in so short a time. Playoff crowds were off by 16 per cent in the BNL and a staggering 30 per cent in the Elite.

With several teams needing the playoffs to make a profit, some must have caught a cold.

The success of a few clubs in attracting bigger crowds was refreshing in a season where the trend was the other way. The total attendance at all senior games crashed 17.5 per cent to 864,676, the worst for 15 years.

The prize for the most success in pulling 'em in goes to Dundee Stars where promotions manager, **Allan Paul**, attracted 44 per cent more followers, almost half as many again as in season 2003-04.

Second prize goes to the Bracknell Bees whose team won two of the major trophies in the BNL, the surest way of stoking up interest. Their crowds went up by a third.

It's not our brief in this column to ponder the wisdom of both these two teams being left without a league at the end of the season (and one without an owner as well).

In Cardiff, the fans seem at last to have forgiven their Devil of an owner, **Bob Phillips**, for whatever it was he was supposed to have done to the once hugely successful Welsh team. (Actually, we've forgotten now, too.)

While their fanbase is much lower than in **John Lawless**'s heyday, the Devils attracted 14 per cent more followers than in 2003-04.

But it was a bad year for the sport's most decorated team, the Sheffield Steelers. Owner **Norton Lea**'s care with the pennies outweighed the best vocal efforts of his unofficial marketing man and Steelers played to the smallest crowds in their history, under 4,000 a game.

Vipers endured far worse gates on Tyneside where they played in front of a dismal average of 1,260 fans in a building that holds over 5,000. New owner **Paddy O'Connor** will have his work cut out if he is not to feel the loneliest owner in British ice hockey.

The controversial Crossover Games received a mixed reaction. While the BNL teams enjoyed the same level of support whichever league was in town, the Elite teams' home crowds dropped off by 18 per cent, almost one in five, when BNL sides visited.

However, the bare figures do not reveal if this reduction was due to a lack of interest in a 'lower' team or just fewer travelling supporters.

Finally, a sobering bit of trivia. Last season, only 11 teams in the country attracted more than 1,000 fans to their league games. In 1990-91, 17 teams (half as many again) attracted that number.

DIARY OF THE SEASON

Season 2004-05 and more especially the summer of 2005 produced the usual crop of surprises in the sport. And we don't mean shock results on the ice.

No, if there's one thing you can be certain of in British ice hockey it is the off-ice politics that cause the fans to jump up and down.

We've summed up the major events in our Review of the Year *later in the* Annual *but it helps to get matters in perspective if you understand the order in which they happened.*

So read on and see just how the last wacky 12 months unfolded.

AUGUST 2004

28th - Several Elite League (EL) teams keep an import spot open for locked-out NHL players.

Some teams have to ice guest players in pre-season friendlies when their imports discover it's not as easy to get into this country as it used to be. The UK immigration department has tightened up its rules and everyone coming to this country from overseas needs an entry visa which means them having to appear in person at a UK Mission in their home country. This can take some time to arrange.

SEPTEMBER

4th - The British National League (BNL) opens with games in the new Winter Cup. The English Premier League (EPL) also starts play.

11th - On the opening weekend of the Elite League, teams play in three competitions: league, Challenge Cup and the Crossover Games against the BNL teams.

8th - Dundee *Evening Telegraph* announces that **Tom Stewart**, the 'mastermind' behind the £300 million Ice Valley project in Monifieth outside Dundee, has been made bankrupt. Mr Stewart ran the Dundee Rockets in the 1980s.

17th - London Racers' first home league game is brought forward from Sunday to Friday. No explanation is given for the late change.

21st - The BNL start their league games (in mid-week). With the Winter Cup continuing, this means the sport's top 14 teams are now playing in five competitions at the same time.

24th - The *Annual* learns that Edinburgh Capitals and Newcastle Vipers have given the statutory 12-month notice to the BNL that they wish to withdraw from the league.

OCTOBER

13th - Steelers' captain **Dion Darling** has a public row with club owner, Norton Lea, over the lack of medical facilities at the club and other issues. Lea responds in the local paper, saying: "This has convinced me it is time for me to leave the club as soon as possible."

NOVEMBER

6th - Ice maintenance problems at Milton Keynes, exacerbated by a long-running dispute between Planet Ice and the local council, result in the abandonment of Lightning's Winter Cup game against Dundee Stars. Stars threaten to sue for compensation for their costs.

10th - At a meeting in Cardiff chaired by Devils' owner **Bob Phillips**, an action committee is formed to try and secure the Elite League team's future as their lease on the Wales National Ice Rink expires in November 2005.

18th - The Sheffield *Star* newspaper reports that the sale of Sheffield Steelers to builder **Gary Apsley** has fallen through. Among the snags are a pending lawsuit from injured former Steeler **Marc Twaite** and a £500,000 bond required by the Arena to whom the team pay rent.

22nd - The *Annual* learns that First Choice Travel, a Newcastle coach company, are owed £10,000 by the Vipers.

28th - **Darryl Illingworth** announces that his Newcastle Vipers have quit the BNL and applied to join the Elite League. He reveals that Edinburgh Capitals will also quit the league.

DECEMBER

8th - At a meeting of the Elite League in Milton Keynes, Dundee Stars, Edinburgh Capitals and Newcastle Vipers are granted membership of the league 'in principle'.

9th - In Steelers' programme, **Norton Lea** says he has put £40,000 of his own money into club.

17th - At a meeting of the five remaining BNL clubs to decide their future, **Eamon Convery** (EL chairman), **Bob Phillips** (Cardiff) and **Roger Black** (London) attend to discuss joining/merging with Elite League. [**John Hepburn** (Guildford) told his fellow BNL clubs he was going to the meeting 'waving a white flag'.] Meeting appears favourable to merger but a decision is deferred to the next Elite League meeting on 10 Jan.

22nd - Newcastle Vipers raise £6,000 with a collection from their fans after announcing at the BNL game against Hull that they had a £12,000 debt to pay off urgently.

JANUARY 2005

2nd - Guildford Flames refuse to travel to their scheduled BNL game at Newcastle, as Vipers are unable to provide proof that their liability insurance is in force. The game is postponed.

10th - Following a meeting of the Elite League, the *Annual* learns that the clubs voted in favour of a 15-team league (including Manchester) for next season.

12th - **John Craighead** resigns from Nottingham Panthers after sitting out a number of games, partly due to him contracting the mumps. This enables him to sign later for another Elite League club, Cardiff Devils, a move normally barred by l eague regulations.

FEBRUARY

1st - **Paul Heavey** takes over from **Rob Stewart** as coach of Sheffield Steelers. This is much the same point of the season at which he took over at Manchester a year ago. He is unable to sign any new players as the deadline has passed.

3rd - Guildford Flames say they have told the Elite League that 'their rules of play and conditions of membership are acceptable and that the Flames are very interested in participating as an Elite League club'.

4th - Official invites are sent to all BNL clubs inviting them to join 'the Elite Ice Hockey League umbrella', but without voting rights on the league's Board. This was apparently not discussed at the meeting on 17 Dec.

5th - In their first game since owner **Neil Black** threatened to sack coach **Paul Adey** in the event of another defeat, Panthers fail to score at home in a 1-0 loss to arch-rivals Sheffield Steelers. It is **Paul Heavey**'s debut as Steelers' coach.

7th - A Public Notice appears in Newcastle papers advising of a creditors' meeting of Newcastle KBS Vipers Ltd.

14th - The BNL clubs accept the Elite League's invite but request, among other things, full voting rights on the league's board.

16th - Former Durham Wasp, **Patrick (Paddy) O'Connor**, takes control of Newcastle Vipers after a creditors' meeting of Newcastle KBS Vipers Ltd reveals substantial debts.

MARCH

3rd - The Elite League declines the BNL's counter-offer of membership with voting rights.

9th - Nottingham Panthers' coach Paul Adey, already struggling with a team depleted by injuries, receives a second 'public warning' from his owner Neil Black after Panthers are shutout 3-0 in Sheffield. "Paul's job is on the line," Black tells the local paper.

14th - **Chris McSorley** quits as coach of the GB senior team, citing pressure of work following his purchase of the Geneva club and the lack of support in Britain for its national team. The

announcement comes just a month before the World Championships.

15th - Newcastle Vipers are accepted as the eighth playing member of the Elite League. Surprisingly, in the light of the terms dictated to the other BNL clubs, owner Paddy O'Connor is granted a seat on the board of directors.

17th - Coventry Blaze coach **Paul Thompson** is the first to publicly throw his hat in the GB coaching ring. He tells the *Coventry Evening Telegraph*: "I can't deny that it is a position that would interest me - who wouldn't want to coach their national team?"

20th - The day before an Elite League board meeting, the *Edinburgh Evening News* confirms that Capitals have applied to join the league. Club boss **Scott Neil** says: "The Capitals have put forward a sensible budget to the Elite League that increases our ... expenditure considerably from last season."

21st - Bracknell Bees' owner, **John Nike**, announces at the club's awards evening that the team will not be entering the BNL next season.

25th - The *Scottish Sun* reports that Edinburgh Capitals have been admitted to the Elite League.

30th - Belfast Giants are knocked out of the Elite playoffs after losing 3-0 in Cardiff. It is their fifth game in seven days.

APRIL

6th - Dundee Stars upset the Flames 3-2 in Guildford to win the BNL playoff championship by two games to one.

9th - At a press conference during the playoff finals weekend the Elite League finally confirms that Edinburgh Capitals have been accepted. Owner **Scott Neil** admits that he does not have a seat on the league's board of directors. **Neil Morris**, owner of the league's Manchester Phoenix, assures the media that they will have news of their new rink 'in a couple of weeks'.

10th - Coventry Blaze win the Elite League playoff championship at Nottingham.

11th - **Martin Weddell**, GM of Bracknell Bees, announces that the Nike Group of Companies will cease to operate the Bees and the basketball team from 6 May.

13th - After a meeting in Bracknell of Bees' sponsors, a restructured side seems likely to apply for entry into the English Premier League.

27th - Hull Stingrays confirm that they have applied to join the English Premier League.

MAY

1st - At a meeting of the English IHA in Hull, three former BNL clubs - Bracknell, Guildford and Hull - apply to join the EPL.

3rd - The *Milton Keynes Citizen* reports that 'weeks of intense negotiations between English Partnerships, Milton Keynes Council, developers

Abbeygate Helical and Planet Ice have been concluded'. The outcome, according to club chairman **Harry Howton**, is that Lightning can play in the rink until a new one is built nearby.

5th - At an Elite League board meeting applications from the remaining BNL clubs - Dundee, Fife and Guildford - are believed *not* to have been discussed. As this leaves the two well-run Scots sides, Dundee and Fife, with no league to play in, fans describe this as Meltdown Day for British ice hockey.

6th - The Elite League releases no information about their meeting but a statement on Nottingham Panthers' website describes it as 'positive and forward thinking'.

Dundee Stars reveal that following the rejection of their application to join the Elite League they are working on plans for 'a six to eight team professional league encompassing teams from Scotland and England.' with four to six imports. The proposed league has a sponsor, according to Stars' announcement.

Guildford Flames confirm 'with regret' that they have been denied membership of the Elite League and say they will now work towards playing in an alternative league.

The *Annual* learns that at an IHUK board meeting, the Elite League were asked to reconsider their decision not to admit the three remaining BNL clubs.

7th - A Belfast paper reports that **Tony Hand** will return to coach and play for the Giants.

9th - Following their rejection by the Elite League, Guildford Flames apply to join the English Premier League.

12th - Dundee Stars, Fife Flyers, Whitley Warriors, Paisley Pirates and representatives from teams in Aberdeen, Dumfries and Ayr (Limekiln Road) attend a meeting in Kirkcaldy to discuss the formation of a three/four-import northern league.

13th - Planet Ice join Manchester Phoenix in their plans for a new 3,000-seat rink in the area in time for the start of the new season.

17th - Belfast Giants confirm that **Tony Hand** will *not* be with the team next season.

18th - New Elite League members, Edinburgh Capitals, announce that **Tony Hand** will be rejoining the club on a two-year contract as player-coach after one season's absence.

20th - Estate agent **David Taylor's** consortium is favoured to take over the Bracknell Bees, according to the *Reading Evening Post*.

26th - The Nottingham *Evening Post* reports 'doubts over the future of Belfast'. The *Annual* discovers that Giants applied for a substantial five-figure subsidy at a recent Elite League board meeting after they lost a major sponsor in *MG Rover*, the collapsed car manufacturer.

27th - The *Annual* learns that London Racers owe between £12,000 and £15,000 to some of their players. There are rumours that the club may not be able to afford to continue.

JUNE

1st - Edinburgh Capitals announce they have reached agreement with the local Heriot-Watt University which will enable their imports to enjoy a year of education as well as hockey.

3rd - Paisley Pirates confirm they have been in discussions over the formation of a four-import league in Scotland/north of England but have decided against joining due to the costs involved.

4th - Whitley Warriors are confirmed as members of the English National League, ruling them out of joining any proposed new league.

7th - Few are surprised when Nottingham Panthers' coach, **Paul Adey**, is released, two months after he took the team to the final of the Elite League playoffs.

8th - Many fans are taken aback, though, when former Sheffield Steelers' coach **Mike Blaisdell** returns from Canada to take over as coach of Panthers, his old team's arch-rivals. The Hall of Famer quit Panthers in 1999, claiming breach of contract and lack of financial backing from owner **Neil Black**. Mr Black said: "Paul Adey had some bad luck and if Mike couldn't come he'd still be coach. But it was time for a change and now Mike is back to complete unfinished business."

10th - Belfast Giants issue a statement to quell rumours that the club is having financial problems, saying that negotiations are ongoing with sponsors, investors and the appointment of a new coach.

11th - At the AGM of the English IHA in Nottingham, Bracknell Bees, Guildford Flames, Hull Stingrays and Sheffield Scimitars are all accepted into the English Premier League, taking the number of teams to 13.

13th - A heated row is reported from a meeting of Ice Hockey UK over the plight of Fife and Dundee. IHUK threaten sanctions against the Elite League if the two are not admitted. There also arguments over the structure of the governing body and who runs their office.

15th - Elite League postpone their scheduled fixtures meeting to the 27th amid reports that Belfast Giants and Manchester Phoenix have not yet made a firm commitment to the league for next season. London Racers still owe wages to some of their players.

16th - Elite League chairman, **Eamon Convery**, tells the *Fife Free Press* that "the idea of bringing Fife and Dundee into the [Elite League] set-up is not stroked out, but it's not stroked in, either".

17th - In a 1,000-word press release (enough to fill one-and-a-half pages of this book), Manchester Phoenix confirm that they will not be icing a team in the Elite League in the coming season, though they believe their new 'semi-permanent' rink could be open by "the late autumn". This leaves the league with nine teams. (Phoenix later confirm that the Elite League have left a place open for them in the 2006-07 season.)

26th - Belfast Giants pull out of the Challenge Cup saying they have very little ice-time in February and March due to a big musical show being staged in the Odyssey.

27th - Telford change their nickname from Wild Foxes to Tigers, becoming the third EPL team in the last 12 months to revert to their original name, following Swindon Lynx (now Wildcats) and Solihull Kings (now Barons).

28th - Belfast Giants announce on their website that they have received an injection of Can$1.5 million (about £750,000) from Canadian software businessman, **Jim Yaworski**.

29th - The Elite League announce that nine teams (last season's plus Edinburgh and Newcastle) will begin the 2005-06 season on 9 September in three separate competitions - Challenge Cup, league and playoffs. This finally slams the door on the season for Dundee Stars and Fife Flyers.

JULY

1st - **Bob Wilkinson** takes over as chairman of Ice Hockey UK for a period of two years.

4th - At a meeting in Sheffield of the Work Permit Criteria committee (see under *League Organisation* for the workings of this body) the EL proposed that the criteria be extended to the United Hockey League and the Central Hockey League in North America, and European countries outside the elite group of the World Championships. The proposal could not be considered by Work Permits UK as the league failed to submit any persuasive evidence to support their proposal.

7th - The Ward brothers, owners of the Stars, tell the fans at a meeting in Dundee, that they are continuing to work with other Scottish clubs, including Fife Flyers, to create an enhanced Scottish National League for the coming season.

8th - Belfast Giants admit that they have been unable to agree terms with their former coach, **Dave Whistle**.

19th - **Bob Phillips**, the leaseholder of the Wales National Ice Rink, announces that his company, Arena Sports Ltd, has purchased Sheffield Steelers.

21st - Belfast Giants finally confirm that their new coach will be Canadian **Ed Courtenay**, 37, a player and assistant coach with the ECHL's South Carolina Stingrays. Courtenay played on a line with Tony Hand at Sheffield and Ayr.

22nd - Dundee *Evening Telegraph* reports that Dundee Stars have formally applied to join the Elite League in 2006-07.

28th - Belfast Giants announce that top former NHLer, **Theo Fleury**, has 'agreed to sign' for the team.

AUGUST

5th - **Rick Strachan** is belatedly confirmed in his post as coach of the GB team. The delighted Hull Stingrays' coach says: "Next year we will be. pushing for a medal. Long term our plan has to be to qualify for the 2010 Olympics."

12th - **Gill Short** is made redundant as secretary of Ice Hockey UK and the governing body's office is closed.

13th - Another Elite League club receives overseas backing as former Scottish Eagles' captain, **Angelo Catenaro**, agrees a 'five-figure sponsorship' of Edinburgh Capitals through his Canadian company, Vecture Inc.

REVIEW OF THE YEAR

The Great Ice War

New fans start here

Since the collapse of the professional, import-dominated Superleague in 2003 with heavy debts, the UK's leading clubs have been struggling to find a level at which they can operate profitably and entertainingly.

The three surviving Superleague sides - Belfast Giants, Nottingham Panthers and Sheffield Steelers - set up the Elite League in 2003-04 (against the wishes of the governing body) and persuaded five smaller clubs to join them. When Manchester Phoenix dropped out in 2004, it left seven teams in the league.

The Elite League - run by the club owners independently of the governing body - had a lower wage cap than Superleague's and talked of encouraging home-grown players. However, seven other major teams preferred to continue playing in the British National League (BNL) which had a guideline of 50 per cent of each club's roster being British born and trained.

In the summer of 2005, the owners of the BNL clubs fell out and the league became the second one to collapse in two years. The Elite League accepted Edinburgh Capitals and Newcastle Vipers giving them nine teams for season 2005-06.

The remaining BNL teams went their separate ways: Bracknell Bees (under new ownership), Guildford Flames and Hull Stingrays joined the English Premier League which is designated as a 'development league' and has a strict limit of four non-British trained players (three on the ice at any one time) on each team.

Dundee Stars and Fife Flyers dropped into the amateur Scottish National League.

Meanwhile, Ice Hockey UK (IHUK) came close to financial meltdown - again. The ineffectual governing body became a battleground as the Elite League and the English Ice Hockey Association fought for control of the sport.

Over the next few pages, the editor looks at the upheavals in our governing bodies and major clubs since the start of season 2004-05. There's more details in our Diary of the Season.

ICE HOCKEY UK
Governing on a shoe-string

We'll start at the top, though these days it's not easy to decide just who is in control of our sport.

The governing body, Ice Hockey UK, was handicapped from its birth in 1999 as it inherited most of the debts left by its predecessor, the British Ice Hockey Association (BIHA).

The BIHA had been severely weakened by the Superleague who insisted that it transfer to them the BIHA's rights to sponsorship and TV income. But as the leagues have failed to negotiate very much on either front in recent years, they have taken to renegotiating the fees downwards. This and the collapse of the BNL has left the governing body's finances in a precarious state.

When it was set up, Ice Hockey UK was told by the government-backed UK Sport (which contributes zilch to ice hockey) to allow all ice hockey's various bodies to put a representative on IHUK. Each rep would become a director of the governing body and elect a chairman annually from among themselves.

It takes little imagination to see how this would lead to squabbling, especially as the governing body had handed control of the 'professional' leagues to the clubs.

In the last five years, four men have held the near impossible position of IHUK chairman. The latest is **Bob Wilkinson**, 62, a retired army sergeant-major who took over on 1 July 2005.

Like **Neville Moralee**, his immediate predecessor, Bob is a director of the English Ice Hockey Association. He lives in the Durham area and has been around the sport most of his life; he and his wife, Val, and son, Robert, are all passionate supporters of home-grown talent.

All three have been active in the English junior programme in various capacities, mainly with the England under-16s which Bob helped to form some 20 years ago. Earlier this year he was Ice Hockey UK's IIHF liaison man with the GB under-20s and under-18s at the World Championships.

He told the *Annual* in August: "I said I'd do the job for two years but I know it's going to be really tough. I didn't think we'd last a month when I first took over. We're not destitute but we're not far away. My aim is simple - for us to come out with a profit after my two years."

Among Mr Wilkinson's early tasks was the unpleasant one of having to tell IHUK's long-time secretary, **Gill Short**, that she was redundant, and to close their Nottingham office. "It was costing us £40,000 a year," said Bob. "We just couldn't afford it."

Surprisingly, in view of the past difficult relations between the bodies, Bob agreed to let the Elite League help them find a new office which they will share. "The league said they will pay the rent in lieu of their fee. If it helps to keep our costs down, I have to agree," he said.

The league also agreed to 'loan' their director of hockey, **Andy French**, to help with processing the International Transfer Cards, the documents needed by incoming foreign players.

This co-operation appeared to finally end what little authority the governing body had over the 'independent' league.

THE MERGER
Elite - only if you do as we say

The final efforts to bring about a merger between the Elite League and the British National League were made during season 2004-05.

After the joint meeting of the leagues with the International Ice Hockey Federation in February 2004, which produced the rather messy but well-meaning Crossover Games, there was some hope that this might be achieved.

But the two bodies were poles apart in their approach to the game. The Elite League believe it should be as 'professional' as possible, meaning they want to use players from any nation in the world - as long as they don't cost too much - and they still cling to the belief that arena hockey is viable, despite massive evidence to the contrary, i.e. Superleague.

From the way the 'negotiations' were conducted (See *Diary of the Season*), there was little goodwill towards a merger, either between the leagues or between the bickering BNL clubs.

The EL took full advantage of their rivals' infighting, picking off Edinburgh Capitals and Newcastle Vipers as early as December.

Then with only five BNL teams left, the Elite moved in for the kill.

After a joint meeting before Christmas which appeared to favour a merger of some kind, the EL issued an invite to all the BNL clubs (including Edinburgh and Newcastle), outlining the Elite's apparently non-negotiable terms.

The *Annual* has acquired a copy of this - it runs to three pages - and the subsequent correspondence between the leagues. Briefly, the invitation created a two-tier membership with the BNL clubs playing in a separate 'conference' and having no directors on the EL board for season 2005-06.

Membership was to cost each BNL club six per cent of their net gate money, with a minimum of £15,000, plus another £5,000 towards 'start-up

---

> **WHY THE 'MERGER' DIDN'T WORK**
> *Two quotes from correspondence between the leagues illustrates the gulf dividing them:*
> **Eamon Convery**, *chairman of the Elite League*: "At no stage were we involved in discussions regarding merger of the leagues. We were trying to find a workable solution in dealing with the position of so many clubs wanting to join the Elite League."
> **Tom Muir**, *chairman of the BNL*: "We recognise that some of the existing Elite League clubs will need assistance in building their businesses for a further year. We are in support of such assistance. We would further state that the clubs from [the BNL] would not be, in any way, a financial drain on the new league."

---

costs'. There was no minimum or start-up fee for the existing clubs.

These terms were unacceptable to the BNL. Their chairman, **Tom Muir** of Fife Flyers, replied to **Eamon Convery**, his opposite number, requesting that all members of the merged league be treated equally and that consideration should be given to dividing the 15 teams regionally, into three conferences if necessary.

Mr Convery's response was, to put it crudely, take it or leave it.

After that, the BNL disintegrated. Bracknell Bees, under a new owner, and Hull Stingrays successfully applied to join the English Premier League (EPL).

But Dundee Stars, Fife Flyers and Guildford Flames swallowed their pride and made another application to the Elite, realising that the only alternatives were the limited import EPL - too weak for the wealthy Flames - or oblivion (sorry, the Scottish National League) for the Flyers and Stars. As far as we heard, the applications were never seriously considered.

In July, the Dundee *Evening Telegraph* revealed that the Stars had applied to join the EL for season 2006-07. **Steve Ward**, the club's co-owner, said: "We went back to the Elite League and had various meetings, but we would not join the league and leave Fife and Guildford out in the cold."

ELITE LEAGUE
How long can it last?

On the face of it, the Elite League enjoyed a successful second season. The playoff finals were the most entertaining witnessed by the *Annual* for years, and the crowds at league games went up by seven per cent, the first increase shown by teams in the top flight for four years. But television coverage, sponsorship or any national marketing of the UK-wide league remained as far away as ever.

The cloud over Sheffield Steelers was lifted when **Norton Lea**, reputedly a stingy owner, handed over control of the club to...er, well, that wasn't such good news. The new boss, **Bob Phillips**, already owns one Elite League team, Cardiff Devils, though he likes to deny it.

Belfast Giants were saved from the brink of collapse in the summer for the second time in two years when a Canadian businessman bailed them out with $1.5 million, and Coventry Blaze sold out the Skydome arena for several games.

The Elite's long-running spat with the rival British National League finally ended with the BNL's collapse. Sadly, however, they failed to integrate the seven clubs into their fold to create a truly national league, something for which Ice Hockey UK; the IIHF, the world governing body; and the fans had been begging for ages. Instead, the EL pleaded that ten teams was all their 'business plan' could support and shut their doors after admitting Capitals and Vipers.

The Elite's business plan is simple - to ensure that the biggest clubs have enough games so that they can afford to continue subsidising their weaker brethren.

Manchester Phoenix, the tenth team, never made it back as their 'semi-permanent' rink was not ready in time. (See *New Rinks News*.)

While three of the five remaining BNL clubs moved into the English Premier League, the Elite's closed door policy also meant the virtual closure of two of the sport's most successful clubs - Dundee Stars and the 67-year-old Fife Flyers - who couldn't find an alternative league to play in. Both had to downsize and drop into the amateur Scottish National League.

Despite the expansion, a number of question marks remained over the Elite League's long term survivability. Basingstoke Bison rarely attracted more than 1,000 fans last season, and at Lee Valley London Racers mostly played in front of 500 or so. Bob Phillips' lease on the Wales National Ice Rink was due to run out at the end of the coming season, and the big clubs' agreement to provide financial support to the small ones was going into its last season.

The new owners of Newcastle Vipers would need pockets as deep as an NHL club's and the marketing expertise of *Coca-Cola* if they were to overcome ten years of indifference to ice hockey in the football-mad city.

No one quite knows how Edinburgh, with their tiny crowds, had survived even this far; the league must have signed them with their fingers crossed behind their back.

The league itself carries on its business with one man handling most of the admin. - **Andy French**, who has done many jobs in the sport.

As capable as he is, it seemed a pity that the 'professional' league couldn't afford to give him some help, especially as he spent his 'spare time' helping Ice Hockey UK, the English Premier League and the referees.

On the ice, the league remained heavily dependent on overseas players and ignored the IIHF's guidelines issued last year that they should reduce the number of 'imports' from eleven to ten for season 2005-06. The number of 'goons' employed - players better at fighting than scoring - increased worryingly.

BRITISH NATIONAL LEAGUE
Shameful collapse

If the Elite League's carefree ignoring of the financial facts was frustrating, it was a crying shame that the owners of the British National League clubs failed to work together.

The BNL should have had it made. The league made sense not only in hockey terms with a strict import limit, but also financially with wealthy owners who rarely overspent. But the owners could never seem to agree on the important matters, like the playoff format which changed almost every year, sponsorship and TV. They were reputed to have squabbled over the *Findus* monies and argued over television. Only a couple of BNL games were ever screened.

Formed in 1997 with nine teams including - believe it or not - Blackburn, Paisley and Telford, the league rose to 12 in 2001-02. But only a year later in 2003, with *Findus* on the last year of their three-year deal, Basingstoke Bison, Cardiff Devils and Coventry Blaze went off to help form the Elite League.

Reduced to a barely sustainable seven teams in 2003-04, the league couldn't carry on after Edinburgh and Newcastle deserted for the EL during last season.

The fallout hit Dundee Stars and Fife Flyers, two of the league's stronger members, the hardest. Flyers were a founder member and the BNL's playoff trophy was named the **John Brady** Bowl in honour of their late rink manager who worked hard to create the league.

The two Scottish teams have never had any serious financial problems (Stars were admittedly only formed in 2001), have won numerous trophies (Stars were the BNL's reigning playoff champs) and regularly attracted crowds of around 1,500.

Stuart Robertson, the Scottish IHA's rep on Ice Hockey UK, told Glasgow's *Daily Record*: "I argued long and hard to have Fife and Dundee included [in the Elite League for 2005-06]. I can't understand why the two teams aren't included but there is just so much one can do."

He went on to make the clearest statement yet that the structure of the governing body was unworkable: "Ice Hockey UK is the national governing body and the Elite League have two representatives on it, but the league is a private limited company and they make their own decisions."

In the light of this, perhaps we shouldn't have been surprised when the Elite League duly refused to accept any responsibility for the Scottish teams, instead going on about how two more clubs would upset their 'business model'.

All we can say is it's a pretty strange model if it doesn't allow for the inclusion of two of this small sport's best clubs.

But in truth, the responsibility for Fife and Dundee really lay with the BNL. How could they have thrown it all away and then expected another league, with whom they'd battled for years, to save them?

This will come back and haunt someone soon.

THE ENGLISH ICE HOCKEY ASSOCIATION
The oldest new kids

With the demise of the BNL, the Elite League still trying to establish themselves and Ice Hockey UK fighting to keep control of their financial puck, the English Ice Hockey Association (EIHA) was becoming the sport's most influential body.

Fans of our major clubs might well be excused for asking who is the EIHA? Established in 1982, it is the sport's oldest and largest organising body, with over 250 men's, women's and junior teams. It turned over £380,000 in the year ended 31 December 2004.

Chaired for most of its existence by **Ken Taggart**, a flamboyant and talkative retired USAF master-sergeant who lives in Colorado, the association controls all ice hockey apart from the Elite League, the GB teams and Scotland.

The EIHA has also provided the two most recent chairmen of Ice Hockey UK, **Neville Moralee** and currently **Bob Wilkinson**.

Its most public duty is looking after the English leagues - the English Premier and the English National. And with the expansion of the EPL to include three former BNL sides, it is likely to become a lot more public in future.

A lot busier, too, with 13 teams in what is now ice hockey's second tier. This is going to give Mr Taggart a few headaches, not just because he lives 4,000 miles away but also because he lost his right hand man, **Bill Britton**, who passed away in the summer. (See *Tributes.*)

Ken told the *Annual* that he would be more hands-on with the EPL, with help coming from league secretary, **Rob Laidler**, and that man of many parts, **Andy French**.

Clubs in and out of trouble

BELFAST GIANTS
The luck of the Irish

From their formation in 2000 by the tricky **Bob Zeller**, via a couple of major trophies and a successful spell in Europe, to a chance meeting with a Canadian millionaire in 2005, everything that can happen to a UK ice hockey team seems to have happened to the Belfast Giants.

Did we mention a close shave with the liquidators? Well, the Giants had that, too, a couple of years ago. It seems they were on the brink again at the end of last season when one of their major sponsors, *MG Rover,* had problems of its own. Title sponsor, *Harp* lager, had ended their backing the previous year.

The club's owners **Albert Maasland**, a Canadian banker living in England, and **Jim Gillespie**, a Texas oilman who helped to rescue

> "The missing link for us is having someone to replace *Harp* lager. We are talking to companies but they have to have the same outlook as us." *John Elliott, Giants' general manager.*

the Giants after their near-collapse in 2003, were understood to be unwilling to inject any more funds into the team.

Then In the nick of time, **Jim Yaworski**, a Calgary-based software developer, rode from out of the west and agreed to a three-year deal to put $1.5 million Canadian (roughly £750,000) into the Giants.

A few years back, so the story goes, team captain, **Shane Johnson**, found himself sitting next to 'Jimmy Y' at the back of his plane home. It turned out that Yaworski was a self-confessed hockey nut and was looking to buy a club.

Later, according to the Giants, 'he saw a documentary on Canadian TV which confirmed Belfast as a truly inclusive sporting team'. He remembered his meeting with Johnson and got in touch with the team.

The luck of the Irish, eh?

But there's more. It turned out that Yaworski was best mates with one of Calgary Flames' greatest ever stars, **Theo Fleury**.

The only drawback was that the 5ft 6in Stanley Cup winning forward had suffered bad times with drugs and was barred from playing in the NHL for not co-operating with their 'substance abuse programme'. This delayed approval of his work permit to play here, but he was finally cleared in August and was due to start playing in October.

When he makes it to the Odyssey, the 37-year-old with 455 goals and 1,088 points in 15

NHL seasons - plus another 79 points in the cup - will be the most famous player to skate on our rinks since **Garry Unger**, the former NHL ironman, was here in the mid-Eighties.

BRACKNELL BEES
New owner and new league

John Nike OBE, the wealthy entrepreneur who built the John Nike Leisuresport Complex, home of the Bracknell Bees, sold the club in the summer of 2005 for one pound.

The purchaser was one of the club's sponsors, **David Taylor**, 41, a local estate agent. Though he had only watched his first game in season 2004-05, he had fallen in love with the sport and the Bees at first sight.

Mr Nike, on the other hand, had been falling out of love with the game ever since his fingers were burned financially in the Superleague, which Bees won in 1999-2000.

He was infuriated this season by the Elite League when Bees, the BNL title-holders, were one of the clubs that the league invited to join - on condition that they had no say in running the league. "The terms were so bad," said his right-hand man, **Martin Weddell**, "that we didn't even bother putting them to our lawyers."

With the chance of a united national league receding fast, Mr Nike announced on 11 April that he was selling both the Bees and the Thames Valley basketball club.

He gave his reasons as: "continued escalating costs, both leagues [ice hockey and basketball] being in complete turmoil and the Inland Revenue who continue to pressurise [me] for having supported these two professional sports."

Only three days later Mr Taylor went public with his three-year project for rescuing the Bees, which included retaining **Mike Ellis**, the league-winning coach.

"The plan is to run the team in the English Premier League for two years," he said. "Once we have built up merchandising rights and increased sponsorship and ticket sales, we will look at taking the club into the Elite League in the third year."

He estimated the cost of running the team in the EPL at £150,000.

A few uncertain weeks followed: Mr Taylor firmed up his plans and put in an application for Bees to join the EPL, while **Tom Stewart**, the eccentric former owner of Dundee Rockets, put in a counter-bid for the Bees, and Ellis waited to see if he would be offered the vacant coaching post at Nottingham Panthers.

Finally, on 11 June, Bees were among four clubs accepted into the EPL, including local BNL rivals, Guildford Flames.

A few days later on 17 June Berkshire Sports Marketing Ltd was incorporated with Mr Taylor, his wife, Sharon, and Mike Ellis as directors. Bees' assistant captain, **Ryan Aldridge**, a former GB under-20 international, was appointed as Ellis's assistant with the team.

BSM will operate the Bees under a one-year licence drawn up after negotiations with Mr Nike's company, Arena Leisuresport Promotions.

NEWCASTLE VIPERS
Seven up

Let's see - Whitley Bay's **Francis Smith**, **Sir John Hall**'s Sporting Club, Ice Hockey Superleague, **Harry Harkimo** of Jokerit, the Eye Group and **Darryl Illingworth**.

That means **Paddy O'Connor**, former ice hockey player turned successful businessman who bought Newcastle Vipers in February 2005, is the seventh owner of the team playing out of Newcastle's *Metro Radio* Arena in ten years.

(We will spare readers of a sensitive nature by not adding up all the losses but they must top a million by now.)

The one-time Durham Wasp took over the club, of which he had been a sponsor, when Darryl Illingworth's company was forced into liquidation with debts of well over £100,000. The owner of Newcastle's speedway team, the KBS Vipers, Mr Illingworth bought the hockey team in 2002, originally in partnership with former GB coach, **Alex Dampier**.

Although Vipers twice won the *Findus* Cup and were league runners-up this season, they finished well down the BNL in their first two years and have yet to reach the playoff finals.

This record contributed to an alarming drop in their crowds which fell by a third during Darryl's stewardship, from an average of 1,882 in his first year to 1,260 last season. The arena holds 5,500 for ice hockey.

One of Newcastle's biggest expenses has always been the arena itself for which the owner is understood to have paid a rental of around £4,000 a game in season 2004-05.

It wasn't just the rental and last season's tiny crowds that undermined the team's finances. In

---

ANYWHERE HE SCORES A HAT IS HOME
Whitley Bay native **David Longstaff** scored a hat-trick in 16 minutes on his return to the rink in Newcastle Vipers' first 'home' playoff game.

December, Mr Illingworth admitted that the club had lost £175,000 in his first season. He told the Newcastle *Journal*: "Our first year... crippled us to the extent that we are still struggling with it now. We are making money and all of it is going to pay off the first year's debts."

He made no secret of the fact that it was his wife's love of the game that had kept him involved. It was rumoured that he had to use money from his successful speedway club to keep the hockey team afloat.

The former owner had applied to join the Elite League in November and Paddy O'Connor swiftly endorsed this. (Stories that the league had offered to help the club pay off their debts could not be confirmed.)

The EL were keen to have another big arena team, despite its horrendous history. They welcomed Vipers with open arms in March 2005, giving Paddy their highest honour, a seat on the board. A new company - Newcastle Vipers (North-East) Ltd - was set up to run the team with O'Connor, player and co-coach **Rob Wilson**, and import forward **Paul Ferone** as its directors.

Wilson was in firm denial over the past. "We're an arena-based team and we feel the Elite League is where we should be," he said. "Newcastle is a big city and we feel it can sustain a top flight team."

The first blow hit the club in July when their general manager and bench coach, **Clyde Tuyl**, a former partner of Dampier at Newcastle and Sheffield, quit saying he was 'emotionally drained' after three years at the helm. Wilson agreed to carry on as player-coach with former Jesters' and Cardiff Devils' mentor, **Glenn Mulvenna**, returning from running a bar in Florida to act as bench coach.

O'Connor's recipe for success where so many others have failed was grand but lacked detail: "I have a hockey background and a business background," he said. "This club's not being run by people who don't understand ice hockey from top to bottom. Our goal is to build the club up in the long term, not try to gain financial reward overnight."

We hope seven is your lucky number, Paddy.

SHEFFIELD STEELERS
Two-club Bob
Talking of owners, Steelers' clocked up their fifth when **Bob Phillips**, the man behind Cardiff Devils, bought the 14-year-old team in July 2005.

ICE HOCKEY'S CHANGING ECONOMICS
From an June 2005 interview in the Sheffield Star *with Steelers' home-grown Brit,* **Ryan Lake**, *who had signed for Hull Stingrays in the EPL:*
"My number one choice is still Sheffield. But I have to think of my finances and my future. Last year, I had to ask my mum for money to meet some of the utility bills. I'm 22 in August and I want to be my own person, not dependent on my parents.

"I work in Hull as a golf course co-ordinator and greensman. Stingrays would allow me to continue to work there while making me the best paid British player at the club. I didn't want to get to 30 and have no career outside hockey to go into, so I have to be realistic."

Despite the financial security at his home city, Lake would come back to Sheffield if management could find the right formula. "**Dave Simms** told me once I could have a five-year deal at Sheffield and that was very flattering.

"I accept that playing with three English Premier League imports seems a massive drop from playing with eleven, but at Sheffield I would be playing on a third line with British guys. There are some decent BNL players in the EPL this coming season so it wouldn't be all that different. I'd be playing 10-15 minutes in the Elite League and 40-50 in the EPL.

"It would be helpful, perhaps, if I could board with a family in Sheffield where the utility bills wouldn't be a problem. Or, if training was in the evening, I could work in the day, but Steelers are never going to move their practice times to suit British players.

"If I end up back at Hull I know I wouldn't get noticed as much, it wouldn't be good for playing for Britain, either. But we'll just have to wait and see."

He beat off rivals bids from two consortia - one led by local businessman and fan, **Robin Edwardes**, which included former GB coach **Chris McSorley** and songwriter **Eliot Kennedy**, and another comprising builder **Gary Apsley** and Coventry Blaze director **Mike Cowley** who lives in Sheffield.

Norton Lea, 78, the unpopular former owner, had been trying to sell the sport's most successful club for some months, partly due to his health and his age.

Hated by the fans for his austere ways and lack of marketing, Mr Lea had gained control of Steelers in 2001 after the epic battle for the club in the wake of **Darren Brown**'s bankruptcy. When he sold it to Bob Phillips, the local *Star* newspaper reported that he received the asking price of £300,000.

Mr Phillips bought the club, which has an annual turnover of £500,000, through his company Arena Sports Ltd, which includes former Devils' and GB defender **Shannon Hope**.

While Steelers were delighted to have the uncertainty over the club's future lifted, there was some controversy over Bob Phillips controlling two teams in the same league.

He brushed this aside in an interview with the Sheffield *Star*, insisting he did not own the Devils. The 53-year-old Welsh businessman explained: "I own Cardiff's rink lease, let Devils play there free and give them £100,000 a year from the takings. When Cardiff play Sheffield, I'll be cringeing, cringeing with both sets of supporters and sponsors."

He could have added that there is nothing in the league's rules to bar one man owning two clubs, though as these have never been published, we cannot be certain.

We can be pretty certain, though, that Mr Phillips is hedging his bets against the possibility that the Devils will have no rink at the end of the coming season. (See *New Rinks News*.)

One snag that will have needed sorting out is the matter of who owns the Steelers' name and logo. According to Bob Phillips, the name is owned by Mike Cowley and Gary Apsley who are asking £150,000 for it. "We will resolve this one way or another," he insisted.

■ **Rob Stewart**'s team struggled at the box office (their league crowds were down by seven per cent) and in the league where they finished fifth, their lowest for six years.

But across the road in iceSheffield, the Scimitars were burning up UK ice hockey's fourth tier, the English National League. In their second season in the two-pad complex, their first under player-coach **Neil Abel**, a former Steeler, Scimitars won the grand slam of league (north), national playoffs and cup. (More details under *English Leagues*.)

In June they 'won promotion' to the now second tier English Premier League when their application was accepted by the English IHA, and signed ex-GB defenceman, **Brent Pope**.

Discipline

The most celebrated case of the rough stuff in season 2004-05 involved one of the Elite League's imported 'goons', a story which was reported on both sides of the Atlantic.

It was an important one on several levels as we will analyse after you've read what happened. Our first report comes from the officials' own website, HockeyRefs.com.

Ref assaulted by NHLer

28 March 2005, London, UK - London Racers' import **Eric Cairns** has shamed himself for attacking a referee in the British Elite Ice Hockey League (EIHL). Cairns, 30, has been playing for London in the UK's top level league during the ongoing NHL lockout. The incident occurred [on 23 March] during a playoff game [in Coventry] against the Coventry Blaze.

Referee **Andy Carson** whistled Cairns - who has 1,053 penalty minutes in 406 NHL games - for a slashing minor less than five minutes into the game. While en route to the penalty box, the role player [we like that - ed.] verbally abused Carson. The verbal displeasure quickly escalated to Cairns physically assaulting the veteran zebra. Carson was slashed once in the legs and once on the hands.

Cairns then refused to leave the ice, despite pressure from teammates and linesmen **Andrew Dalton** and **Tom Darnell** - and proceeded to initiate a bench clearing fight that included a tilt with Blaze's NHLer **Wade Belak**.

Carson handed Cairns a match penalty, which resulted in an automatic one-game suspension. A further suspension is likely, as the EIHL disciplinary committee will review the incident.

Coventry won the game, 5-2.

The Coventry Evening Telegraph *reported* - 'In the first period a bench clearing brawl saw Cairns and Blaze coach **Paul Thompson** ejected from the game. Pursuing referee **Andy Carson** around the ice - an act sure to earn him a big ban - he was given a match penalty and was being escorted off the ice by three of his team-mates when he lunged at **Andre Payette** on the Blaze bench. That prompted a bench clearance, with **Wade Belak** taking on Cairns in a heavyweight bout at centre ice.'

*Cairns' boss **Roger Black**, defended his player in the* Toronto Sun - "Unfortunately, the refs are not of a sufficient standard over here. Basically, they lose control of games. The players see that hand come up too many times to call a penalty and they get frustrated."

The Annual *comments* - The first and most obvious question is why do the Elite League bring in players like Eric Cairns. The answer is that they treat the game as 'entertainment' first and a 'sport' second. This is a hangover from the discredited Superleague with which we disagree; the game seems entertaining enough to us without sexing it up.

Leaving that aside, however, even if you take the league's view that the game is simply WWF on ice, then surely it makes sense for the refs to be trained to deal with such situations. We're sure it isn't in any training manual read by Andy 'veteran zebra' Carson who, we will add as no

Above: Cardiff Devils' fans protest against the imminent closure of the Wales National Ice Rink; *below, right:* locked out NHL defenceman, **ERIC CAIRNS**, London Racers' enforcer, who was hit with a long suspension during the Elite League playoffs.

Photos: Diane Davey, Dave Page

one else will, has served British ice hockey loyally and well for a number of years.

The league's second omission was failing to make a firm and clear public statement about Cairns' punishment, probably adding the rider (albeit tongue-in-cheek) that it would not be tolerated in future. Instead, not a peep.

For the record, Cairns was suspended from all games played under IIHF auspices for the rest of the season and all of season 2005-06. As he is contracted to play in the NHL, who are not IIHF members, this was scarcely any punishment at all for an offence of this severity.

At the end of the season, the 6ft, 6in defenceman returned to the NHL's Florida Panthers for whom he had signed before the lockout in July 2004.

Third is Roger Black's statement. Slagging off your officials, your league and, by extension, UK ice hockey in one of Canada's most widely read newspapers deserves nothing but contempt. Still, maybe you were misquoted, Rog.

Television

Not much on the box this year

This was not a vintage year for our sport on television. What little ice hockey was broadcast went out on *Sky Sports* and *NASN*, the North American Sports Network. Both channels are pay-TV.

Sky Sports screened the Elite League playoff finals weekend and one EPL game. With the NHL closed down for the entire campaign, NASN was reduced to screening a few games from the American Hockey League (AHL), but they treated us to the first showing for several years of the World Championships (elite pool, sadly, not GB).

The Elite League's playoff games were broadcast in a one-hour highlights show on *Sky Sports* on the Tuesday and Wednesday evenings following the games. Veteran hockey broadcasters **Paul Ferguson** (play-by-play) and **Richard Boprey** (colour) - both former players - were the commentators.

This was the second year in a row that *Sky* had shown the finals and it must have been reasonably successful because the TV boys sat down to talk turkey about showing regular EL games in season 2005-06. More on this in a moment.

At the end of October, Slough Jets' EPL game at home to Romford Raiders was shown on *Sky Sports Extra.* We missed this but we understand that the game was entertainingly produced, presumably on similar lines to the one shown two years ago.

The AHL games on NASN were so few and far between that we never did catch one. The channel told us they had tied up a two-year deal with the league to screen up to 80 games, including the Calder Cup playoffs, but most of the stations from which they expected to get a satellite feed (MSG, Rogers SportsNet, etc.) didn't show the games, after all.

When you think of it, one of the main reasons for the NHL's troubles was the lack of TV coverage. So why would a minor league game be more attractive on the box?

NASN also broadcast one or two games each week from the NCAA (USA college league) but unfortunately for British fans, these came in the season after GB international **Colin Shields** had left the University of Maine.

Plug: As you can see from our advert for the channel elsewhere in the *Annual*, NASN are contracted to show the NHL again in season 2005-06. For details, go to www.nasn.com.

NASN's 'live and exclusive' coverage of the World Championships in Austria was taken from the Canadian channel, CBC. Consequently, it was concerned mostly with the Canadian team's games. Bit of a bummer for them when the Czechs won.

Finally, we thought you should see this message from an obviously well-connected poster on www.thehockeyforum.com, the UK's ice hockey internet chat-room. Posted on 20 May 2005, it refers to the negotiations between the Elite League and *Sky Sports* for coverage of the league in season 2005-06. Some of the comments have been edited.

'As the person who sat in on the meeting with **Sue Ashworth**, the acquisitions and corporate management editor at *Sky Sports*, I can categorically state that she said (and I quote): "One of our main requirements is that we need a minimum of ten Elite teams to provide the variety that our viewers would expect."

'As it stands at the moment, the league are attempting to sort out sponsorship funding as they have to pay for [*Sky*'s coverage] or it's a no-go.

'It's quite a complicated deal compared to the usual TV ... deals, but the gist is that the league have to pay most of the production costs for the first year. ....There has been very little progress because certain owners ... would prefer that this sponsorship went direct to individual clubs.

'To make TV a viable project, we need a minimum of £240,000 to pay for production costs (approximately £8,000 to £10,000 per programme multiplied by 30 programmes). Even at that figure, it's still heavily subsidised by the production company. ➢ *page 42*

Book Reviews

DOUG MCEWEN
The Magnificent Number Seven

To his many accolades as one of the most skilful and popular imports to play in this country, **Doug McEwen** can add the rare honour of having a book written about him.

That is not the only unique event in the life of this colourful Canadian with Scots, Irish and Objiwa Indian ancestry who was raised in a uranium mining boom town and went on to play ice hockey for his adopted country against his native one.

Ian McFarlane, a one-time director of Peterborough Pirates for whom Dougie played his first season here in 1986-87, has produced a fine portrait of the forward who was voted Player of the Year by Pirates - and then sacked, a decision McFarlane describes as 'the single biggest man-management boob in the club's history'.

McEwen has recently scored his 1,000th goal after 19 seasons in Britain with four different teams, most successfully with Cardiff Devils. It was Devils' player-coach, **John Lawless**, who first brought him to this country and he helped the team win numerous trophies in the Nineties.

Doug was on the GB team that won promotion to the World A Pool in 1993 and played against his native Canada and Russia in 1994. He scored once in Italy and had a goal disallowed that an unofficial replay later showed was legal.

Written in the first person, this is an entertaining book which does full justice to its subject. A must have for every ice hockey fan.

Copies are available from Doug McEwen, 32 Swift Close, Deeping St James, Peterborough PE6 8QR, price £10 plus £2.50 post and packing.

THE DOUG McEWEN STORY

HOCKEY IN THE MOVIES
Hollywood On Ice

Did you know that Cardiff Devils' enforcer, **Mike McWilliam**, appeared in the movie *Miracle on Ice*? This and numerous other intriguing behind-the-scenes stories of ice hockey and the movies, including the all-time classic, *Slap Shot*, are in this latest book by veteran sports journalist, **Phil Drackett**, a former netminder and writer and editor with *Ice Hockey World*. With many rare photos and a complete filmography, this is a true collectors' item.

Copies are available, price £6 including p&p, from The Ice Hockey Annual.

FED UP FANS FORM LOBBY GROUP

Weary of the infighting and uncertainty in British ice hockey, a group of fans got together in the summer of 2005 and formed the Ice Hockey Supporters Association UK (IHSAUK).

The fans, led by **Rob Hitchen**, a former Manchester Storm supporter, were particularly moved by the plight of Fife Flyers and Dundee Stars who were left without a league to play in when the British National League collapsed.

According to their website, www.icefans.co.uk, the association's aim is 'to give all fans a voice that will communicate directly with the sport's owners and governing body'.

Anyone wishing to join the association should e-mail Mr Hitchen at ihsauk@learnedrobb.co.uk.

A more realistic figure would be £20,000 per programme - i.e. £600,000.

'The irony is that in the Superleague days *Sky Sports* funded the TV coverage in full. Then the league decided that they'd get a better deal if they went to another broadcaster. [*Channel Four* and a comic, as we recall - ed.]

'The conditions of this new deal are in effect so that the Elite League prove themselves to *Sky*. They don't want another Superleague debacle. They also don't want clubs going under financially halfway through the season so that they don't have ten teams to show on TV.'

This has a horrible ring of truth, doesn't it? We can only add that as the league hasn't got ten teams, this is all academic, anyway. But it also begs another question. Why didn't the league try harder to add a tenth team? And don't say Manchester. That was always a long-shot.
▪ The internet continued to be the Elite League's medium of choice. In December 2004 they announced that one game each week would be broadcast live on internet radio. Starting with BBC Radio Sheffield and Steelers' home games, the league hoped to extend this to broadcasts from all their clubs' local BBC radio stations.

The 85th Varsity Match

Oxford University avenged last year's defeat in the Varsity Match by trouncing old rivals, Cambridge University, 6-1 at Milton Keynes on 6 March 2005.

The Dark Blues took control of this latest battle for the Patton Cup during the second period with unanswered goals from **Kyle Hickey**, **Gregoire Webber**, **Ryan Topping** and **Daniel Koldyk**.

Andreas Rauschecker had opened Oxford's tally after 15 minutes and man of the match,

Noah Honch, scored in the dying seconds. Oxford outshot Cambridge 53-22.

Cambridge's lone goal came at the start of the last session from **John Kedrowski** who took the Cawthra Cup as their best player. **Jakob Schultz** won the Pearson Cup as Oxford's player of the game.

This was the 85th game in the series which dates back to 1900, the longest running rivalry in European ice hockey. Oxford, the Dark Blues, have now won 56 games to the Light Blues 27. Two games have been drawn.

We are indebted to the Oxford captain, **Lalit Aggarwal**, for sending us details of the match.
▪ The Patton Cup was donated by **Major B M (Peter) Patton**, one of the early pioneers of hockey in this country, who is a member of both the British and IIHF Halls of Fame.

Overseas visitors

NHL TOURISTS

Hockey Stars for Hope, a team of fringe NHLers who play for charity, toured the UK and Europe at the beginning and end of season 2004-05.

Playing six games in seven days in September, the British leg took HSH to Fife (8th), Sheffield (9th) and Lee Valley (10th). The 15-strong side included veteran Canadian NHLer **John Chabot**, 42, who has played for many years in Germany.

The team returned in May to play five more games, this time at Dundee (5th), Cardiff (7th), Coventry (8th), Sheffield again (9th) and Nottingham (10th). HSH included Vancouver Canucks' hard man **Brad May**, and **Sebastien Charpentier**, a Washington Capitals' goalie.

With the games being played as strictly non-contact, the organisers were able to select several home-grown British players, senior and junior, to play on the opposing teams. Part of the proceeds from the games were donated to British clubs.

SUNY CANTON

A team of university players from the State University of New York (Canton) played two games in England - the Cardiff under-19 side on 5 January and Oxford City Stars on 13 January.

MORE QUOTES

The tragedy of Fife and Dundee

"There's a .... number of reasons, but basically the existing clubs were concerned over the number of games. It would have had implications on the derbies that teams such as Nottingham and Sheffield have had going over the past few seasons. There would also be an additional cost involved in supporting a further three teams. Each team would need to facilitate a further three home and away matches into the fixture schedule. The sheer logistics wouldn't have worked." *Eamon Convery, chairman of the Elite League, explaining why the league's board turned down applications from BNL teams, Dundee Stars, Fife Flyers and Guildford Flames.*

"It's a disgraceful situation that three of the strongest and most stable teams in British hockey are struggling to find a league, while teams far less stable seem to be embraced into the Elite League." *Mike Pack, owner of Hull Stingrays, commenting on the rejection of his fellow clubs.*

"I've 27 years' experience and I'm convinced I'm right - a 12, 13 or 15-team league will kill British ice hockey. I'm not opposed to bringing everyone under one umbrella, but it will not work as one league. It's lunacy. It's pandering to the needs of the lowest." *Dave Simms, Sheffield Steelers' spokesman, on 14 December.*

"If Dave Simms is so smart why not own a team? I'm sick of him shooting his mouth off. If we kept all the little teams out of ice hockey there'd only be three sides in the whole country. Without the little teams there would be no league." *Rick Strachan, Hull Stingrays' coach, 15 December.*

"We have the fan base, good facilities and a history of recruiting players of the highest quality. The only issue was with Plexiglas which would have been rectified over the summer. The Elite League had an opportunity to secure a long term future not only for themselves but for British ice hockey as a whole." *Stuart Scott, Fife Flyers' spokesman.*

"We would not vote for anything that would take the league over ten teams. Once we go to eleven, there would be only two home games against our derby rivals [Nottingham Panthers], who are big draws, but with ten teams we could have three." *Simms again.*

"How can they [the Elite League] say no to a team that is probably more financially secure than most in this country? What's happening is an insult to the game and to the people who have put their lives into the game, played and been in the game as a family tradition. They will kill the game in Scotland. Fife and Dundee need top level hockey for kids to watch so that they can then aspire to play at that level." *Mark Morrison, Fife Flyers' player-coach.*

'The EPL consists of 13 teams, a massive increase in opponent variety compared to the past couple of seasons, [and] very welcome news in terms of competition. [Flames will compete] against clubs who are geographically better placed than many of their opponents of the past several seasons.' *Press release from the more fortunate Guildford Flames who were able to join the English Premier League.*

The Elite League's finances

"The way things stand at the moment it is not possible to play in the Elite League without a major sponsor who is prepared to lose £500,000 a year. And if you have just one backer like the Bees ... did last year then you are totally at the whim of that person or company and the whole house of cards can come crashing down." *David Taylor, the new owner of Bracknell Bees.*

"The model in Lee Valley seems to be that you can agree a high expenditure regardless of income, build a totally irrational image, and if it doesn't get the results on the ice spend some more money until it does." *Mike Pack again, responding to his fellow BNL club owners regarding the Elite League's terms for joining the league. The EL subsidises its smaller teams.*

"Our move into the Elite League means we'll have to ice three lines which opens the door for local talent. We're allowed 11 imports but I don't know if I'll use all my quota. The budget for the Elite League is the same as the BNL - about £5,000 a week - but we were nowhere near that last season and I aim to run a tight ship again." *Scott Neil, boss of Edinburgh Capitals, waxing optimistic about their chances in the top league. [Ed's note: the Elite League's wage cap in season 2004-05 was supposed to be about £7,000 a week, though the league has not published a figure. Capitals finished last in the BNL and in the Crossover Games.]*

Newcastle Vipers

"It's a creditors' meeting. Nothing to be worried about." *Darryl Illingworth, boss of the BNL's Newcastle Vipers.*

"Paddy [O'Connor] is a top class guy and has turned into a diligent and astute businessman. If any man can make Newcastle viable, it is he." *Dave Simms on the new owner who decided to take the bankrupt team into the Elite League.*

Selling the Elite League

"We are confident that hockey fans around the UK will not be disappointed when they hear the news. On the contrary, we are confident that the news will genuinely excite people about the particular direction the league is taking in its efforts to grow the sport in this country." *Eamon Convery, in a release asking the media 'to reserve space for the imminent announcement of a major new initiative'. TV coverage? Merger of leagues? Major sponsorship? No. An internet link for the league to the website, nhl.com.*

"... the biggest signing in British hockey history since the Thirties and Forties." *Roger Black, London Racers' owner, describing his signing of locked-out NHLer Scott Nichol, overlooking the likes of Garry Unger, Mike Blaisdell, Doug Smail, etc., etc.*

'The Racers' season is set to take flight this Friday [17 September] and expect fists to fly. The Basingstoke Bison and their mammoth new forward **Jeff (Shrek) Ewasko** will be at Lee Valley Ice Centre when the puck drops at 8 p.m. Racers' tough guy **Jeremy Cornish** is sure to take this opportunity to drop his gloves for the first time at the Bike Shed and take on the monster Bison.' *Promo. for London Racers' opening game. For once, it wasn't more bull from Rog. Both players duly fought each other.*

'I'd just popped home for lunch, when the phone rang. It was **Mark Bernard** wishing me and the family a happy Christmas from the Bison. Now that's what I call good customer relations.' *Basingstoke season ticket-holder.*

'Prayers Answered – Steelers Sign a Christian. 'Sheffield Steelers have signed former NHLer **Jeff Christian**, and coach **Rob Stewart** is delighted. "This is the Man we have been waiting for," he said. "We said our prayers and a Christian has come to us..."' *Steelers' press release.*

'*Thomson* Cardiff Devils took a skeleton team of just ten senior squad members to London to play a game where neither side could gain. Both the Devils and the Racers have secured their playoff positions and didn't want to risk any more injuries. London dropped their NHL stars for the night and Devils left behind **Jon Cullen, Jason Becker** and **Warren Tait** plus injured **Dave Matsos** and **Jonathan Phillips**. They took with them some of their English National League squad including **Jamie Dancey** and **Steve Fisher**, ...**Mike Brabon** taking his place between the pipes.' *Cardiff Devils' press release after their 'game' in Lee Valley on 8 March. Devils lost 5-2.*

"What the people running this sport (I use the term loosely) seem to do best is make the fans lose their enthusiasm for it." *London Racers' fan.*

The playoffs

"I didn't watch when **Ashley [Tait]** went clear. I turned away, shut my eyes and crossed my fingers and my legs. As I turned, **Andre Payette** turned to face me. The next thing I knew, someone was trying to break my back. It was Payette giving me a bear hug, and I could tell that we'd won! *Paul Thompson, after the Elite League playoff final.*

"It's the stupidest idea I've heard of. Why don't we have a skills competition - or even a beer-drinking competition?" *Dion Darling, Sheffield Steelers, giving the media his carefully considered opinion on the third place playoff after Steelers lost their semi-final.*

'In my opinion, the best and most consistent team is the one that wins the league. The team that wins the playoffs has done well over a short space of time but might not be the best team over a season. I don't like the playoffs. Never have, never will. Yes, they're exciting, so are league games, so are cup games.

'One thing I hate even more is teams that plan only for the playoffs and use the league as a warm-up. That robs the fans of the competitive games they deserve, being loyal enough to buy a season ticket.' *A fan on the web. Playoff crowds were down last season by between 16 and 30 per cent.*

English Introverts Association

'Please note that there are deliberately no contact e-mail addresses for EIHA directors, other EIHA officials or any clubs on this site. All contact should be done via the official club contact at your local rink as they have all the necessary contact information.

'NOTE: There is no point requesting the contact details from **Malcolm Preen** [webmaster], as due to the Data Protection Act he is unable to supply that information.' *Notice on the home page of www.eiha.co.uk, the website of the English Ice Hockey Association , the largest body in UK ice hockey.*

Major Teams 2004-05

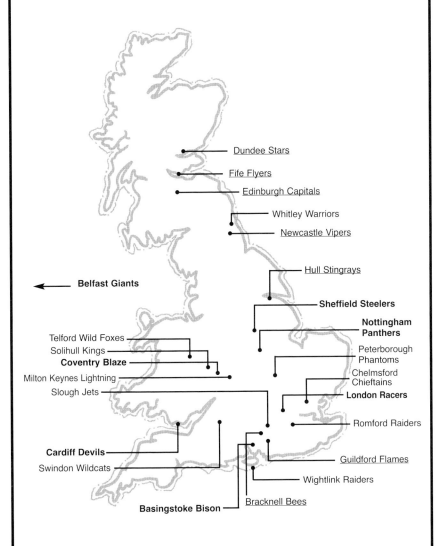

Dundee Stars

Fife Flyers

Edinburgh Capitals

Whitley Warriors

Newcastle Vipers

Hull Stingrays

Belfast Giants

Sheffield Steelers

Nottingham Panthers

Telford Wild Foxes

Solihull Kings

Coventry Blaze

Milton Keynes Lightning

Slough Jets

Peterborough Phantoms

Chelmsford Chieftains

London Racers

Romford Raiders

Cardiff Devils

Swindon Wildcats

Guildford Flames

Wightlink Raiders

Bracknell Bees

Basingstoke Bison

Elite League   British National League   English/Scottish Leagues

BASINGSTOKE BISON

PLAYER	ALL COMPETITIONS					ELITE LEAGUE				
Scorers	GP	G	A	Pts	Pim	GP	G	A	Pts	Pim
Shawn Maltby (I)	47	22	37	59	60	47	22	37	59	60
Doug Sheppard (I)	50	27	30	57	28	50	27	30	57	28
Mike Ford (I)	50	19	27	46	56	50	19	27	46	56
Jeff Ewasko (I)	45	7	15	22	130	45	7	15	22	130
Duncan Dalmao (I)	35	9	12	21	28	35	9	12	21	28
Jerry Galway (I)	50	6	14	20	38	50	6	14	20	38
Steve Gallace 6	18	7	8	15	6	18	7	8	15	6
Jason Norrie (I)	18	5	8	13	70	18	5	8	13	70
Tony Redmond	42	2	11	13	20	42	2	11	13	20
Owen Walter (I)	48	2	10	12	88	48	2	10	12	88
Brent Pope 5	30	1	7	8	56	30	1	7	8	56
Shaun Thompson	46	3	3	6	10	46	3	3	6	10
Jeff Corey (I)	19	2	4	6	10	19	2	4	6	10
Pavol Reiciciar 4	13	3	1	4	0	13	3	1	4	0
Jozef Lukac (I) 7	30	3	1	4	22	30	3	1	4	22
Steve Ellis (I)	17	1	3	4	6	17	1	3	4	6
Ricky Skene	49	1	2	3	38	49	1	2	3	38
Michael Wales 3	3	2	0	2	18	3	2	0	2	18
Lewis Buckman 2	22	2	0	2	6	22	2	0	2	6
Greg Wood	30	2	0	2	2	30	2	0	2	2
Dominic Hopkins 1	14	1	1	2	2	14	1	1	2	2
Adam Hyman	9	1	0	1	0	9	1	0	1	0
Ronnie Vogel (N) (I)	50	0	1	1	20	50	0	1	1	20
Jimmy Day	1	0	0	0	2	1	0	0	0	2
Richard Hardy	2	0	0	0	25	2	0	0	0	25
Shane Moore	9	0	0	0	8	9	0	0	0	8
Dean Phillimore	10	0	0	0	4	10	0	0	0	4
Dean Skinns (N)	49	0	0	0	2	49	0	0	0	2
Bench Penalties					72					72
TEAM TOTALS	50	128	195	323	827	50	128	195	323	827
Netminders	GPI	Mins	SOG	GA	Sv%	GPI	Mins	SOG	GA	Sv%
Ronnie Vogel (I)	49	2788	1626	155	90.5	49	2788	1626	155	90.5
Dean Skinns	8	242	138	16	88.4	8	242	138	16	88.4
Empty Net Goals			7	7				7	7	
TEAM TOTALS	50	3030	1771	178	89.9	50	3030	1771	178	89.9

Also appeared: Brian Worrall, Ryan Wyatt, Greg Randall 3, Ashley Skinns 1.

Also played for: 1 Wightlink Raiders; 2 Milton Keynes Lightning, .
Nottingham Panthers, Peterborough Phantoms;
3 Milton Keynes Lightning; 4 Peterborough Phantoms;
5 London Racers, Peterborough Phantoms; 6 Newcastle Vipers;
7 Coventry Blaze.

Shutouts: Vogel - league: 9 Oct at Belfast Giants (24 saves).

League, Challenge Cup and Crossover Games

BASINGSTOKE BISON *left to right, back row:* Tony Skinns (equipment), Jerry Galway, Jeff Corey, Owen Walter, Mike Ford, Jeff Ewasko, Dominic Hopkins, Josef Lucak, Steve Ellis, Ricky Skene, Doug Sheppard, Alan Parrott (equipment); *front row:* Ron Vogel, Lewis Buckman, Duncan Dalmao, Mark Bernard (coach), Shawn Maltby, Tony Redmond, Shaun Thompson, Dean Skinns.

Photo: David Taylor

One-liners

GRAHAM MERRY

Once again it was all change in the Bison Herd as **Mark Bernard**, a former Superleague goalie at Bracknell and Manchester Storm, took over as general manager and head coach. Of the previous season's players, only British teenagers **Dean Skinns** and **Shaun Thompson** returned.

Bernard, fresh from coaching in America's United League, recruited 6ft 7in Canadian **Jeff Ewasko**, the tallest player to wear a Basingstoke jersey, and their first Slovakian, defenceman **Jozef Lukac**. Both were new to this country, as were seven others of the 11 Bison imports.

However, Scottish forward **Tony Redmond** returned from Guildford for a ninth year and during the season set a new record for the most league appearances for the club.

The season started brightly with a draw against eventual Elite League champions Coventry, but, as in 2003-04, Bison suffered from firing on only one line offensively.

That was the impressive Canadian trio of **Shawn Maltby, Doug Sheppard** and **Mike Ford** who produced the goals all season.

With results not going their way Bernard released Canadian **Steve Ellis** and Brit **Dominic Hopkins**, and a week later there was an injury crisis as five top players were ruled out.

Ironically, with a makeshift side they drew 3-3 with Belfast but that was one of the few high spots before Christmas.

Canadian **Jeff Corey** was forced out for the season with a knee injury just when he was running into form. **Brent Pope** joined on a trial basis but his partnership with **Duncan Dalmao** worked so well that once everyone was fit, it was Lukac who was released and sent to Coventry.

Meanwhile Slovakian **Pavol Rieciciar** had replaced Ellis but he was not the answer, even if Bison never lost when he scored.

The arrival of **Steve Gallace** from Newcastle and **Jason Norrie** from North America in the first week of January made an immediate impact as the Herd upset Panthers 5-3 in Nottingham.

At last the squad were firing on two lines and they ended the campaign with nine wins and one overtime loss in their last 18 games, after having secured only six victories from their previous 32 outings. But the damage was already done and the most unwanted statistic from the season was a new club record of eight league shutouts.

On the plus side, Bernard proved to be a breath of fresh air, attracting many new sponsors. Most supporters ended the season smiling even though their team finished bottom of the league and failed to make the playoffs.

PLAYER AWARDS

Players' Player	Shawn Maltby
Most Valuable Player	Doug Sheppard
Coach's Player	Shawn Maltby
Captain's Player	Doug Sheppard
Best British Player	Tony Redmond

LEADING PLAYERS

Shawn Maltby *born 22 July 1976*

The Cambridge, Ontario born captain was the team's top points scorer and formed a lethal partnership with fellow Canadian **Doug Sheppard**, his senior by just three days. Showed fine leadership qualities on and off the ice. Younger brother of Detroit Redwing **Kirk Maltby**.

Doug Sheppard *born 19 July 1976*

In his first year in Britain like his linemate Maltby, the native of Georgetown, Ontario was the Herd's leading goal scorer. Finding the net was not his only attribute as he was also a solid all-round player.

MOST PROMISING PLAYER

Shaun Thompson *born 13 July 1987*

The teenage forward from Slough was given a regular spot on the third line and did not disappoint. He was called up to play for Great Britain's under-18 and under-20 teams.

FACT FILE 2004-05

Elite League:	Seventh
Playoffs:	Did not qualify
Challenge Cup:	Third in group

HISTORY

Founded 1988 as Beavers. Name changed to Bison in May 1995.

Leagues Elite League 2003-05; British National League 1998-2003; Superleague 1996-98; British League, Premier Div 1993-96; British League, Div One 1990-93; English League 1988-90.

Honours: British League, Div One & playoffs 1992-93; English League (promotion) playoffs 1989-90. *Benson and Hedges* Plate 1999-2000 & 2000-01.

BELFAST GIANTS

PLAYER	ALL COMPETITIONS					ELITE LEAGUE					PLAYOFFS				
Scorers	GP	G	A	Pts	Pim	GP	G	A	Pts	Pim	GP	G	A	Pts	Pim
Tony Hand	58	19	55	74	94	50	19	49	68	60	8	0	6	6	34
George Awada (I)	58	34	27	61	54	50	32	23	55	40	8	2	4	6	14
Curtis Huppe (I)	56	27	32	59	48	48	24	30	54	42	8	3	2	5	6
Curtis Bowen (I)	58	26	29	55	80	50	24	26	50	70	8	2	3	5	10
Fredrik Nasvall (I)	58	26	28	54	86	50	23	25	48	56	8	3	3	6	30
Shane Johnson	53	16	23	39	73	46	14	23	37	57	7	2	0	2	16
Todd Kelman (I)	46	9	16	25	12	38	9	14	23	10	8	0	2	2	2
Diarmuid Kelly (I)	57	3	16	19	42	49	3	16	19	40	8	0	0	0	2
Marc Levers	56	10	8	18	46	48	10	8	18	46	8	0	0	0	0
Jason Bowen (I)	58	5	13	18	94	50	3	12	15	76	8	2	1	3	18
Mel Angelstad (I)	57	3	10	13	295	49	3	9	12	253	8	0	1	1	42
Roman Gavalier (I)	55	3	8	11	36	47	3	6	9	36	8	0	2	2	0
Mark Morrison	58	3	4	7	8	50	3	4	7	8	8	0	0	0	0
Leigh Jamieson	53	0	5	5	32	45	0	5	5	32	8	0	0	0	0
Graeme Walton	58	0	5	5	10	50	0	5	5	10	8	0	0	0	0
Martin Klempa (N) (I)	57	0	0	0	25	49	0	0	0	25	8	0	0	0	0
Bench Penalties					6					6					0
TEAM TOTALS	58	184	279	463	1,041	50	170	255	425	867	8	14	24	38	174
Netminders	GPI	Mins	SOG	GA	Sv%	GPI	Mins	SOG	GA	Sv%	GPI	Mins	SOG	GA	Sv%
Martin Klempa (I)	55	3260	1420	115	91.9	47	2810	1206	92	92.4	8	450	214	23	89.3
Chris McGimpsey	8	275	124	12	90.3	7	245	117	9	92.3	1	30	7	3	57.1
Empty Net Goals			4	4				3	3				1	1	
TEAM TOTALS	58	3535	1548	131	91.8	50	3055	1326	104	92.4	8	480	222	27	88.2

Also appeared: Hugh Smyth (N).

Shutouts: Klempa (7) - league: 11 Sep at Sheffield Steelers (23 saves), 25 Sept v London Racers (22), 2 Oct v Coventry Blaze (30), 30 Oct v Dundee Stars (23), 3 Dec at London Racers (18), 17 Dec v Hull Stingrays (13), *11 Feb v Basingstoke Bison (18); McGimpsey (2) - league: 14 Jan v Basingstoke Bison (21 saves), □ *11 Feb v Basingstoke Bison (5).
  * shared shutout

All Competitions = league and playoffs
Elite League includes Challenge Cup and Crossover Games

Klempa closes 'em down

MICHELLE CARSON

"It's going to go right down to the wire," said Giants' new player-coach, **Tony Hand**, at the start of the Elite League season. And, boy, was he right.

It was a roller-coaster of a ride for the Giants as the Scotsman led them to the runners-up place, only six points adrift of champions Coventry after 50 games.

Giants gave early notice that they would be a force to be reckoned with. Starting on the road against the defending titleists, Sheffield Steelers, and Coventry Blaze, Steelers' eventual successors, Giants enjoyed a whitewash in Sheffield Arena - **Martin Klempa** had the first of his seven shutouts - and took a point in the Skydome.

Fast forward to their first home game and the Belfast side were on winning form again, Klempa pulling off some incredible saves for his second shutout, this time a 5-0 result over London Racers.

Hand's new signings, **George Awada**, the former Manchester forward, and **Curtis Huppe**, became were one of the league's most powerful offensive duos and ended the season with a grand total of 61 goals between them.

As the season continued, Giants remained on top form, leading the league, and in their first Crossover Game in the Odyssey, local netminder, **Chris McGimpsey**, narrowly missed getting his own shutout in a 6-1 defeat of Edinburgh Capitals.

But for **Todd Kelman**, one of only three original Giants left on the squad (**Jason** and **Curt Bowen** were the others), it was a season of injuries, the first a broken bone in his foot and then a serious facial injury when he was caught by an opponent's high stick.

Into the New Year and the team were tied for top spot in both the league and the Crossover Games. In March they duly won the Crossover title, **Roman Gavalier** bagging the winning goal in overtime against the Guildford Flames in front of a packed Odyssey crowd. Sadly, though, no silverware was on offer.

Belfast battled hard for the title for the remainder of the season, but it was not to be.

In a difficult start to the Playoffs, the Giants managed to pick up only one point in their first three games. Amazingly, and to Hand's and his team's immense frustration, the schedule called for them to play their next five games within a week. Unsurprisingly, they fared poorly, picking up only two more points and failing to reach the Final Four weekend.

PLAYER AWARDS

Player's Player	**Martin Klempa**
Coach's Player	**George Awada**
Most Valuable Player	**Martin Klempa**

LEADING PLAYERS

George Awada *born 2 June 1975*

The team's top goal scorer with 34 in all games, he was a respected team player on and off the ice. A former USA minor leaguer, he was in his second season in the Elite League after a year with Manchester Phoenix.

Martin Klempa *born 20 July 1973*

Technically excellent and very agile, he fools some opposition shooters as, unusually, he wears a glove on his right hand.

Played in the Slovak Extraleague for his home town of Poprad but joined Giants after a season in the Russian Elite League. He represented Slovakia in the 1996 World Championships and has been capped 11 times for his country.

MOST PROMISING PLAYER

Marc Levers *born 30 June 1981*

Joining Giants after making his Elite League debut last year with Nottingham Panthers, his best qualities are his speed and agility. Despite missing quite a bit of the season with a shoulder injury, he still scored 18 points (ten goals). One of GB's hottest young players on his debut in Hungary this year.

FACT FILE 2004-05

Elite League:	Runners-up
Playoffs:	Third in qr-final gp.
Challenge Cup:	Third in qual. group
Crossover Games	Winners

HISTORY

Founded: 2000.

Leagues: Elite League 2003-05, Superleague 2000-03.

Honours: Crossover Games 2004-05; Superleague Playoffs 2002-03; Superleague 2001-02.

BELFAST GIANTS *left to right*, *back row*: Jason Ellery (equipment), Graeme Walton, Roman Gavalier, Curtis Huppe, Leigh Jamieson, Jason Bowen, Diarmuid Kelly, Mel Angelstadt, Fredrik Nasvall, Marc Levers, Mark Morrison; *front row*: Chris McGimpsey, George Awada, John Elliott (general manager), Tony Hand, Shane Johnson, Curtis Bowen, Todd Kelman, Martin Klempa.

Photo: Michael Cooper.

BRACKNELL BEES

PLAYER	ALL COMPETITIONS					BRITISH NATIONAL LEAGUE					PLAYOFFS				
Scorers	GP	G	A	Pts	Pim	GP	G	A	Pts	Pim	GP	G	A	Pts	Pim
Peter Campbell (I)	69	60	57	117	84	38	30	31	61	70	12	8	7	15	6
Lukas Smital (I)	67	46	62	108	78	35	25	30	55	22	12	10	9	19	38
Matus Petricko (I)	70	34	58	92	82	37	22	24	46	42	12	5	8	13	16
Martin Masa (I)	65	37	47	84	74	34	19	27	46	20	10	5	5	10	34
Greg Owen	60	24	31	55	12	35	10	19	29	10	3	0	0	0	0
Mark Richardson	64	22	29	51	12	35	10	18	28	4	11	2	3	5	2
Mike Ellis	69	22	25	47	26	36	10	11	21	12	12	4	6	10	8
Danny Meyers	69	8	22	30	58	35	5	13	18	26	12	0	2	2	16
Lee Richardson	70	13	15	28	20	38	7	7	14	16	11	2	3	5	2
Mike Rees (I)	71	10	17	27	153	37	2	7	9	60	12	1	3	4	45
Dwight Parrish 3	49	6	21	27	66	26	0	7	7	22	10	3	2	5	4
Serge Dube (I)	17	7	11	18	0	11	4	5	9	0					
Ryan Aldridge	70	4	14	18	95	38	1	6	7	32	12	0	2	2	2
Steve Weidlich (I)	18	3	13	16	79	11	2	6	8	57					
Jan Krulis (I) 1	24	1	12	13	102	8	1	2	3	36	12	0	6	6	54
Danny Hughes 2	36	4	5	9	6	17	4	1	5	2	4	0	0	0	2
Ross McDougall	69	2	6	8	24	38	0	3	3	4	9	1	0	1	4
Mark Galazzi	48	2	4	6	18	28	1	2	3	10	7	1	0	1	2
Brendan Witt (I)	3	1	4	5	0	3	1	4	5	0					
Luke Reynolds	45	0	3	3	2	20	0	0	0	2	8	0	0	0	0
Stevie Lyle (N)	70	0	2	2	12	37	0	1	1	10	12	0	1	1	0
Scott Spearing	12	0	0	0	2	3	0	0	0	0					
Richard Hardy	36	0	0	0	6	17	0	0	0	6	12	0	0	0	0
Bench Penalties					8					0					6
TEAM TOTALS	70	308	458	766	1019	38	154	224	378	463	12	43	57	100	241
Netminders	GP	Mins	SOG	GA	Sv%	GP	Mins	SOG	GA	Sv%	GP	Mins	SOG	GA	Sv%
Stevie Lyle 3	67	3986	1945	140	92.8	38	2164	1107	76	93.1	12	760	413	31	92.5
Dan Green	11	393	218	29	86.7	4	158	94	12	87.2					
David Wride	1	27	14	3	78.6										
Empty Net Goals		5	1	1			5	1	1						
TEAM TOTALS	70	4411	2178	173	92.1	38	2322	1202	89	92.6	12	760	413	31	92.5

Also appeared: Tony Barclay, Greg Martyn.

Also played for: 1 Nottingham Panthers; 2 Chelmsford Chieftains; 3 Sheffield Steelers.

Shutouts: Lyle (8) - cup: 6 Nov v Newcastle Vipers (24 saves), 28 Nov at Hull Stingrays (30),
final: 23 Feb v Newcastle Vipers (29); league: 26 Dec at Guildford Flames (29).
*30 Dec v Edinburgh Capitals (9), 6 Feb v Hull Stingrays (18),
9 Feb at Hull Stingrays (23), 13 Feb v Sheffield Steelers (26).
Green - league: *30 Dec v Edinburgh Capitals (4 saves).
* shared.

League includes Crossover Games with Elite League teams
All Competitions = league, playoffs and Winter Cup

BRACKNELL BEES *left to right, back row:* Ross McDougall, Danny Hughes, Greg Martyn, Luke Reynolds, Scott Spearing, Lee Richardson; *middle row:* Danny Meyers, Serge Dube, Martin Masa, Mike Rees, Matus Petricko, Steve Weidlich, Lukas Smital; *front row:* Stevie Lyle, Greg Owen, Mark Richardson, Mike Ellis, Peter Campbell, Ryan Aldridge, Dan Green.

Photo: Robert Swann.

Brack to the future

ALAN MANICOM

Club founder **John Nike** hailed his British National League and Cup double winners as the best team in Bees' 18-year history. Certainly only **Dave Whistle**'s 1999-2000 Superleague champions could dispute that claim, having battled it out in the country's top flight. But **Mike Ellis**'s exciting squad enjoyed more success than their predecessors, albeit in the second tier.

Bees began the season in sizzling style, going on a 12-match winning run in the Winter Cup, while their march to the title included notable scalps in the Crossover Games against eventual Elite League champions Coventry, playoff finalists Nottingham, arch rivals London and - sweetest of all - home and away derby triumphs over Basingstoke.

The highlight of a stunning 10-3 home win over their nearest neighbours was a hat-trick in under two minutes by little-known British forward **Danny Hughes**, remarkably all within seconds of him taking the ice.

Even when in October **Serge Dube** and **Steve Weidlich** stunned their team-mates by announcing they were going back to play for their former club in Texas, Bees took it in their stride.

Captain **Mike Rees**, the undoubted unsung hero of the team, and his British protégé **Danny Meyers**, voted the top British defenceman, shouldered the extra responsibilities with ease.

Former Manchester Storm defenceman **Dwight Parrish** was added before the much-heralded arrival of **Brendan Witt**, courtesy of the NHL lock-out. But the Washington Capitals' star contributed little more than briefly raising the profile of the club. After a fire at his new Florida home forced him to quit, Bees brought in Nottingham's **Jan Krulis** on the transfer deadline.

Within days, thanks to a 2-0 win at Hull Stingrays, Bees had clinched the BNL title with six games to spare.

The Winter Cup final was another one-sided affair, Bees beating Newcastle 8-1 in the north-east before running out 8-3 winners on aggregate. But despite making it through to the semi-finals of the playoffs, the treble proved beyond them.

For the second year running, influential British forward **Greg Owen** was ruled out of the climax to the season with a knee injury. And, amid growing signs of complacency, they were dumped out of the competition after twice losing penalty shoot-outs to eventual playoff champions Dundee Stars.

PLAYER AWARDS

Players' Player	Lukas Smital
Coach's Award	Stevie Lyle
Player of the Year	Peter Campbell
Best Forward	Martin Masa
Best Defensive Player	Stevie Lyle
Most Improved Player	Mark Richardson
Best British Player	Danny Meyers

LEADING PLAYERS
Peter Campbell *born 7 September 1979*
The league's top goalscorer with almost a goal a game. The centreman's ability to spot a chance and put the puck away with ruthless efficiency earned him a call-up for Team Canada just before Christmas.

Stevie Lyle *born 4 December 1979*
Possibly the club's most important signing. He not only had the best record of any netminder in the league, he was also British which freed up an import slot. Posted eight shutouts, including four in February alone.

Lukas Smital: *born 15 August 1974*
The league's player of the year got better with every game and was Bees' outstanding player in the playoffs. The right-winger had an almost telepathic understanding with Czech mate **Martin Masa** which they put to great effect in setting each other up for some superb goals.

MOST PROMISING PLAYER
Mark Richardson *born 3 October 1986*
Smooth-skating, hugely talented forward with the vision to spot and create chances, he iced on a formidable line with exciting Czech imports Martin Masa and Lukas Smital, and ended a terrific season by playing for GB. Winner of the **Vic Batchelder** Award for best young British player.

FACT FILE 2004-05
British National League:	Fourth
Playoffs:	Runners-up
***Findus* Cup**:	Runners-up

HISTORY
Founded: 1987.
Leagues: British National League 2003-05; Superleague 1996-2003; British League, Premier Div. 1991-95; British League, Div. One 1995-96, 1990-91; English League 1987-90.
Honours: British National League and Winter Cup 2004-05; Superleague 1999-2000, Promotion Playoffs 1991-92, English League 1989-90.

CARDIFF DEVILS

PLAYER	ALL COMPETITIONS					ELITE LEAGUE					PLAYOFFS				
Scorers	GP	G	A	Pts	Pim	GP	G	A	Pts	Pim	GP	G	A	Pts	Pim
Vezio Sacratini (I)	64	28	48	76	82	50	23	43	66	68	10	4	3	7	2
Jon Cullen (I)	60	32	42	74	34	46	26	34	60	32	10	5	6	11	2
Dave Matsos (I)	57	22	32	54	10	46	20	27	47	10	7	0	3	3	0
Nathan Rempel (I)	64	24	28	52	58	50	19	21	40	40	10	2	6	8	2
Russ Romaniuk (I)	62	14	25	39	95	49	11	20	31	81	10	3	3	6	2
Ed Patterson (I)	24	8	20	28	32	24	8	20	28	32					
John Craighead (I)1	28	13	11	24	97	16	7	6	13	20	9	5	5	10	36
Jeff Burgoyne (I)	64	6	18	24	46	50	6	16	22	38	10	0	0	0	4
Jonathan Phillips	48	6	16	22	46	43	6	15	21	44	1	0	0	0	0
Kirk Dewaele (I)	64	2	15	17	106	50	2	13	15	72	10	0	0	0	6
Rob Davison (I)	52	8	8	16	160	40	6	7	13	138	10	1	1	2	12
Jason Becker (I)	57	8	8	16	6	47	8	6	14	6	10	0	2	2	0
Warren Tait	62	3	9	12	12	48	3	7	10	12	10	0	1	1	0
Phil Hill	63	5	6	11	12	49	3	6	9	10	10	1	0	1	2
Jason Stone	57	1	4	5	12	47	1	4	5	12	10	0	0	0	0
Phil Manny	53	2	0	2	14	45	2	0	2	14	8	0	0	0	0
Neil Francis	44	0	2	2	34	30	0	2	2	22	10	0	0	0	0
Steve Fisher	1	1	0	1	0	1	1	0	1	0					
Dan Blakemore	1	0	1	1	0	1	0	1	1	0					
Jamie Dancey	1	0	0	0	2	1	0	0	0	2					
Jason Cugnet (N) (I)	64	0	0	0	45	50	0	0	0	45	10	0	0	0	0
Bench Penalties					16					14					0
TEAM TOTALS	64	183	293	476	919	50	152	248	400	712	10	21	30	51	68
Netminders	GPI	Mins	SOG	GA	Sv%	GPI	Mins	SOG	GA	Sv%	GPI	Mins	SOG	GA	Sv%
Jason Cugnet (I)	61	3579	1686	131	92.2	49	2859	1361	106	92.2	8	480	202	11	94.6
Mike Brabon	9	300	168	18	89.3	7	180	99	12	87.9	2	120	69	6	91.3
Empty Net Goals			5	5				3	3				2	2	
TEAM TOTALS	64	3879	1859	154	91.7	50	3039	1463	121	91.9	10	600	273	19	93.0

Also appeared: Steve Fisher.

Also played for: 1 Nottingham Panthers.

Shutouts: Cugnet (6) - league: 24 Sept at London Racers (29 saves), 24 Oct v☐ Belfast Giants (18), 30 Oct v London Racers (21), *4 Dec v London Racers (12), 30 Jan v Sheffield Steelers (30); playoffs: 30 Mar v Belfast Giants (17). ☐ Brabon - league: *4 Dec v London Racers (1).
*shared shutout

All Competitions = league, playoffs and Challenge Cup playoffs
Elite League includes Challenge Cup (excluding playoffs) and Crossover Games

The final Whistle

TERRY PHILLIPS

Thomson Cardiff Devils made vast strides during the 2004-05 season.

Trust between owner **Bob Phillips** and the fans was re-established and attendances grew steadily as head coach **Dave Whistle** built a team to challenge the best.

But on the ice it was a season of frustration for the team who finished in the top four of all four competitions but, unusually for a Whistle-coached side, lacked the finishing touch.

Devils led the Elite League for some time before fading to an eventual third spot. They went one better in the Crossover Games, moving past league rivals Coventry Blaze to end only two points behind Belfast Giants.

They reached the finals of the Challenge Cup, giving Coventry Blaze a fright at home in the second leg after crashing 6-1 at the Skydome.

At 4-1 ahead, only two goals behind on aggregate, Cardiff had Coventry in a panic. But the Blaze, to their credit, worked hard, got the breaks and eventually killed off the Cardiff comeback.

In the playoffs, Devils powered into the semi-finals as group winners, but they were destined to more disappointment, going down to a gutsy Nottingham Panthers and then losing a near-farcical third place playoff to old rivals Sheffield Steelers.

In Whistle's first full season in charge, he lost high scoring **Dennis Maxwell** (to London Racers), GB international **Matt Myers** (Nottingham Panthers) and long-serving Devils, **Ivan Matulik** (Varese, Italy) and retired bruiser **Mike Ware**.

But netminder **Jason Cugnet** and defender **Jeff Burgoyne** returned, while among the newcomers were American **Jon Cullen**, who proved to be one of Whis's best signings, **Dave Matsos** (from Bracknell), **Kirk DeWaele** (Sheffield) and Bracknell Bees' top scorer **Nathan Rempel**.

Vezio Sacratini took over the captaincy during his testimonial season and enjoyed a strong campaign repeating as the team's leading pointsman with 76 (28 goals) in 64 games.

San Jose Sharks' defenceman **Rob Davison** was the first NHL player signed by an Elite team and feisty forward **John Craighead** joined from Panthers in mid-season.

• Defenceman **Jason Stone**, 32, played his 16th season for the club. He has made more than 500 appearances for his home city team, only moving on for one season when he played for Guildford Flames.

PLAYER AWARDS

Player of the Year	**Jon Cullen**
Players' Player	**Dave Matsos**
Best British Player (Norman Memorial Award)	**Warren Tait**
Most Improved Player	**Phil Hill**

LEADING PLAYERS

Jeff Burgoyne *born 26 February 1977*

The All-Star defenceman is one of the fittest guys on the team and one of the most skilled in the league. Flirted with retirement during the summer after he was offered an office job in Costa Rica!

Jon Cullen *born 25 October 1977*

The American centreman from Atlantic City Boardwalk Bullies arrived as Devils' second choice but finished as the team's second top scorer with 74 points (32 goals) in 60 games. Among the league's smallest players, his mix of guts, grit and sheer skill put him head and shoulders above most of his opponents.

MOST PROMISING PLAYER

Phil Hill *born 23 May 1982*

The 6ft 3ins Cardiff-born forward established himself on the third line and was first choice as their most improved player.

Gutsy, intense and consistent shifts marked him out as a player who will make continue to make an impact.

Best mates with GB international **Jonathan Phillips** with whom he graduated from Devils' youth system.

FACT FILE 2004-05

Elite League	Third
Playoffs	Semi-finalists
Challenge Cup	Finalists
Crossover Games	Runners-up

HISTORY

Founded 1986.

Leagues Elite League 2003-05; British National League 2001-03; Superleague 1996-2001; British League, Premier Div. 1989-96; British League, Div. One 1987-89; British League, Div. Two 1986-87.

Honours Superleague Playoff Champions 1999; British League and Championship winners 1993-94, 1992-93, 1989-90; British League winners 1996-97; *Benson and Hedges Cup winners 1992.*

CARDIFF DEVILS *left to right, back row:* Neil Francis, Jeff Burgoyne, Nathan Rempel, Rob Davison, Jason Becker, Phil Hill, Kirk DeWaele, Phil Manny, Jonathan Philips, Jon Cullen, Warren Tait, Tony Day (equipment); *front row:* Jason Cugnet, Russ Romaniuk, Dave Matsos, Ed Patterson, Dave Whistle (coach), Vezio Sacratini, Jason Stone, Mike Brabon.

Photo: Adrian Rapps

CHELMSFORD CHIEFTAINS

PLAYER	ALL COMPETITIONS					ENGLISH PREMIER LEAGUE					PLAYOFFS				
Scorers	GP	G	A	Pts	Pim	GP	G	A	Pts	Pim	GP	G	A	Pts	Pim
Duane Ward (l)	49	48	56	104	177	28	25	35	60	87	5	5	4	9	56
Scott McKenzie	47	33	32	65	30	29	22	24	46	12	6	4	4	8	0
Duncan Cook (l)	24	29	27	56	44	18	23	20	43	36	6	6	7	13	8
Carl Greenhous	52	12	28	40	66	32	7	15	22	28	5	0	5	5	22
Andy Hannah	39	17	17	34	79	24	10	12	22	28	6	2	1	3	45
Michael Timms	52	17	12	29	34	31	9	3	12	22	6	0	1	1	4
Elliot Andrews	24	7	17	24	6	13	3	2	5	4					
Danny Wright	54	6	15	21	16	32	6	13	19	6	6	0	1	1	0
Marc Long (l) 1	15	7	10	17	36	6	1	2	3	16					
Danny Hughes 2	20	10	6	16	2	11	4	3	7	0	6	5	2	7	2
Michael Bowman 3	24	5	11	16	10	15	3	6	9	8	6	0	4	4	2
Jake French	46	2	13	15	50	28	2	10	12	24	6	0	0	0	2
Shaun Wallis	41	9	5	14	65	22	5	4	9	24	6	1	1	2	12
Ross Jones	30	6	8	14	22	14	2	2	4	4					
Mark McCoy	19	0	13	13	64	10	0	3	3	56	1	0	0	0	0
Anthony Leone	36	4	4	8	2	17	3	0	3	2	6	0	0	0	0
Andy Clements	25	3	3	6	2	10	0	1	1	0					
Lee Brears	48	1	5	6	20	28	0	5	5	18	6	0	0	0	0
Karl Rogers	16	1	3	4	24	16	1	3	4	24					
Brian McLaughlin(l)4	11	0	2	2	44	5	0	2	2	34					
Gregg Rockman (N)	50	0	2	2	4	29	0	2	2	0	6	0	0	0	0
Adam Gray (l) 4	9	1	0	1	38	4	1	0	1	24					
Sean Easton	33	1	0	1	4	20	1	0	1	2	2	0	0	0	0
Richard Gunn	5	0	1	1	0	5	0	1	1	0					
Alex Green	37	0	0	0	18	20	0	0	0	16	5	0	0	0	0
Bench Penalties					16					12					0
TEAM TOTALS	54	219	290	509	873	32	128	168	296	487	6	23	30	53	153
Netminders	GPI	Mins	SOG	GA	Sv%	GPI	Mins	SOG	GA	Sv%	GPI	Mins	SOG	GA	Sv%
Michael Robinson	1	60	57	6	91.2	1	4	3	1	66.7					
Gregg Rockman	50	2980	1805	194	89.2	29	1726	1005	115	88.6	6	359	270	25	90.7
Carl Ambler	13	187	123	14	88.6	4	187	123	14	88.6					
Steven Clements	1	4	8	3	62.5										
Empty Net Goals		9	1	1			3	0	0			1	1	1	
TEAM TOTALS	54	3240	1994	218	89.1	32	1920	1131	130	88.5	6	360	271	26	90.4

Also appeared: Darren Brown, Gary Brown, Chris Brummit, Dan Cabby, Ben Clements, Daniel Hammond, Matt Turner, Derek Whitbread.

Also played for: 1 Peterborough Phantoms; 2 Bracknell Bees; 3 Peterborough Phantoms, Sheffield Steelers; 4 Slough Jets.

Shutouts: Rockman - league: 3 Jan at Solihull Kings (24 saves).

All Competitions = league, playoffs and Premier Cup

CHELMSFORD CHIEFTAINS *left to right, back row:* Mick Gunn (manager), Elliot Andrews, Greg Rockman, Darren Brown, Gary Brown, Derek Whitbread, Andy Hannah, Duane Ward, Shaun Wallis, Daniel Hammond, Carl Ambler, Sean Easton, Alex Green, K Davis (equipment); *front row:* Anthony Leone, Danny Wright, Carl Greenhous, Steve Lipinski (club owner), Jake French, Scott McKenzie, Michael Timms, mascot.

Photo: Chris Webber

Gregg is Chiefs' rock, man

IVOR HOBSON

It was a turbulent summer for Chieftains as their owner, **Ollie Oliver**, departed after nine seasons to take charge at Romford. Head coach **Dean Birrell** followed, taking seven players with him and leaving the squad without five of their top seven points scorers.

The new management team, Chelmsford Promotions, was headed by local businessmen **Steve Lipinski** and **Mick Gunn**, and their first signing was Chieftain stalwart, **Andy Hannah**, who doubled as player and coach.

Hannah's line-up was mostly inexperienced with ten under-19's icing during the season. The imports were led by captain **Carl Greenhous** who returned for his third spell in Essex, but ex-Haringey Racer, **Brian McLaughlin**, lasted only 11 games before he was replaced by former Elite Leaguer, **Mark McCoy**.

Leading the British contingent were former Swindon goalie, **Gregg Rockman**, and **Elliot Andrews**, who recorded 24 points in as many games. But Andrews' season was brought to an early conclusion after he suffered a broken arm playing against *Wightlink* Raiders.

The season opened with a promising 5-3 win at Slough in the Premier Cup and the Tribe could well have finished top of the qualifying group had it not been for two costly losses against the ENL's Invicta Dynamos.

Duane Ward's 18 goals helped Chieftains to nine wins in 16 Cup games, in stark contrast to their league form where they gained only two points in their opening seven fixtures. A 6-4 victory at Slough snapped the winless streak in mid-October but they struggled at home with only 11 wins in 27 games, and their first victory didn't come until early November.

The loss of **Scott McKenzie** with a broken collar bone, and **Andy Clements** with a hernia didn't help. But **Karl Rogers** made a surprise comeback, four years after his serious eye injury.

January heralded a change of fortunes with Andrews becoming bench coach and former Peterborough Phantom, **Duncan Cook**, hitting five against Solihull in a 14-0 win which sparked a season-best five-game winning streak. But Chieftains lacked aggression - a deficiency reflected when they won the Fair Play trophy - and they finished three notches below last term.

The playoffs began well with a win at Slough, the double over *Wightlink* and six goals from Cook. But after holding Jets scoreless for 40 minutes in their crucial final home game, the Tribe came up short, dropping a heartbreaking 3-0 decision in the closing period.

PLAYER AWARDS

Player of the Year	**Duane Ward**
Players' Player	**Jake French**
Coach's Player	**Gregg Rockman**
Best Young Player	**Alex Green**

LEADING PLAYERS

Gregg Rockman *born 24 May 1982*
His goaltending kept Chieftains in contention during their difficult playoff run as he faced over 55 shots a game. Had shutouts in two consecutive games against Solihull during the season.

Duane Ward *born 20 February 1976*
'Wardo' scored over 100 points and averaged almost a goal a game with 48 in 49 to finish among the league leaders again. A popular player despite a season of ups and downs.

MOST PROMISING PLAYER

Lee Brears *born 29 May 1985*
A determined forward with fine potential who became a regular in the line-up in only his second season at senior level. A graduate of the junior ranks at Chelmsford and Guildford, he has represented England at under-17 level.

FACT FILE 2004-05

English Premier League: Seventh
Playoffs: Third in group
Premier Cup: Group runners-up

CLUB HISTORY

Founded: 1987.
Leagues: English Premier League 2002-05, 1998-2001; English (National) League 2001-02, 1996-98 and 1988-93; British League, Div One 1993-96; British League, Div. Two 1987-88.
Honours: League winners, Playoff champions and *DataVision* Millennium Cup winners 1999-2000.

COVENTRY BLAZE

PLAYER	ALL COMPETITIONS					ELITE LEAGUE					PLAYOFFS				
Scorers	GP	G	A	Pts	Pim	GP	G	A	Pts	Pim	GP	G	A	Pts	Pim
Dan Carlson (I)	63	29	49	78	56	50	22	42	64	48	10	7	5	12	4
Adam Calder (I)	58	37	31	68	215	44	32	26	58	183	10	3	4	7	16
Ashley Tait	64	30	33	63	56	50	20	28	48	50	10	6	3	9	4
Chris McNamara (I)	57	27	30	57	66	43	21	22	43	28	10	5	3	8	10
Joel Poirier (I)	62	24	31	55	66	48	22	20	42	60	10	2	6	8	2
Neal Martin (I)	62	6	31	37	28	48	6	28	34	24	10	0	3	3	0
Doug Schueller (I)	62	9	27	36	96	49	6	20	26	88	10	2	6	8	8
Andre Payette (I)	60	15	20	35	492	46	14	17	31	369	4	1	1	2	64
Russ Cowley	59	12	17	29	20	45	8	14	22	16	10	3	3	6	4
Graham Schlender (I)	64	10	14	24	137	50	8	9	17	100	10	2	3	5	6
Tom Watkins	61	10	13	23	24	48	7	8	15	20	10	1	5	6	4
Wade Belak (I)	44	7	11	18	176	30	5	9	14	129	10	1	2	3	16
Jozef Lukac (I) 3	31	8	6	14	8	18	5	4	9	8	10	1	2	3	0
Pavol Mihalik (I)	29	4	10	14	86	28	4	10	14	86					
Michal Vrabel (I)	17	2	4	6	16	17	1	4	5	16					
James Pease	61	0	5	5	10	47	0	5	5	6	10	0	0	0	4
Jody Lehman (N) (I)	64	0	2	2	4	50	0	2	2	0	10	0	0	0	2
Bari McKenzie 2	7	1	0	1	0	5	0	0	0	0					
Nathanael Williams	51	0	1	1	20	37	0	0	0	0	10	0	0	0	20
Bench Penalties					28					6					22
TEAM TOTALS	64	231	335	566	1604	50	181	268	449	1237	10	34	46	80	186

Netminders	GPI	Mins	SOG	GA	Sv%	GPI	Mins	SOG	GA	Sv%	GPI	Mins	SOG	GA	Sv%
Jody Lehman (I)	61	3648	1772	109	93.8	48	2870	1315	89	93.2	9	538	288	11	96.2
Dan Shea	9	267	130	18	86.2	7	201	100	13	87.0	2	66	30	5	83.3
Empty Net Goals			2	2				2	2				0	0	
TEAM TOTALS	64	3915	1904	129	93.3	50	3071	1417	104	92.8	10	604	318	16	94.9

Also appeared: Adam Brittle 1, Tom Carlon 1.

Also played for: 1 Telford Wild Foxes; 2 Milton Keynes Lightning; 3 Basingstoke Bison.

Shutouts: Lehman (6) - league: 21 Nov at London Racers (29 saves), 12 Dec v Bracknell Bees
(23), 16 Jan v Cardiff Devils (32), 26 Feb at Nottingham Panthers (30);
playoffs: 31 Mar v London Racers (29), semi-final: 9 Apr v Sheffield Steelers (41).

All Competitions = league, playoffs and Challenge Cup playoffs
Elite League includes Challenge Cup (excluding playoffs) and Crossover Games

Thommo's triple

ANTONY HOPKER

Coventry Blaze fans won't forget the 2004-05 season for a long time when their team won the Elite League's Grand Slam in only their second campaign at the top level.

After Blaze had finished a surprising third on their league debut, coach **Paul Thompson** had a clear-out as he had pretty much a British National League roster.

While stalwarts such as goalie **Jody Lehman**, **Ashley Tait** and **Joel Poirier** returned, 'Thommo' recruited a brand new defence plus forwards **Dan Carlson, Adam Calder, Andre Payette** and **Chris McNamara.**

All proved big contributors. Carlson's speed and work ethic made him the league's best two-way centreman, Calder's finishing made him joint top goal scorer while Payette outraged opposition fans with antics that saw him clock up a record number of penalty minutes.

Blaze struggled occasionally in the early section of the season. The turning point came in November when **Michal Vrabel** was replaced by **Wade Belak** of the NHL's Toronto Maple Leafs. He paired up with **Neal Martin**, voted the league's best player, to form an impenetrable wall in front of Lehman and Blaze stopped leaking goals and losing matches.

"This team is becoming addicted to winning," declared Thompson.

But Coventry were still locked in a three-way battle for the league. Cardiff, like Nottingham, fared poorly against the Blaze and eventually dropped off the pace, but the league was only resolved in Blaze's favour with two games left.

They were already trophy holders by then, having lifted the Challenge Cup in February. A **Doug Schueller** slapshot saw them through a tight semi-final against Nottingham, and they ran riot in the first leg of the final, beating Cardiff 6-1.

In a fight-strewn second leg, the Devils almost achieved the unthinkable. But despite having three players ejected, Calder off with concussion and Martin barely able to hold his stick, Blaze somehow brought the game back to win on the night and on aggregate.

After qualifying easily for the semi-finals, they won a war of attrition against Sheffield, and in the final against Panthers, GB captain **Ashley Tait** scored the sudden-death winner against his old club to give Blaze the Grand Slam.

Thompson, who had coached the team since their English League days, and his directors, led the celebrations of a remarkable success story. "The pressure has been amazing. I've never known a season like it," he said.

PLAYER AWARDS

Player of the Year	**Neal Martin**
Players' Player	**Jody Lehman**
Best Defenceman	**Neal Martin**
Best Forward	**Adam Calder**
Coach's Player	**Tom Watkins**
British Player of the Year	**Ashley Tait**
Most Improved Player	**James Pease**
Clubman of the Year	**Dan Shea**
Best Plus/Minus	**Doug Schueller**

LEADING PLAYERS

Adam Calder *born 28 March 1976*

The former University of North Dakota right winger played on his off-wing with Blaze and was able to cause havoc in the defence when he cut inside. A deceptively lazy player, his 32 goals tied him for first in the league.

Neal Martin *born 8 September 1975*

The former London Knight joined Blaze after three seasons in the German DEL and Austria. His speed of thought and passing earned the Sudbury, Ontario defenceman plaudits as the league's best player. His vision, penalty killing and positional play were also exemplary.

MOST PROMISING PLAYER

Russ Cowley *born 12 August 1983*

The left-winger came of age as a senior player on the Blaze's third line which made a difference in the tight games during the run-in. Stronger than in the past, his speed was also a vital asset. Also a promising GB forward.

FACT FILE 2004-05

Elite League:	Winners
Playoffs:	Champions
Challenge Cup:	Winners
Crossover Games	Fourth

HISTORY

Founded: 2000, after club moved from Solihull.

Leagues: Elite League 2003-05; British National League 2000-03.

Honours: Elite League, Challenge Cup and Elite League Playoff Championship 2004-05; British National League & Playoff Championship 2002-03;

COVENTRY BLAZE *left to right, back row:* Nikki Sherlock (physio), Dan Carlson, Pavol Mihalik, Doug Schueller, James Pease, Michal Vrabel, Chris McNamara, Andre Payette, Graham Schlender, Nathanael Williams, Adam Calder, Andy Henry (fitness coach), Steve Small (manager); *front row:* Jody Lehman, Russell Cowley, Joel Poirier, Paul Thompson (coach), Ashley Tait, Luc Chabot (asst. coach), Neal Martin, Tom Watkins, Dan Shea.

DUNDEE STARS

PLAYER	ALL COMPETITIONS					BRITISH NATIONAL LEAGUE					PLAYOFFS				
Scorers	GP	G	A	Pts	Pim	GP	G	A	Pts	Pim	GP	G	A	Pts	Pim
Cory Morgan (I)	46	28	30	58	78	31	18	21	39	60	15	10	9	19	18
Scott Barnes (I)	49	25	26	51	185	34	15	18	33	123	15	10	8	18	62
Patric Lochi (I)	47	24	21	45	32	33	17	10	27	26	14	7	11	18	6
Cristiano Borgatello (I)	50	12	33	45	60	37	11	26	37	40	13	1	7	8	20
Gary Wishart	49	15	29	44	36	34	12	20	32	14	15	3	9	12	22
Jason Shmyr (I)	51	10	29	39	243	36	7	20	27	201	15	3	9	12	42
Jeff Marshall (I)	49	11	15	26	30	34	6	12	18	22	15	5	3	8	8
John Dolan	49	11	14	25	20	34	3	8	11	16	15	8	6	14	4
Paul Berrington	32	6	16	22	34	32	6	16	22	34					
David Smith	52	9	12	21	37	37	8	6	14	33	15	1	6	7	4
Scott Corbett (I)	24	7	14	21	6	12	4	5	9	6	12	3	9	12	0
Mark Scott (I)	28	4	14	18	22	22	2	13	15	10	6	2	1	3	12
Andy Samuel	34	7	4	11	8	19	3	3	6	4	15	4	1	5	4
Paddy Ward	48	0	10	10	42	33	0	9	9	16	15	0	1	1	26
James Hutchinson	41	1	7	8	10	37	1	7	8	10	4	0	0	0	0
Derek Bekar (I)	3	2	1	3	4	3	2	1	3	4					
Ali Haddanou	38	1	2	3	45	26	0	1	1	41	12	1	1	2	4
Daymen Bencharski (I)	3	0	3	3	20	3	0	3	3	20					
Chad Reekie	47	0	1	1	10	32	0	1	1	8	15	0	0	0	2
Evan Lindsay (N) (I)	48	0	1	1	0	33	0	0	0	0	15	0	1	1	0
Colin Downie (N) 1	48	0	0	0	2	37	0	0	0	2	11	0	0	0	0
Bench Penalties					8					6					2
TEAM TOTALS	53	173	282	455	932	38	117	200	317	696	15	56	82	138	236
Netminders	GP	Mins	SOG	GA	Sv%	GP	Mins	SOG	GA	Sv%	GP	Mins	SOG	GA	Sv%
Evan Lindsay (I)	46	2746	1697	157	90.7	32	1874	1185	115	90.3	14	872	512	42	91.8
Colin Downie 1	7	329	179	21	88.3	6	269	140	15	89.3	1	60	39	6	84.6
Glenn Ridler (I)	5	267	151	21	86.1	5	267	151	21	86.1					
Empty Net Goals		4	4				4	4				0	0		
TEAM TOTALS	53	3342	2031	203	90.0	38	2410	1480	155	89.5	15	932	551	48	91.3

Also appeared: Kyle Doig, Billy Fisher (N), Andy Hannah, Craig Johnston, Alan Mashton, Stephen Murphy (N), Chris Petrie, Charlie Ward (N).

Also played for: 1 Fife Flyers.

Shutouts: Lindsay (3) - cup: *14 Nov at Peterborough Phantoms (7 saves);
league: 6 Feb v Coventry Blaze (46);
playoffs: 2 Apr at Guildford Flames (19).
Downie - cup: *14 Nov at Peterborough Phantoms (13 saves).
* shared.

League includes Crossover Games with Elite League teams

All Competitions = league and playoffs (Winter Cup statistics incomplete)

DUNDEE STARS *left to right, top row:* Ali Haddenou, Mike Ward (club co-owner), Niall Elliot (club doctor), Andy Dell (physio), Chad Reekie; *middle row:* David Smith, Patric Lochi, John Dolan, James Hutchinson, Mark Scott, Jeff Marshall, Scott Barnes, Cristiano Borgatello; *front row:* Evan Lindsay, Gary Wishart, Paddy Ward, Paul Berrington, Roger Hunt (coach), Jason Shmyr, Cory Morgan, Colin Downie.

Photo: Godfrey Mordente

Late shiners

KATHERINE TRAIL

The Dundee *Texol* Stars may have finished a mediocre fifth in the league but **Roger Hunt's** side stormed to a resounding and somewhat unexpected Playoff Championship.

Stars had a strong presence at the back, with young Italian **Cristiano Borgatello** and **Jeff Marshall**, and a formidable forward line with imposing captain **Jason Shmyr**, another Italian in speedy winger **Patric Lochi**, feisty **Scott Barnes** and goalscorer **Scott Corbett**.

They also had a strong British contingent with veteran **Davie Smith**, young forwards **Gary Wishart** and **John Dolan** and defencemen **Paddy Ward**, **James Hutchinson** and **Chad Reekie**.

After a rocky start to the season, Hunt made a bold move by cutting 21-year-old Canadian netminder **Glenn Ridler** and bringing in former London Racer **Evan Lindsay**. The gamble paid off, with Lindsay putting in outstanding performances, particularly in the playoffs.

The squad were plagued with injuries, assistant captain **Paul Berrington** suffering a bad groin injury and **James Hutchinson** hurting his leg. Both missed the last couple of months of the league as well as the playoffs.

Experienced netminder **Colin Downie**, who acted as back-up to Lindsay until the last few games of the playoffs, underwent a knee operation and was replaced by former Stars' netminder **Stephen Murphy** who returned from Sweden.

The turning point to the season came with the acquisition of Canadian forward **Cory Morgan**, who proved himself an asset both on the ice and in the dressing room.

However, they lost Corbett who returned home to Canada with a recurring knee injury and he was replaced with another ex-Racer, ironman **Mark Scott**. Corbett returned to the team for the playoffs but this forced Scott to sit out most of the post-season.

After a nailbiting round-robin campaign in the playoffs, Stars grabbed the last semi-final spot ahead of Newcastle and never looked back.

The league-winning Bracknell Bees were disposed of in two games, with both going to penalty shots. Dolan, a local youngster, scored the winning shot and the Stars progressed to the best-of-five final series against the Guildford Flames.

Three back-to-back victories saw them lift the John Brady Bowl at the Spectrum for the second time in four years.

PLAYER AWARDS

Player of the Year	**Jeff Marshall**
Players' Player	**Cristiano Borgatello**
Most Improved Player	**Scott Barnes**
Clubman of the Year	**Paul Berrington**

Scott Barnes *born 29 October 1978*

Usually for an import, he won the most improved player award for his feisty play and unfailing effort after a slow start. Although not a big man, he stood up for himself and his teammates and ended as runner-up in the club's scoring.

Jeff Marshall *born 20 February 1978*

The defenceman from Newmarket, Ontario impressed with his smooth backward skating and puckhandling skills and was an integral part of the team during their playoff run. Joined Stars from the North American minor leagues after two seasons on university and college teams.

MOST PROMISING PLAYER

John Dolan

The young Dundonian really came into his own in the playoffs when he fired home the penalty shot against Bracknell to send Stars into the final. Came up through the Dundee junior system with the Tigers and later the Camperdown Stars.

FACT FILE 2004-05

British National League:	Fifth
Playoffs:	Champions
Winter Cup:	Fifth in qual.round
Crossover Games	Tenth

HISTORY

Founded: 2001.
Leagues: British National League 2001-05.
Honours: British National League Playoff Champions 2004-05 & 2001-02; British National League 2001-02; Caledonian Cup 2002.

EDINBURGH CAPITALS

PLAYER	ALL COMPETITIONS					BRITISH NATIONAL LEAGUE				
Scorers	GP	G	A	Pts	Pim	GP	G	A	Pts	Pim
Dino Bauba	51	37	58	95	164	35	19	36	55	91
Marty Johnston (I)	39	27	46	73	57	28	18	27	45	45
Martin Cingel (I)	54	26	45	71	62	38	16	28	44	42
Miroslav Droppa (I)	54	18	26	44	24	38	8	15	23	14
Jan Krajicek (I)	42	12	14	26	56	33	8	11	19	40
Ratislav Bohme (I)	54	9	17	26	22	38	7	11	18	14
Neil Hay	49	10	15	25	38	33	8	8	16	14
Laurie Dunbar	54	9	16	25	32	38	7	9	16	16
Steven Lynch	53	6	19	25	38	37	4	15	19	24
Craig Wilson	46	4	6	10	57	33	3	3	6	33
Mindaugas Kieras (I)	39	2	8	10	50	27	1	4	5	20
Ross Hay	48	0	3	3	2	32	0	3	3	2
Steven Francey	10	1	1	2	0	2	0	0	0	0
Daniel McIntyre	49	0	2	2	36	33	0	2	2	18
Ross Dalgleish	21	1	0	1	0	13	0	0	0	0
Ian Beattie	26	1	0	1	4	18	1	0	1	0
Blair Daly (N)	6	0	1	1	0	5	0	0	0	0
Dave Trofimenkoff (N) (I)	51	0	1	1	78	36	0	1	1	56
Andrew Robinson 1	1	0	0	0	2	1	0	0	0	2
David Beatson	39	0	0	0	31	27	0	0	0	27
Ryan Ford (N)	42	0	0	0	4	28	0	0	0	2
Grant McPherson	42	0	0	0	14	26	0	0	0	0
Bench Penalties					8					6
TEAM TOTALS	54	166	278	444	779	38	102	173	275	466
Netminders	GP	Mins	SOG	GA	Sv%	GP	Mins	SOG	GA	Sv%
Blair Daly	2	5	1	0	100.0	2	5	1	0	100.0
Dave Trofimenkoff (I)	51	3044	2023	229	88.7	37	2220	1495	173	88.4
Ryan Ford	7	241	164	30	81.7	3	78	67	15	77.6
Empty Net Goals			1	1				1	1	
TEAM TOTALS	54	3290	2189	260	88.1	38	2298	1563	189	87.9

Also appeared: Colin Bennett (N), C J Blackburn, Alistair Flockhart (N), Kevin Forshall (N), James Goodman, Gavin Jackson (N), Ryan Johnstone, Paul Jones (N), Shaun Littlewood, Graham Newell, Ashley Skinns 1, Danny Wood.

Also played for: 1 Wightlink Raiders.

Shutouts: None

League includes Crossover Games with Elite League teams

All Competitions = league and Winter Cup

Hand's out, Caps smacked

NIGEL DUNCAN & MARK EASTON

Scott Neil praised his *Carlsberg* Capitals despite them signing off with the British National League's wooden spoon. His men also failed to qualify for the next stage of the Winter Cup.

This was in marked contrast to the year before when Capitals came third - their highest ever position - and made the final four of the playoffs guided by Britain's best home-bred player, **Tony Hand**.

The departure of Hand to Belfast Giants naturally left a massive hole, but Neil worked tirelessly with his small budget.

He built his side around Murrayfield regulars **Steven Lynch** (the captain), **Laurie Dunbar**, **Craig Wilson** and brothers **Neil** and **Ross Hay** who all returned to the club along with imports **Jan Krajicek**, **Martin Cingel** and **Miroslav Droppa**.

It was the new guys who grabbed the headlines, though. **Dino Bauba** and netminder **Dave Trofimenkoff** jumped from close rivals Dundee Stars, **Marty Johnston** came from the ECHL's Peoria Rivermen, and two steady defencemen joined from Eastern Europe - Slovakian **Rastislav Bohme** and Lithuanian **Mindaugas Kieras**. Bauba, Johnston and Cingel produced over 200 points between them.

Injuries played a big part. Krajicek could not make the first few months due to a knee injury suffered the previous season, leaving the team an import short and contributing to their sixth place in the Winter Cup. The league and Crossover Games did not make happy reading, either, with only six wins in 38 games.

Neil argued: "We were a better team than the statistics suggested. The guys played really well in spells and only went down by narrow margins to top teams in many games. We entertained and pushed a lot of teams to the wire.

"People may criticise us for not bringing in players before the deadline, but we had to be mindful of our budget. We'll never compromise this club by handing out cash for the sake of it.

"We had encouraging interest from sponsors. *Carlsberg* came in and *The Evening News* and *Scotsman* backed us again and also provided us with much-needed media coverage."

The club did taste success in two minor cups. They won the Keyline Cup competition on their home ice which brought the curtain up on the season. And at the close, former Great Britain international **Jock Hay** steered the Scottish National League side to the Spring Cup by beating Solway Sharks.

PLAYER AWARDS

Player of the Year	**Martin Cingel**
Players' Player	**Dave Trofimenkoff**
Supporters' Player	**Dino Bauba**
Best British Player	**Daniel McIntyre**
Scottish Nat'l Lge Player	**Grant McPherson**

LEADING PLAYERS

Dino Bauba *born 10 January 1972*

The veteran Lithuanian still has the skill and eye for goal and ended as the team's top scorer by over 20 points. Equally successful against teams from his own league and the Elite League.

Dave Trofimenkoff *born 20 January 1975*

Another solid season for the Canadian stopper who won games single-handedly at times, though he didn't always have a strong defence in front of him.

MOST PROMISING PLAYER

Daniel McIntyre *born 25 July 1984*

Son of **Duncan McIntyre**, an Edinburgh player of an earlier generation, he made his first appearance for the seniors at the age of 18. What he lacks in height and weight he makes up for with his will to win, never backing down from anyone.

FACT FILE 2004-05

British National League:	Seventh
Playoffs:	Did not qualify
Winter Cup:	Sixth
Crossover Games:	14th

HISTORY

Founded: 1998. Previous teams in the Murrayfield rink were: *Murrayfield Royals* 1995-98 and 1952-66, *Edinburgh Racers* 1994-95; *Murrayfield Racers* 1966-94. *Edinburgh also enter a team called Capitals in the Scottish National League.*

Leagues: *Capitals* - British National Lge 1998-2005; *Royals* - British National Lge 1997-98, Northern Premier Lge 1996-97, British Lge, Div One 1995-96, British Lge 1954-55, Scottish National Lge 1952-54; *Racers* - British Lge, Premier Div 1982-95, Northern Lge 1966-82.

Past Honours: *Racers* - See *The Ice Hockey Annual 1998-99.*

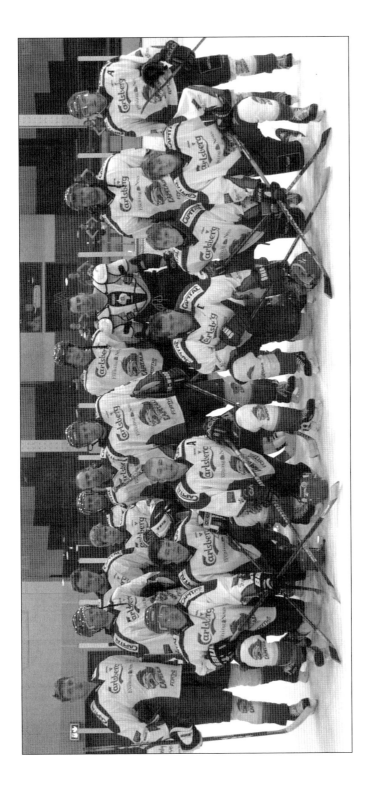

EDINBURGH CAPITALS *left to right, back row:* David Beatson, Neil Hay, Craig Wilson, Blair Daly, Laurie Dunbar, Dave Trofimenkoff, Ratislav Bohme, Jan Krajicek, Miroslav Droppa, Dino Bauba, Martin Cingel; *front row:* Ross Hay, Daniel McIntyre, Marty Johnston, Steven Lynch, Iain Beattie, Grant McPherson.

FIFE FLYERS

PLAYER	ALL COMPETITIONS					BRITISH NATIONAL LEAGUE					PLAYOFFS				
Scorers	GP	G	A	Pts	Pim	GP	G	A	Pts	Pim	GP	G	A	Pts	Pim
Todd Dutiaume (I)	61	40	46	86	79	31	20	21	41	59	13	5	8	13	4
Adrian Saul (I)	68	26	54	80	72	37	9	26	35	42	13	7	8	15	6
Karry Biette (I)	35	24	29	53	28	19	9	16	25	14					
Mark Morrison (I)	61	18	34	52	70	33	13	15	28	30	11	2	5	7	14
Steven King	63	14	33	47	28	34	6	13	19	18	13	4	5	9	6
Greg Kuznik (I)	67	15	30	45	96	36	7	16	23	22	13	3	5	8	16
John Haig	66	15	27	42	46	35	6	18	24	36	13	1	1	2	2
Judd Medak (I)	29	14	23	37	42	14	8	11	19	6	13	5	12	17	36
Kent Davyduke (I)	22	14	14	28	32	9	8	7	15	16	13	6	7	13	16
Kyle Horne	68	12	15	27	56	37	7	10	17	32	13	1	1	2	12
Paul Spadafora (I)	20	10	6	16	35	7	4	4	8	6	13	6	2	8	30
Lee Mitchell	60	8	6	14	14	33	5	3	8	6	12	1	0	1	2
Dreu Volk (I)	41	6	7	13	89	24	3	5	8	65					
Chris Sebastian (I)	10	5	7	12	2	5	1	1	2	2					
Derek King	58	1	11	12	26	33	0	5	5	18	12	0	3	3	8
Euan Forsyth	58	2	3	5	20	31	2	3	5	10	13	0	0	0	0
Liam Greig	46	2	2	4	124	26	2	1	3	74	10	0	1	1	14
Daryl Venters	23	1	3	4	6	13	0	0	0	4					
Frank Morris	5	1	0	1	25	5	1	0	1	25					
Chris Linton	4	0	1	1	4	3	0	0	0	0					
Jamie Wilson	16	0	1	1	8	11	0	1	1	4	1	0	0	0	0
Scott Hay (N) (I)	41	0	1	1	51	23	0	0	0	29					
Thomas Muir	17	0	0	0	29	8	0	0	0	27	2	0	0	0	0
Steve Briere (N) (I)	26	0	0	0	6	13	0	0	0	2	13	0	0	0	4
Bench Penalties					12					2					8
TEAM TOTALS	69	229	353	582	1000	38	112	176	288	549	13	41	58	99	178
Netminders	GP	Mins	SOG	GA	Sv%	GP	Mins	SOG	GA	Sv%	GP	Mins	SOG	GA	Sv%
Scott Hay (I)	41	2460	1530	137	91.0	23	1362	917	88	90.4					
Colin Downie 1	1	60	37	4	89.2	1	60	37	4	89.2					
Steve Briere (I)	26	1580	1000	112	88.8	13	791	529	71	86.6	13	789	471	41	91.3
Craig Arthur	3	43	26	3	88.5	1	20	9	1	88.9					
Empty Net Goals			10	10				7	7				2	2	
TEAM TOTALS	69	4143	2603	266	89.8	38	2233	1499	171	88.6	13	789	473	43	90.9

Also appeared: Mike Haston (N), Steve McDonald, Chris Wands.
Also played for: 1 Dundee Stars.
Shutouts: None

League includes Crossover Games with Elite League teams
All Competitions = league, playoffs and Winter Cup

That Saul for the oldest club

STUART SCOTT

It was a season which promised much, yet sadly delivered only disappointment for the UK's oldest team. Coming off a championship season, expectations were high, but a spectacular series of injuries to key players and the obligatory mid-season roster changes combined to ensure that the Flyers would be unable to ice a full team for several weeks.

One of the players most missed was assistant coach **Karry Biette**. The gritty forward suffered the double whammy of a knee injury and a puck to the face during a game in Edinburgh which left him with temporarily restricted vision in one eye.

Among the others were **Todd Dutiaume**, who was in the middle of his best season in some time, and **Dreu Volk**, who had joined the team during the summer. They were ruled out for the season, though Dutiaume confounded expectations and resumed playing after only a few weeks.

The early signs had been good. The return of Fife hero, **Greg Kuznik**, was hailed as one of the best signings of the summer, and he was joined by former Edinburgh golden boy, **Adrian Saul**.

Incoming netminder **Scott Hay** was hampered by a slow start but he picked up his form as the season progressed, but **Chris Sebastian**, supposedly the final cog in Flyers' attack, failed to settle and was released back to Canada.

After a good start with 14 points from their first 8 games, the team dissolved into a mire of inconsistency. One week they would be at the top of their game, beating the likes of Belfast, Nottingham and Sheffield from the Elite League, the next they would be shipping goals in double figures against runaway league champions Bracknell, Newcastle and the Elite's Cardiff.

Soon the losses outweighed the wins and Fife were at the wrong end of the table.

Coach **Mark Morrison** made changes to his roster, some expected, some surprising. Most surprising was his decision to axe goalie Hay and bring back **Steve Briere**, who had been stagnating in Texas. Morrison hoped he would galvanise the defence which had been short of experience since Volk's departure.

The return of **Paul Spadafora**, another cult hero, and the arrival of attackers **Judd Medak** and **Kent Davyduke** from the ECHL had an instant impact. Flyers' fortunes turned around and they marched to the Playoff semi-finals.

But this was halted when Morrison suffered an horrific spiral fracture in his leg during Game One of the three-game series. The team were unable to regroup and fell to the Flames.

PLAYER AWARDS

Mirror of Merit	**Todd Dutiaume**
Player of the Year	**Greg Kuznik**
Players' Player	**Greg Kuznik**
Best British Player	**John Haig**
Best Young Player	**Lee Mitchell**

LEADING PLAYERS

Todd Dutiaume *born 26 May 1973*
In his seventh season with the club, he typifies Flyers' hockey - fast, slick and entertaining. His two-way play was inspirational in an outstanding season. Worthy winner of the coveted Mirror of Merit trophy.

Greg Kuznik *born 12 June 1978*
Widely considered one of the best defencemen in the UK, his grit and determination, combined with his athleticism and reading of the game, made him a standout for the second year running.

MOST PROMISING PLAYER

Lee Mitchell *born 10 April 1987*
'Mitch' was only 17 but he settled into life in the BNL like a veteran. A member of the GB under-18 and under-20 squads, he threw himself into every shift and was rewarded with slots on the second line and regular ice-time.

FACT FILE 2004-05
British National League:	Sixth
Playoffs:	Semi-finalists
Winter Cup	Semi-finalists

HISTORY
Founded: 1938.
Leagues: (*Findus*) British National League (BNL) 1997-2005; Northern Premier League (NPL) 1996-97; British League 1982-96, 1954-55; Northern League (NL) 1966-82; Scottish National League (SNL) 1981-82, 1946-54, 1938-40.
Major Honours:
British Champions 1985.
Leagues: BNL 2003-04, 1999-2000; NPL 1997-98, 1996-97; British Lge, Div. One 1991-92; NL 1976-78; SNL 1951-52, 1939-40. *Playoffs:* BNL 1999-2000, 1998-99.
Findus Challenge Cup: 2001-02; *Autumn Cup:* 1978, 1976, 1975; Scottish - 1950, 1948. *Scottish Cup:* 2001, 2000, 1999, 1998, 1995, 1994.

GUILDFORD FLAMES

PLAYER	ALL COMPETITIONS					BRITISH NATIONAL LEAGUE					PLAYOFFS				
Scorers	GP	G	A	Pts	Pim	GP	G	A	Pts	Pim	GP	G	A	Pts	Pim
Jozef Kohut (I)	67	39	35	74	143	36	21	21	42	40	15	9	7	16	38
Milos Melicherik (I)	70	19	55	74	94	38	11	27	38	70	16	4	13	17	18
Peter Konder (I)	69	25	46	71	72	38	15	22	37	46	16	4	10	14	12
Ratislav Palov (I)	68	34	35	69	8	37	16	15	31	4	15	6	12	18	4
Paul Dixon	68	6	37	43	22	37	3	23	26	12	16	1	5	6	2
Nick Cross	70	12	24	36	126	38	9	15	24	28	16	2	5	7	41
Marian Smerciak (I)	67	11	20	31	56	37	4	6	10	24	15	5	2	7	6
David Oliver (I)	31	12	17	29	35	16	8	13	21	4	15	4	4	8	31
Stuart Potts	59	13	11	24	12	33	6	4	10	8	10	0	2	2	0
Neil Liddiard	69	7	16	23	100	37	5	8	13	58	16	1	3	4	18
Jason Baird (I)	15	8	12	20	108	8	4	7	11	50					
Juraj Durco (I)	44	5	12	17	38	25	3	7	10	30	16	2	5	7	6
Jason Reilly 1	56	4	13	17	18	29	2	6	8	4	16	2	6	8	8
Nicky Chinn 1	40	7	9	16	102	24	3	5	8	86	16	4	4	8	16
Dusan Pohorelec (I)	19	7	6	13	2	12	1	2	3	2					
Adam Walker	64	2	3	5	2	34	0	1	1	2	15	1	0	1	0
Peter Michnac (I)	24	1	3	4	61	12	1	1	2	22					
Stan Marple	11	1	2	3	12	6	1	1	2	6	3	0	0	0	0
David Savage	25	1	0	1	0	13	0	0	0	0					
Jamie McLennan (N) (I)	10	0	1	1	4	3	0	0	0	0	7	0	1	1	4
Miroslav Bielik (N) (I)	58	0	0	0	4	33	0	0	0	4	9	0	0	0	0
Bench Penalties					10					6					2
TEAM TOTALS	70	213	357	570	1029	38	113	184	297	506	16	44	79	123	206
Netminders	GP	Mins	SOG	GA	Sv%	GP	Mins	SOG	GA	Sv%	GP	Mins	SOG	GA	Sv%
Jamie McLennan (I)	10	571	288	21	92.7	3	186	96	8	91.7	7	385	192	13	93.2
Miroslav Bielik (I)	58	3466	1901	162	91.3	34	2041	1089	92	91.5	9	540	324	25	92.3
Tom Annetts	7	214	99	13	86.9	4	142	65	12	81.5	1	40	23	1	95.7
Empty Net Goals			5	5											
TEAM TOTALS	70	4251	2293	201	91.2	38	2369	1250	112	91.0	16	965	539	39	92.8

Also appeared: Neil Adams 2, Alan Boney, Andrew Hemmings, Gavin Jackson (N), Simon Lavis (N), Chris Wiggins, James Wiggins 1.

Also played for: 1 Slough Jets; 2 Solihull Kings.

Shutouts: Bielik (6) - league: 25 Sept at Edinburgh Capitals (26 saves), 13 Nov at Fife Flyers (4
1 Jan v Basingstoke Bison (17), 23 Jan v Fife Flyers (17), 16 Feb v
Sheffield Steelers (46); playoffs: 13 Mar at Bracknell Bees (36).

League includes Crossover Games with Elite League teams

All Competitions = league, playoffs and Winter Cup

GUILDFORD FLAMES *left to right, back row:* Stan Marple, David Savage, Peter Konder, Jozef Kohut, Adam Walker, Peter Michnac, Ratislav Palov, Dusan Pohorelec, Andrew Hemmings, Jason Reilly, Dave Wiggins (asst. manager); *front row:* Simon Lavis, Stuart Potts, Nick Cross, Milos Melicherik, Miroslav Bielik, Paul Dixon, Marian Smerciak, Neil Liddiard, Tom Annetts.

Near miss Marple

ANDY SMITH

Guildford Flames' season built slowly, ending with them reaching the Playoff final where they were swept in three games by Dundee Stars.

It was coach **Stan Marple**'s second season using a Slovakian-influenced side but Flames did not have the strength in depth they that enjoyed in season 2003-04.

Marple made the fewest number of changes at the club for many years. The netminding duo of **Stevie Lyle** (to Bracknell) and **Joe Dollin** (Swindon) were replaced by 20-year-old Slovak **Miroslav Beilik** and Bracknell junior **Tom Annetts**. Brits **Stuart Potts** and **Adam Walker** came in for **Tony Redmond** (Basingstoke) and **Mark Galazzi** (Bracknell) while the sole North American, Central League All-Star **Jason Baird**, took over **Ryan Vince**'s spot.

Flames missed out of the Cup semis by just one point and more disappointment came when the Central League started in mid-October and Baird, who had never lived up to expectations, left for 'personal reasons'. In came former Slovak international **Dusan Pohorelec**.

Flames' 5-2 defeat of local rivals, Basingstoke Bison of the Elite League, in their opening clash in the Crossover Games was a much needed morale boost against the 'superior league'.

In the 14-game competition they also achieved success against Sheffield and London, and later they completed the double over the Bison. A draw in the House of Steel and an overtime loss on their first visit to Belfast's Odyssey Arena gave them a total of ten points with only Bees topping them among BNL teams.

But in a disastrous December Flames beat only the English Premier League side Milton Keynes in an eight-game run.

The dearth of off-season changes caught up with Flames when championship winning defenceman **Peter Michnac** was surprisingly replaced by fellow Slovak **Juraj Durco**. But, as in his first stint at the club, the signing of **Nicky Chinn** from Slough Jets at Christmas proved a turning point. In January, Flames won more than they lost for the first time in the season.

Marple's final signings were two NHLers: forward **David Oliver** (Dallas Stars) and **Jamie McLennan** (New York Rangers) who shared the netminding duties with Beilik.

In the drawn-out Playoffs, Flames topped the table after their round-robin games, finishing in a tie with Bees. Then followed two trips to Scotland. They polished off Flyers in the semis but lost Smericak and Durco to injury and couldn't hold the rejuvenated Stars in the final.

PLAYER AWARDS

Player of the Year	**Paul Dixon**
Coach's award	**Nick Cross**
Sportsmanship Award	**Marian Smerciak**
Supporters' Club Player	**Miroslav Beilik**
Supporters' Club Best Brit	**Nick Cross**

LEADING PLAYERS

Miroslav Beilik *born 18 December 1983*

The Slovakian netminder joined with little Extraleague experience but great recommendations. Tall and with an unconventional style, his team's winning record owes a lot to his ability as they leaked over 30 shots a game.

Nick Cross *born 7 April 1976*

A physical forward, he accepted his promotion to assistant captain by producing levels of responsibility, aggression and skill he had not previously shown. Led Flames' third line and was used effectively on special teams.

Paul Dixon *born 4 August 1973*

In his second season partnering **Marian Smerciak** at the back, Flames' captain and assistant coach showed yet again why he is one of the top British defencemen of all-time. Led by example with patient defence and a rushing offence. His blueline slapshot was one that opponents were wary of.

FACT FILE 2004-05

British National League:	Third
Playoffs:	Finalists
Winter Cup	Seventh
Crossover Games	Ninth

HISTORY

Founded: 1992.

Leagues: British National League (BNL) 1997-2005; Premier League (PL) 1996-97; British League, Div. One 1993-96; English League 1992-93.

Honours: BNL and Playoffs 2000-01, 1997-98; *ntl* Cup 2000-01; *B&H* Plate 1998-99.

HULL STINGRAYS

PLAYER	ALL COMPETITIONS					BRITISH NATIONAL LEAGUE					PLAYOFFS				
Scorers	GP	G	A	Pts	Pim	GP	G	A	Pts	Pim	GP	G	A	Pts	Pim
Jeff Glowa (I)	63	30	41	71	69	37	20	19	39	41	10	5	8	13	12
Dru Burgess (I)	65	24	32	56	28	37	11	18	29	12	10	3	6	9	0
Slava Koulikov	61	23	31	54	44	36	14	20	34	28	10	3	1	4	2
Andrei Nikolaev (I)	65	23	29	51	22	38	14	17	31	6	10	2	4	6	4
Scott Wray (I)	29	17	24	41	42	14	4	13	17	30					
Evgeny Alipov (I)	63	12	25	37	72	37	7	16	23	38	10	1	1	2	10
Pavel Gomenyuk (I)	53	4	22	26	131	32	3	10	13	95	3	0	3	3	4
Sergei Rublivsky (I)	25	13	7	20	16	16	9	4	13	12	7	4	2	6	2
Craig Minard (I)	20	2	14	16	20	11	1	5	6	6					
Adam Radmall	66	3	10	14	20	38	2	9	11	18	10	0	1	1	2
Kevin Phillips	63	2	8	10	36	37	2	5	7	28	10	0	0	0	0
David Phillips	53	4	4	8	34	32	2	2	4	22	10	1	1	2	8
David Pyatt	64	5	2	7	8	36	1	1	2	8	10	1	0	1	0
Vladimir Chernenko (I)	37	1	6	7	40	23	1	5	6	24	8	0	0	0	0
Tim McKay	17	4	1	5	2	9	2	0	2	0					
Luke Boothroyd	63	4	1	5	16	37	1	1	2	8	10	1	0	1	2
Ladislav Kudrna (N) (I) 1	66	0	1	1	22	38	0	1	1	8	10	0	0	0	2
Sam Roberts (N)	55	0	0	0	4	32	0	0	0	2	10	0	0	0	0
Dave Ritchie	56	0	0	0	2	31	0	0	0	0	9	0	0	0	2
Bench Penalties					8					8					8
TEAM TOTALS	66	173	258	431	636	38	96	146	242	394	10	21	27	48	58
Netminders	GP	Mins	SOG	GA	Sv%	GP	Mins	SOG	GA	Sv%	GP	Mins	SOG	GA	Sv%
Ladislav Kudrna (I) 1	64	3802	2233	194	91.3	38	2249	1337	113	91.5	9	533	310	32	89.7
Sam Roberts	8	215	123	15	87.8	5	75	49	7	85.7	2	80	41	3	92.7
Empty Net Goals			2	2				1	1				1	1	
TEAM TOTALS	66	4017	2358	211	91.1	38	2324	1387	121	91.3	10	613	352	36	89.8

Also appeared: Andrew Brown, Mark Florence 2, Karl Holmes, Stephen Lee, Tristan Rogers (N).

Also played for: 1 Nottingham Panthers; 2 Sheffield Steelers.

Shutouts: Kudrna - cup: 21 Nov at Guildford Flames (36 saves).

League includes Crossover Games with Elite League teams
All Competitions = league, playoffs and Winter Cup

Kudrna done it without Ladi

CATHY WIGHAM

When Stingrays' coach **Rick Strachan** gazed into his crystal ball, it told him the side he had put together would finish in the top four. It turned out his predictions were not ambitious enough.

Stingrays were only overtaken for second place in the last fortnight by Newcastle and Guildford, made a Winter Cup semi-final appearance and gained a playoff place.

Armed with a new Canadian first line of **Dru Burgess**, **Jeff Glowa** and **Scott Wray**, and Czech netminder **Ladislav Kudrna**, Stingrays quickly collected three Elite League scalps - Sheffield (2-1), Coventry (4-3ot), London (3-1).

The surprising turn-around from a team that finished bottom by 20 points last season was due mainly to the first line and netminder functioning well. Strachan had also blended a second line of Europeans in **Slava Koulikov**, **Evgeny Alipov** and **Andrei Nikolaev**, and a third of Hull youngsters **Dave Phillips**, **Luke Boothroyd** and **Dave Pyatt**. Add in the rock-solid defence of **Adam Radmall**, **Pavel Gomenyuk**, **Craig Minard** and **Kevin Phillips**, a serious work ethic and good coaching and Stingrays had cracked it.

Unfortunately, the first crack appeared in November when Canadian Minard left. A bitter blow, it left Gomenyuk to marshall an young Brit defence until Ukrainian **Vladimir Chernenko** replaced him.

Stingrays strung together four wins over Christmas to book their Cup semi-final place. Sadly, top points scorer Wray departed just after Chernenko had arrived, to be replaced after Christmas by Ukrainian **Sergiy Rublivsky**.

After drawing 3-3 in the first leg of the Cup semi-final against Bracknell, Stingrays lost the second 6-1. Strachan's men then reached their most difficult run with away fixtures against most of the Elite sides plus repeated matches against BNL leaders, Bracknell.

After six wins and a draw in nine games, that Winter Cup semi-final ushered in a run of only two victories in 12. Stingrays were short-benched and not physically strong enough to deal with the import-heavy Elite teams.

Pastings in Coventry, London and Basingstoke sapped their energy, particularly without Gomenyuk who sat out much of the late season with knee ligament damage, thanks to **David Longstaff**'s slash.

And ten playoff matches in 19 days proved a bridge too far. "We've got nothing to be ashamed of," concluded Strachan. "The bus is going in the right direction."

PLAYER AWARDS

Player of the Year	**Ladislav Kudrna**
Best Forward	**Jeff Glowa**
Best Defenceman	**Pavel Gomenyuk**
Coach's Player	**Evgeny Alipov**
Fans' Player	**Evgeny Alipov**
Most Improved Player	**Adam Radmall**

LEADING PLAYERS

Pavel Gomenyuk *born 21 April 1978*

The rock solid Ukrainian held the defence together and took over the captaincy after the shock exit of Craig Minard. A big loss after injury and then an infected foot kept him of the last few league games and the playoffs.

Ladislav Kudrna *born 10 January 1977*

Signed from Edinburgh, the outstanding Czech keeper was the cornerstone of his team's title challenge with the second highest save percentage. Ladi's inspired performances also helped them collect the Elite League scalps of Sheffield, London, Coventry and Cardiff.

MOST PROMISING PLAYER

Luke Boothroyd *born 4 April 1987*

The former Bradford and Hull junior spent much of the season as a forward but looked more comfortable on defence (his role with the GB under-20s) where he filled in for Minard and the injured Gomenyuk and Vladimir Chernenko.

FACT FILE 2004-05

British National League:	Fourth
Playoffs:	Sixth in qr-final grp.
Winter Cup:	Semi-finalists
Crossover Games:	Eleventh

HISTORY

Founded: April 2003 by **Mike** and **Sue Pack**. The first club in Hull was *Humberside Seahawks* 1988-96 (known as Humberside Hawks 1993-96). Second club was *Kingston Hawks* 1996-99 (briefly Hull City Hawks 1998-99). Third club was *Hull Thunder* 1999-2003.

Leagues: *Stingrays* - British National League 2003-05; *Thunder* - British National League 1999-2003; *Kingston* - British National League 1997-99, Premier Lge 1996-97; *Humberside* - British Lge, Premier Div. 1991-96, British Lge, Div. One 1989-91, English Lge 1988-89.

Honours: *Humberside Hawks:* British League, Div. One 1990-91; English League 1988-89.

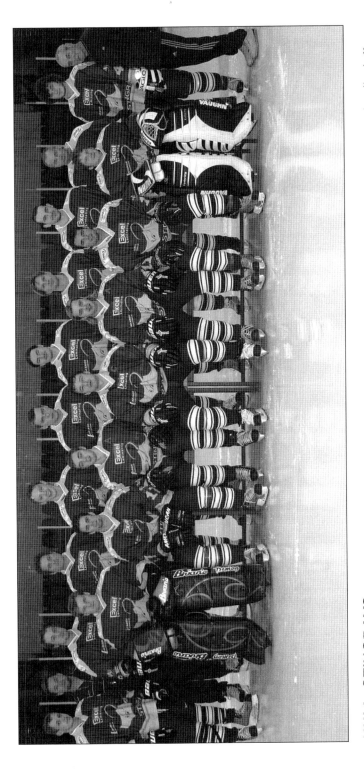

HULL STINGRAYS *left to right, back row:* Dave Ritchie, Rick Strachan (coach), Adam Radmall, Jeff Glowa, Dave Phillips, Vladimir Chernenko, Dave Pyatt, Andrei Nikolaev, Tim McKay, Evgeny Alipov, Luke Boothroyd, Ken Jennison (equipment); *front row:* Ladislav Kudrna, Scott Wray, Kevin Phillips, Pavel Gomenyuk, Slava Koulikov, Dru Burgess, Sam Roberts.

Photo: Arthur Foster.

LONDON RACERS

PLAYER	ALL COMPETITIONS					ELITE LEAGUE					PLAYOFFS				
Scorers	GP	G	A	Pts	Pim	GP	G	A	Pts	Pim	GP	G	A	Pts	Pim
Steve Moria	57	23	25	48	20	49	20	22	42	20	8	3	3	6	0
Dennis Maxwell (I)	56	18	26	44	197	48	16	22	38	179	8	2	4	6	18
Scott Nichol (I)	24	9	18	27	114	16	7	11	18	88	8	2	7	9	26
Jim Vickers (I)	56	10	16	26	38	48	9	14	23	36	8	1	2	3	2
Ian McIntyre (I)	39	8	15	23	40	31	7	12	19	24	8	1	3	4	16
Joe Ciccarello (I) 1	27	5	16	21	8	19	5	13	18	6	8	0	3	3	2
Mark Gouett (I)	56	7	12	19	42	48	4	11	15	34	8	3	1	4	8
Jason Robinson (I)	57	2	13	15	118	49	2	11	13	96	8	0	2	2	22
Eric Cairns (I)	34	3	9	12	140	32	3	9	12	113	2	0	0	0	27
Dusan Halloun (I) 4	30	8	3	11	20	30	8	3	11	20					
Denis Ladouceur (I)	32	8	3	11	8	24	4	2	6	8	8	4	1	5	0
Jason Hewitt	50	8	2	10	77	49	8	2	10	75	1	0	0	0	2
Yannick Tremblay (I)	21	5	5	10	36	21	5	5	10	36					
Richard Hargreaves 4	55	1	9	10	56	47	1	6	7	54	8	0	3	3	2
Jeremy Cornish (I)	57	5	4	9	180	49	4	3	7	174	8	1	1	2	6
Mark Thomas	54	4	2	6	89	46	3	0	3	79	8	1	2	3	10
Matt Foord 4	33	3	2	5	20	25	2	0	2	14	8	1	2	3	6
Darren Cotton 2	22	2	3	5	8	22	2	3	5	8					
Brent Pope 3	14	0	4	4	26	14	0	4	4	26					
J J McGrath	51	1	1	2	12	43	1	1	2	12	8	0	0	0	0
Joe Watkins (N) (I)	27	0	1	1	6	19	0	0	0	6	8	0	1	1	0
Sylvain Daigle (N) (I)	30	0	0	0	6	30	0	0	0	6					
Adam Dobson (N)	56	0	0	0	2	48	0	0	0	2	8	0	0	0	0
Bench Penalties					36					36					.0
TEAM TOTALS	57	130	189	319	1299	49	111	154	265	1152	8	19	35	54	147
Netminders	GPI	Mins	SOG	GA	Sv%	GPI	Mins	SOG	GA	Sv%	GPI	Mins	SOG	GA	Sv%
Sylvain Daigle (I)	30	1836	1036	70	93.2	30	1836	1036	70	93.2					
Adam Dobson	7	322	149	13	91.3	6	262	128	10	92.2	1	60	21	3	85.7
Joe Watkins (I)	23	1318	628	58	90.8	16	898	411	37	91.0	7	420	217	21	90.3
Empty Net Goals			8	8				7	7				1	1	
TEAM TOTALS	57	3476	1821	149	91.8	49	2996	1582	124	92.2	8	480	239	25	89.5

Also appeared: Tom Wills (N) 4.

Also played for: 1 Sheffield Steelers; 2 Peterborough Phantoms, Slough Jets;
3 Basingstoke Bison, Peterborough Phantoms; 4 Slough Jets.

Shutouts: Daigle (2) - league: 1 Oct v Sheffield Steelers (18 saves), 18 Dec at Basingstoke
Bison (52). Watkins - *13 Feb v Hull Stingrays (11 saves).
Dobson - *13 Feb v Hull Stingrays (6 saves)
*shared shutout

All Competitions = league and playoffs
Elite League includes Challenge Cup (excluding playoffs) and Crossover Games

LONDON RACERS *left to right, back row:* Jali Wahlsten (technical advisor), Matt Foord, Mark Thomas, Dennis Maxwell, Eric Cairns, Jim Vickers, Jeremy Cornish, JJ McGrath, Rick Strang (medical officer); *middle row (standing):* Roger Black (chairman), Scott Nicholl, Mark Gouett, Jason Hewitt, Ian McIntyre, Jason Robinson; *front row (kneeling):* Adam Dobson, Denis Ladouceur, Richard Hargreaves, Joe Ciccarello, Steve Moria, Joe Watkins.

Photo: Diane Davey

Goon too far

DAN WARD

Season Two for the London Racers lived up to owner **Roger Black**'s promise of improvements, with increasing attendances and respect from opponents.

With a last place finish in 2003-04, the Racers really had only one direction in which to travel and the signing of former London Knights' favourite, **Dennis Maxwell**, as player-coach, set the tone.

'Maxie' retained just one of the previous year's cohort, his predeccessor as player-coach, the tough import defenceman **Jason Robinson**. Though Robinson kept the dual role, he deferred to Maxwell as they put together a competitive team that packed a punch.

Maxwell's reputation as a reliable contributor with goals and assists was eclipsed in many fans' eyes by his success without the gloves and his first season as coach bore these hallmarks, too. Success came, but so did a focus on a robustness that contrasted with the flailing Finns of Season One.

Two French-Canadians, goalie **Sylvain Daigle** and forward **Yannick Tremblay**, departed at Christmas, which left a hole in scoring punch and, crucially, between the pipes as Daigle compiled the league's best save percentage during his short stay in the capital. The gaps were filled, but the team suffered a knock at losing their first-choice players.

A sixth place finish took the Racers into the off-season ahead of Basingstoke Bison, but despite a good run of form heading into the playoffs, they had a mountain to climb in a group comprising the eventual finalists.

Maxwell acknowledged that in his first year as coach he would be on a steep learning curve, but there's no doubt that he made progress while his own play picked up.

Opposition fans grew to understand that the Racers were no strangers to controversy. The local rivalry with Basingstoke was given plenty of fuel but it was probably New York Islander **Eric Cairns** who cemented his reputation as the most (in)famous man to wear Racers Red.

Involved in a heated exchange with referee **Andy Carson** during a playoff game in March, the 6ft, 6in defenceman was adjudged by the league to have crossed the line and he was banned from the playoffs and beyond.

It was a shame to see him leave under a cloud as he was one of the two locked-out NHLers, alongside Chicago Blackhawk **Scott Nichol**, who had given their all in London's cause.

PLAYER AWARDS

Players' Player	**Mark Gouett**
Most Valuable Player	**Jason Robinson**
Coach's Award	**Jeremy Cornish**
Best Forward	**Steve Moria**
Best Defenceman	**Jason Robinson**
Unsung Hero	**Adam Dobson**
Most Improved British Player	**Matt Foord**
Evolution Fightwear Top Enforcer	
	Jeremy Cornish

LEADING PLAYERS

Jeremy Cornish *born 7 December 1979*
Recruited as a tough-guy role-player, the big forward stood up for his team against some real heavyweights. But he also made a contribution with his gloves on as he was given plenty of ice-time.

Steve Moria *born 3 February 1961*
Brought leadership and experience and proved there is still plenty left in the league's oldest player. Topping his team in goals and points for a second straight season (previously with Bison), 'Mo' was a leader in every way.

MOST PROMISING PLAYER

Matt Foord *born 9 September 1981*
'Foordy' made the transition from Slough Jets' loanee to Elite League regular look easy. Originally drafted as a stop-gap, the home-grown forward showed grit, tenacity and fear for no one.

FACT FILE 2004-05
Elite League: Sixth
Playoffs: Third in qualifying group
Challenge Cup: Fourth in qualifying group
Crossover Games: Sixth

HISTORY
Founded: 2003. Previous team at Lee Valley was the Lions in 1984-95.
League: Elite League 2003-05.
Honours: None.

MILTON KEYNES LIGHTNING

PLAYER	ALL COMPETITIONS					ENGLISH PREMIER LEAGUE					PLAYOFFS				
Scorers	GP	G	A	Pts	Pim	GP	G	A	Pts	Pim	GP	G	A	Pts	Pim
Nick Poole	46	31	68	99	34	23	19	42	61	26	8	7	16	23	4
Gary Clarke	38	49	24	73	46	16	27	8	35	26	8	13	7	20	4
Mikko Skinnari (I)	49	21	33	54	6	30	15	17	32	4	6	5	4	9	0
Greg Randall	53	21	27	48	14	30	16	14	30	10	8	2	7	9	4
Steve Carpenter	48	13	30	43	186	28	9	23	32	110	6	1	4	5	24
Michael Wales 2	52	16	23	39	276	30	10	16	26	145	7	2	2	4	59
Dwayne Newman (I)	52	12	18	30	106	30	8	10	18	36	8	2	6	8	39
Bari McKenzie 3	49	15	12	27	26	29	12	10	22	12	7	1	0	1	6
Adam Carr	46	13	14	27	26	26	7	10	17	4	8	2	3	5	2
Chris McEwan	51	8	14	22	24	29	5	9	14	14	8	3	3	6	4
Kurt Irvine	40	5	16	21	244	18	2	11	13	105	8	2	3	5	88
Dean Campbell	47	9	11	20	14	28	4	10	14	2	7	3	1	4	6
Simon Howard	39	6	13	19	16	22	3	10	13	14	3	0	0	0	2
Ross Bowers	42	8	7	15	24	26	6	5	11	18	8	1	1	2	6
Jamie Randall	54	4	11	15	4	31	3	8	11	2	7	1	2	3	2
Phil Wooderson	26	3	0	3	2	13	3	0	3	2					
Michael Knights	3	0	1	1	2	3	0	1	1	2					
Allen Sutton (N)	49	0	0	0	4	29	0	0	0	2	8	0	0	0	2
Bench Penalties					8					6					2
TEAM TOTALS	54	235	322	557	1046	31	149	204	353	540	8	45	59	104	254
Netminders	GPI	Mins	SOG	GA	Sv%	GPI	Mins	SOG	GA	Sv%	GPI	Mins	SOG	GA	Sv%
Mark Woolf	6	219	93	6	93.5	5	212	88	6	93.2	1	7	5	0	100.0
Allen Sutton	29	1693	716	68	90.5	21	1220	486	45	90.7	8	473	230	23	90.0
Matt vd Velden	7	420	150	16	89.3	7	420	150	16	89.3					
Oliver Blythe	2	6	3	2	33.3	2	6	3	2	33.3					
Empty Net Goal	2	1	1			2	1	1							
TEAM TOTALS	39	2340	963	93	90.3	31	1860	728	70	90.4	8	480	235	23	90.2

Also appeared: Lewis Buckman 1, Tom Castle, Dan Chaplin, Lewis Clifford, David Coffey, Kieron Goody, Paul Gore, Paul Jamieson, Tom Ledgard, Andrew Moore (N). James Roberts, Matt Roberts, Tom Roles, Arum Todd, Ben White, Josh White.

Also played for: 1 Basingstoke Bison, Nottingham Panthers, Peterborough Phantoms; 2 Basingstoke Bison; 3 Coventry Blaze.

Shutouts: van der Velden (5) - league: 28 Nov at Chelmsford Chieftains (27 saves), Sutton - *8 Jan v Solihull Kings (11 saves), 15 Jan v Telford Wild Foxes (22), 26 Feb v Swindon Wildcats (14); cup: 7 Nov at Peterboro' Phantoms (20). Wolfe - *8 Jan v Solihull Kings (11 saves), 27 Feb at Swindon Wildcats (11), 5 March v Peterboro' Phantoms (29).
* shared.

All Competitions = league, playoffs and BNL Winter Cup (goalie statistics show league and playoffs only)

Lightning strike twice

PAUL BROOKMAN

English Premier League champions for the second year in succession and playoff winners for the third year in a row, Milton Keynes Lightning were a class apart from most of their competition.

Coach **Nick Poole** made few changes to the previous season's squad, adding fourth import **Steve Carpenter** from Coventry Blaze and replacing departing goalie **Barry Hollyhead** with **Matt van der Velden**, while also bringing in **Jamie Randall** from Romford Raiders.

Lewis Buckman also signed from Peterborough Phantoms on a two-way contract with the Elite League's Basingstoke Bison but he played only a handful of games before returning to Phantoms. Van der Velden departed at Christmas, giving **Allen Sutton** the number one goalie spot.

Lightning opted out of the EPL Cup and instead tested the ice in the British National League's Winter Cup. It was not a particular success with only two victories in the qualifying stages, both coming against EPL rivals, Phantoms. It didn't boost the crowds, either, despite the prospect of better opposition.

However, Lightning were rarely disgraced with most of the cup losses being by only two or three goals.

In the league it was a different story as Lightning had a seven-game unbeaten start before their first defeat, 6-5 at home to Telford Wild Foxes.

They suffered one more league loss before going on a nine-match undefeated streak and by Christmas they were third in the table, five points behind the leaders, *Wightlink*, but with three games in hand.

By mid-January they were top, but then a major injury crisis put five key players out of action, including top scorer **Gary Clarke**. However, the rest of Poole's army rallied to the cause to ensure the title was lifted with a 4-0 win at Swindon Wildcats at the end of February.

Lightning started their playoff group with a shock 5-4 home defeat by Romford but that was their only reverse as they qualified for the finals weekend at the Coventry Skydome.

There they just overcame Slough Jets 2-1 in the semi-final, thanks to a Clarke goal less than two minutes from the buzzer.

In the final against Phantoms, Lightning crashed in five goals before their old rivals got off the mark. But two late MK efforts ensured a 7-2 victory and the retention of their title.

PLAYER AWARDS

Player of the Year	**Greg Randall**
Most Valuable Player	**Dwayne Newman**
Players' Player	**Dwayne Newman**
Coach's Award	**Jamie Randall**
Club Man of The Year	**Mikko Skinnari**
Best Defenceman	**Dwayne Newman**
Best British Player	**Chris McEwan**

Most Improved Player (Les McCarthy Trophy)
Bari McKenzie/Ross Bowers *(tie)*

LEADING PLAYERS

Steve Carpenter *born 30 March 1971*

Canadian 'Carps' was in his final season before hanging up his skates but he still made a major contribution as the wall in Lightning's defence. His hard but fair body checks made him a firm favourite.

Chris McEwan *born 5 October 1982*

Few rivals could match the Reading-born defenceman for speed. He proved a key player during the team's injury crisis, even scoring twice in a man-of-the-match performance against *Wightlink* in February.

Michael Wales *born 26 August 1982*

Became an increasingly tough opponent to play against. While never being afraid to back down from a fight, he also showed prowess with his scoring touch.

FACT FILE 2004-05

English Premier League	Winners
Playoffs	Champions
BNL Winter Cup	8th in qual. round

HISTORY

Founded: 2002. Original club founded 1990 as *Kings*. Rink closed 1996-98.

Leagues: *Lightning* English Premier League 2002-05; *Kings* Findus British National League 1999-2002; English League (Premier Div) 1998-99, 1990-91; British League, Premier Div 1994-96; British League, Div One 1991-94.

Honours: *Lightning* English Premier League Playoffs 2002-05; English Premier League 2003-05; *Kings* English Cup 1990-99; British League, Div. One 1993-94.

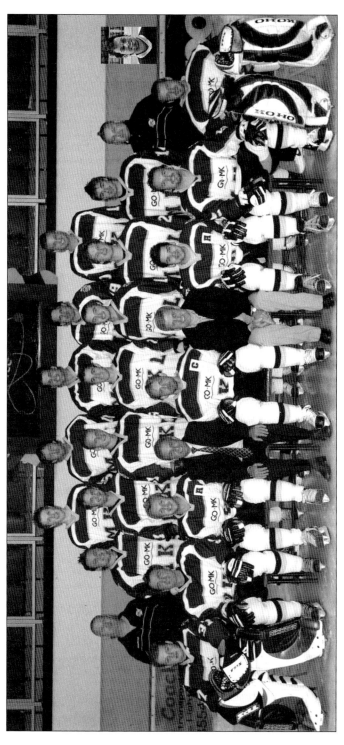

MILTON KEYNES LIGHTNING *left to right, back row:* Bari McKenzie, Kurt Irvine, Steve Carpenter, Jamie Randall, Lewis Buckman; *middle row:* Colin Moore (management), Phil Wooderson, Chris McEwen, Ross Bowers, Michael Wales, Adam Carr, Mikko Skinnari, Gary Clarke, Andy Jolly (equipment); *inset:* Mark Woolf; *front row:* Allen Sutton, Nick Poole (coach), Dean Campbell, Vito Rausa (general manager), Dwayne Newman, Harry Howton (chairman), Greg Randall, Simon Howard (asst. coach), Matt van der Velden.

Photo: Keith Perry Sport Photography.

NEWCASTLE VIPERS

PLAYER	ALL COMPETITIONS					BRITISH NATIONAL LEAGUE					PLAYOFFS				
Scorers	GP	G	A	Pts	Pim	GP	G	A	Pts	Pim	GP	G	A	Pts	Pim
Jonathan Weaver	66	24	57	81	64	36	15	32	47	42	10	1	11	12	2
Matt Beveridge (I)	66	28	47	75	52	36	11	30	41	24	10	5	4	9	2
David Longstaff	63	31	52	63	79	33	13	30	43	22	10	8	7	15	6
Shaun Johnson	63	15	42	57	12	35	7	23	30	6	8	1	5	6	2
Paul Ferone (I)	59	26	25	51	67	29	15	13	28	47	10	5	3	8	6
Hilton Ruggles	63	25	25	50	132	34	16	17	33	48	10	3	1	4	12
Rob Wilson	64	13	30	43	94	36	9	16	25	66	10	0	2	2	6
Steve Gallace (I) 1	34	12	23	35	56	18	8	10	18	44					
Rob Trumbley (I)	59	15	15	30	192	29	12	10	22	92	10	1	1	2	10
Simon Leach	44	4	16	20	88	23	1	11	12	52	10	0	1	1	6
Michael Tasker	41	10	9	19	44	17	4	5	9	24	10	3	2	5	4
Stephen Wallace	40	3	14	17	14	22	1	3	4	6					
Chris McAllister (I)	30	0	8	8	62	16	0	5	5	36	10	0	3	3	10
Karl Culley	64	6	1	7	12	36	6	1	7	8	8	0	0	0	0
Robin Delacour (I)	21	3	2	5	26	8	0	0	0	8					
Kevin Bucas	61	0	5	5	20	34	0	5	5	12	8	0	0	0	0
Scott Moody 2	16	1	2	3	8	5	1	0	1	0					
Doug Teskey (N) (I)	65	0	2	2	6	35	0	1	1	6	10	0	1	1	0
Robert Wilson 3	13	0	0	0	6	6	0	0	0	0					
Richie Thornton	24	0	0	0	38	10	0	0	0	0					
Bench Penalties					18					8					4
TEAM TOTALS	67	219	375	574	1090	37	123	212	335	551	10	27	41	68	70
Netminders	GP	Mins	SOG	GA	Sv%	GP	Mins	SOG	GA	Sv%	GP	Mins	SOG	GA	Sv%
Doug Teskey (I)	67	3937	2332	220	90.6	37	2170	1307	132	89.9	10	570	328	33	89.9
Mark Lee	7	121	66	8	87.9	5	78	48	7	85.4	1	40	17	1	94.1
Empty Net Goals			2	2									1	1	
TEAM TOTALS	67	4058	2400	230	90.4	37	2248	1355	139	89.7	10	610	346	35	89.9

Also appeared: Andrew Thornton.

Also played for: 1 Basingstoke Bison; 2 Slough Jets; 3 Whitley Warriors.

Shutouts: Teskey (2) - cup: 4 Dec at Milton Keynes Lightning (25 saves);
league: 26 Feb at Hull Stingrays (40).

League includes Crossover Games with Elite League teams

All Competitions = league, playoffs and Winter Cup

NEWCASTLE VIPERS *left to right, back row:* Andrew Thornton, Shaun Johnson, Stephen Wallace, Richie Thornton, Robert Wilson, Rob Trumbley, Matt Beveridge; *middle row:* Michael Tasker, Hilton Ruggles, Kevin Bucas, Scott Moody, David Longstaff, Robin Delacoure, Karl Culley, Steve Gallace, Tim Blake (equipment); *front row:* Mark Lee, Clyde Tuyl (general manager), Jonathan Weaver, Darryl Illingworth (owner), Paul Ferone, Rob Wilson (coach), Doug Teskey.

Here we go again

PETER ADAMS

Ice hockey in Newcastle was engulfed in turmoil yet again as **Darryl Illingworth** became the latest owner forced to put his business into liquidation due to losses incurred by the team.

But despite the off-ice agony there was ecstasy on it as Vipers finished as runners-up to the all-conquering Bracknell Bees in both the British National League and the Winter Cup.

Rob Wilson's squad failed to reach the later stages of the playoffs, but many fans will recall the season's most dramatic moment as being their Cup semi against Fife Flyers.

David Longstaff and **Hilton Ruggles** gave Vipers a 2-1 lead in the first leg in Kirkcaldy and the home leg ended in sudden death penalty shots with **Doug Teskey**'s save from **Judd Medak**, and **Matt Beveridge**'s 'five-hole' success against **Scott Hay** being decisive.

Vipers duly reached their third successive Cup final but were thoroughly beaten by the Bees.

In truth, though, the real drama was enacted off the ice. After rumours of unpaid bills circulated before Christmas, a mystery businessman was believed to have bailed out the team. The first sign of trouble on the ice came when import defenceman **Steve Gallace** was allowed to join Basingstoke of the Elite League.

On New Year's weekend, Guildford Flames refused to travel north when it emerged that Vipers had not paid their insurance premium. This was only settled thanks to the fans who raised around £6,000.

Amazingly, the club chose the night of the fund-raiser to announce the signing of a locked-out NHL defender, **Chris McAllister**, whose wages and accommodation were paid for by a sponsor.

After Illingworth's creditors met in February, revealing a sorry state of affairs, the club was reborn with a new owner, the 'mystery businessman', **Paddy O'Connor**, a former player turned telecomms magnate.

His first major decision was to apply to take the club into the Elite League for season 2005-06.

There was more controversy in the playoffs when Vipers were forced to play four of their five home games in Whitley Bay when the renamed *Metro Radio* Arena was unavailable. There were questions over the safety of the Whitley Bay rink.

The season ended with the resignation of respected general manager and bench coach **Clyde Tuyl**, claiming that he was "emotionally drained" after three years with the team.

After a season like this, who can blame him?

PLAYER AWARDS

Player of the Year	**Doug Teskey**
Players' Player	**Shaun Johnson**
Coach's Award	**Kevin Bucas/Karl Culley**
Best Forward	**Paul Ferone**
Best Defenceman	**Rob Wilson**
Most Improved Player	**Kevin Bucas**
Correspondents' Cup	**Doug Teskey**

LEADING PLAYERS

Shaun Johnson *born 22 March 1973*

The Durham-born forward played bravely and skilfully, giving total commitment to the team during a difficult season.

Rob Wilson *born 18 June 1968*

The former GB international was Vipers' 'rock'. At the start of the season he added coaching to his defensive duties and after the off-ice debacle, he took on a management role as well.

MOST PROMISING PLAYER

Stephen Wallace *born 25 October 1986*

Much was expected from the young Billingham forward but he only occasionally lived up to his promise as he was hampered by persistent injury.

FACT FILE 2004-05

British National League	Runners-up
Playoffs	Fifth in qr-final grp
Winter Cup	Runners-up

CLUB HISTORY

Founded: Summer 2002 on formation of Newcastle KBS Vipers Ltd by speedway promoter **Darryl Illingworth** and former GB and Riverkings' coach **Alex Dampier**. Taken over by new company, Newcastle Vipers (North East) Ltd, formed by **Paddy O'Connor**, **Rob Wilson** and **Paul Ferone** in February 2005.

Previous Clubs at the *Telewest* Arena were *Jesters*, *Riverkings*, *Cobras* and **Warriors**. No team 2001-02 after bankruptcy of *Jesters*.

Leagues: *Vipers* British National League 2002-04; *Jesters* Superleague 2000-01; *Riverkings* Superleague 1998-2000; *Cobras* Superleague 1990-98, *Warriors* British League, Premier Div 1995-96.

Honours: *Vipers* Findus Cup 2003 and 2002.

NOTTINGHAM PANTHERS

PLAYER	ALL COMPETITIONS					ELITE LEAGUE					PLAYOFFS				
Scorers	GP	G	A	Pts	Pim	GP	G	A	Pts	Pim	GP	G	A	Pts	Pim
David Clarke	62	32	30	62	30	50	27	19	46	24	10	5	9	14	4
Marek Ivan (I)	53	25	22	47	139	47	24	17	41	121	4	0	3	3	2
Mark Cadotte (I)	54	11	35	46	16	50	7	34	41	10	2	2	0	2	4
Konstantin Kalmikov (I)	60	26	18	44	20	48	20	15	35	6	10	6	3	9	0
Matt Myers	61	5	23	28	85	49	3	15	18	75	10	2	8	10	4
Kim Ahlroos (I)	32	10	17	27	8	30	9	17	26	6					
Calle Carlsson (I)	62	5	21	26	36	52	4	16	20	22	10	1	4	5	6
Steve McKenna (I)	51	8	13	21	28	39	6	11	17	12	10	2	2	4	2
Scott Ricci (I)	62	3	18	21	10	50	3	15	18	4	10	0	2	2	0
John Craighead (I) 1	20	8	10	18	89	20	8	10	18	89					
Jan Krulis (I) 2	40	7	8	15	60	38	7	7	14	44					
Paul Moran	52	6	8	14	46	40	5	6	11	30	10	1	2	3	10
Richard Wojciak	52	6	4	10	10	50	6	4	10	10	1	0	0	0	0
Ian Moran (I)	21	2	7	9	10	14	2	6	8	8	7	0	1	1	2
Nick Boynton (I)	20	3	5	8	28	12	1	3	4	6	8	2	2	4	22
Roman Tvrdon (I)	9	2	5	7	6	9	2	5	7	6					
Jan Magdosko (I)	34	2	4	6	103	34	2	4	6	34					
Mikhail Nemirovsky (I)	3	3	2	5	8	2	0	0	0	0	9	3	2	5	8
Daniel Scott	56	0	3	3	14	48	0	2	2	8	6	0	1	1	6
Rhys McWilliams 3	16	1	0	1	0	7	0	0	0	0	9	1	0	1	0
Lewis Buckman 4	1	0	1	1	0	4	0	1	1	0	6	0	0	0	0
James Neil	4	0	1	1	0	3	0	0	0	0	1	0	1	1	0
Jason Buckman 5	14	0	1	1	0	9	0	1	1	0	5	0	0	0	0
Geoff Woolhouse (N)	41	0	1	1	0	31	0	1	1	0	10	0	0	0	0
C Cruickshank (N) (I)	53	0	1	1	10	50	0	1	1	2	1	0	0	0	0
Bench Penalties					48					42					0
TEAM TOTALS	62	165	258	423	804	50	136	210	346	559	10	25	40	65	70

Netminders	GPI	Mins	SOG	GA	Sv%	GPI	Mins	SOG	GA	Sv%	GPI	Mins	SOG	GA	Sv%
Ladislav Kudrna (I) 6	8	452	280	17	93.9						8	452	280	17	93.9
Curtis Cruickshank (I)	51	2992	1331	102	92.3	48	2867	1279	97	92.4	1	5	1	0	100.0
Geoff Woolhouse	10	325	155	17	89.0	7	180	70	2	97.1	3	145	85	15	82.4
Empty Net Goals			2	2				2	2						
TEAM TOTALS	62	3769	1768	138	92.2	50	3047	1351	101	92.5	10	602	366	32	91.3

Also appeared: Alan Levers (N) 3, Andrew Jaszczyk (N), Euan King (N) 5, Michael Snook (N), Stephen Lewis (N), Jamie Moore (N) 5, James Cooke, Shaun Yardley 5.

Also played for: 1 Cardiff Devils; 2 Bracknell Bees; 3 Solihull Kings; 4 Basingstoke Bison, . Milton Keynes Lightning, Peterborough Phantoms; 5 Peterborough Phantoms; 6 Hull Stingrays.

Shutouts: Cruickshank (5) - league: 11 Sept v Hull Stingrays (30 saves), 7 Nov at Basingstoke Bison (31), 23 Dec at Cardiff Devils (26), 29 Jan at Basingstoke Bison (31), 12 Mar v Cardiff Devils (17). Woolhouse - league: 16 Feb v Basingstoke Bison (29 saves).

All Competitions = league, playoffs and Challenge Cup playoffs
Elite League includes Challenge Cup (excluding playoffs) and Crossover Games

Nurse, nurse!

MICK HOLLAND Nottingham Evening Post

Panthers suffered through one of the most injury-prone seasons they've ever known but still fought their way to the Elite League playoff final where they took Coventry Blaze, the Grand Slam champs, into overtime before conceding.

As ever, it was a new line-up which started the season. In came All-Star goalie Cruickshank from Basingstoke, along with fellow imports **Scott Ricci, Konstantin Kalmikov, Marek Ivan, Jan Magdosko** and **Jan Krulis**. Calle Carlsson returned as captain and the new Brits included Nottingham student **Matt Myers** (from home town Cardiff) and **Richard Wojciak** (Swindon).

They started with one former NHL player, **Roman Tvrdon**, and ended up with three: All-Star defenceman **Nick Boynton**, his Boston team-mate **Ian Moran** and Pittsburgh giant **Steve McKenna**.

Three quite superb performances on their unbeaten Continental Cup quest in France - with goaltender **Curtis Cruickshank** the player of the tournament - should have sparked a first league title since the late 1950s.

CRAIGHEAD GETS THE MUMPS

But both Tvrdon and **Paul Moran** collected knocks in Amiens and that was just the beginning of Panthers' horrendous injury woes that left them short-handed for all but two games.

Magdosko was next in the hospital which left the side depleted until December. And that's when the 'fun' started as coach **Paul Adey** brought in Russian-Canadian **Mikhail Nemirovsky** on deadline day and begged and borrowed players from Peterborough and Solihull.

The controversial **John Craighead** contracted mumps and then quit for Cardiff, claiming he was being victimised by coach Adey. Though Panthers had managed to reach the Challenge Cup semi-final, they didn't beat another Elite League side at home until February.

With hopes of the league title long gone, team owner **Neil Black** warned Adey that if they didn't beat Cardiff in the last league game, he would be sacked. The transformation was immediate . . . well, almost.

In their first play-off game against the rampant Blaze, the jinx struck again with Wojciak and Cruickshank suffering season-ending injuries.

Fortunately, they were given special dispensation to draft in Hull goalie **Ladislav Kudrna** and he performed miracles to lead Panthers to a memorable final. But Adey's battered battlers found it a bridge too far.

PLAYER AWARDS

Player of the Year	Calle Carlsson
Most Valuable Player	David Clarke
Players' Player	
Konstantin Kalmikov/David Clarke (tie)	
Best British Player	David Clarke
NHL Player of the Year	Nick Boynton
Gary Rippingale Team Spirit award:	
	Calle Carlsson
Most consistent	Konstantin Kalmikov
Most entertaining	Matt Myers

LEADING PLAYERS

Calle Carlsson born 2 May 2 1972

The amiable Swedish defender thrived on his additional responsibility as captain. Though his least productive year in goals - he was lethal on the powerplay in the past - he made up for that with his effort and consistency.

David Clarke born 5 August 1981

Once a bit-part player in the old Superleague with London and Newcastle, the winger really blossomed under the guidance of coach Adey, and his goal output and armful of awards show how much he enjoyed his senior role.

MOST PROMISING PLAYER

Matt Myers born 6 November 1984

One of the league's most reliable centremen, he is another Brit to flourish because of the responsibilty and additional ice-time given to him by the coach. One can only imagine what kind of impact the student might have made had he been able to practice full time throughout the season.

FACT FILE 2004-05

Elite League	Fourth
Playoffs	Finalists
Challenge Cup	Semi-finalists
Crossover Games	Third

HISTORY

Founded 1946. Re-formed 1980. Club suspended operations 1960-80. Purchased by Aladdin Sports Management in 1997. Moved to the National Ice Centre in August 2000. Leagues Elite League 2003-05; Superleague 1996-2003; British Lge (BL) (Premier Div) 1982-96 and 1954-60; English Nat Lge (ENL) 1981-82 and 1946-54; Inter-City Lge 1980-82. **Honours**: See *The Ice Hockey Annual* 2004-05.

NOTTINGHAM PANTHERS *left to right,* *back row:* Mark Cadotte, Mikhail Nemirovsky, Kim Ahlroos, Ian Moran, Richard Wojciak, Paul Moran; *middle row:* Paul Adey (coach), Daniel Scott, Konstantin Kalmikov, Steve McKenna, Marek Ivan, Nick Boynton, Matt Myers, Scott Poundall (trainer); *front row:* Adam Goodridge (equipment), Curtis Cruickshank, David Clarke, Calle Carlsson, Scott Ricci, Geoff Woolhouse.

Photo: Dave Page

PETERBOROUGH PHANTOMS

PLAYER	ALL COMPETITIONS					ENGLISH PREMIER LEAGUE					PLAYOFFS				
Scorers	GP	G	A	Pts	Pim	GP	G	A	Pts	Pim	GP	G	A	Pts	Pim
Doug McEwen	52	16	44	60	83	30	13	23	36	54	8	1	9	10	2
Marc Long 2	36	20	29	49	85	25	17	19	36	71	8	3	7	10	14
James Morgan	45	19	28	47	245	27	16	21	37	139	7	2	4	6	40
Jesse Hammill	40	14	24	38	173	21	11	15	26	95	8	2	6	8	6
Antti Kohvakka (I)	55	10	28	38	155	31	9	19	28	87	8	0	0	0	16
Jon Cotton	32	17	20	37	44	21	13	17	30	36	7	3	2	5	6
Shaun Yardley 7	46	24	12	36	46	24	11	9	20		7	5	2	7	4
Darren Cotton 4	29	19	16	35	26	20	8	14	22	26	8	7	2	9	0
Lewis Buckman 6	22	14	11	25	48	15	10	9	19	46	7	4	2	6	2
James Ellwood	52	9	11	20	16	28	6	5	11	10	8	1	4	5	2
Jake Armstrong 5	36	4	16	20	44	24	4	13	17	34	8	0	3	3	10
Pavel Rieciciar (I) 8	19	7	10	17	6	7	3	7	10	4					
Jason Buckman 2	54	11	2	13	60	31	6	2	8	32	7	2	0	2	6
Karl Hopper	54	2	9	11	102	32	2	6	8	70	8	0	1	1	10
James Archer	46	4	5	9	8	28	4	1	5	8	6	0	1	1	0
Michael Bowman 1	16	2	4	6	6	5	1	2	3	0					
Andy Munroe	54	2	4	6	60	31	1	4	5	32	8	1	0	1	18
Mark Williams 3	14	1	1	2	82	5	1	0	1	64					
Steven Maile	45	1	1	2	67	27	0	1	1	53	3	0	0	0	0
Grant Hendry	53	0	2	2	24	30	0	2	2	20	8	0	0	0	0
Stephen Wall (N)	55	0	2	2	29	32	0	2	2	4	8	0	0	0	25
Andrejs Lavrenovs (I)	20	1	0	1	24	5	0	0	0	14					
James Ferrara	30	0	1	1	10	16	0	0	0	10	4	0	0	0	0
Julian Smith	32	0	1	1	6	17	0	1	1	6	4	0	0	0	0
Craig Peacock	33	0	1	1	0	16	0	1	1	0	6	0	0	0	0
Brent Pope 9	2	0	0	0	4										
Bench Penalties					28										2
TEAM TOTALS	56	197	282	479	1481	32	136	193	329	947	8	31	43	74	163

Netminders	GPI	Mins	SOG	GA	Sv%	GPI	Mins	SOG	GA	Sv%	GPI	Mins	SOG	GA	Sv%
Stephen Wall		55	2980	1608	188	88.3	32	1842	884	90	89.8	8	414	226	23	89.8
James Moore 7		12	350	176	30	82.9	3	78	27	5	81.5	2	66	33	3	90.9
Euan King 7		1	30	15	3	80.0										
TEAM TOTALS		56	3360	1799	221	87.7	32	1920	911	95	89.6	8	480	259	26	90.0

Also appeared: Adam Holloway.

Also played for: 1 Chelmsford Chieftains, Sheffield Steelers; 2 Chelmsford Chieftains;
                   3 Romford Raiders; 4 London Racers, Slough Jets; 5 Solihull Kings;
                   6 Basingstoke Bison, Milton Keynes Lightning, Nottingham Panthers;
                   7 Nottingham Panthers; 8 Basingstoke Bison; 9 Basingstoke Bison, London Racers.

Shutouts (league   *Wall/Moore - league: 2 Oct v Solihull Kings (14 saves);
and playoffs):   Wall - league: 19 Dec v Slough Jets (23 saves).
All Competitions = league, playoffs and BNL Winter Cup

PETERBOROUGH PHANTOMS *left to right, back row:* James Archer, James Ferrara, Jason Buckman, Craig Peacock, Steven Maile, Euan King; *middle row:* Grant Hendry, Julian Smith, Karl Hopper, Mark Williams, James Morgan, Andrew Munroe, Andrejs Lavrenovs, Rob Horsfall (equipment); *front row:* James Moore, James Ellwood, Pavel Rieciciar, Doug McEwen, Kevin King (coach), Jesse Hammill, Jon Kynaston (coach), Antti Kohvakka, Michael Bowman, Shaun Yardley, Stephen Wall.

Photo: Dave Page

King's no more

SIMON POTTER

Peterborough's fans demand a lot, so second place in the English Premier League and a berth in the final of the Playoffs wasn't nearly enough for many of them.

Mind you, it was the first season in the club's three-year history that their trophy cabinet had been bare.

As the end of November approached, it was little wonder that there was an air of gloom over the Planet Ice rink, with 19 defeats, a tie and just three victories.

In defence of beleaguered coach **Kevin King**, this was perhaps no surprise with 13 of those defeats at the hands of British National League clubs in Winter Cup ties and a further two against Elite League sides in exhibition games.

At the end of the day, though, a loss is a loss, and veteran **Doug McEwen**, in his 42nd year and 19th season of British hockey, went public in saying that all those defeats had dented Phantoms' confidence.

Perhaps it had been a mistake for them to turn their backs on the Premier Cup they had won two years running to enter the Winter Cup instead.

"KEVIN CAN'T DRIVE TEAM ANY MORE"

Or perhaps it was a masterstroke that made better players out of the youngsters sent out against senior opposition.

Eventually, their fortunes picked up and they achieved a victory over a disinterested and below-par Newcastle Vipers in their final cup game.

They went on to clamber their way up the league table, beat Milton Keynes twice to lift the Planet Ice Shield, and topped their playoff group.

By then, though, King had quit as coach - one match short of his 100th in charge - with joint general manager **Phil Wing** saying: "Kevin feels he can't drive the team forward as coach any more."

His 59-30-10 career record was pretty impressive by anyone's standards, especially considering that 13 of those 30 defeats had been against the BNL clubs.

As at any club in any season, there were heroes as well as villains.

Former Hull youngster **Andy Munroe** sparkled and swept the board at the end-of-season awards night while McEwen remained a class act, despite being old enough to have fathered half of the team.

His sheer brilliance as a playmaker, though, was countered by the club's repeated failure to turn their constant shots into more goals.

PLAYER AWARDS

Player of the Year	Andy Munroe
Players' Player :	Andy Munroe
Best Forward	Marc Long
Best Defenceman	Andy Munroe
Most Improved Player	Jason Buckman
Best Young Player	James Archer
Best Clubman (Maggie Macfarlane Award)	
	Andy Munroe

LEADING PLAYERS

Doug McEwen born 2 October 1963
The Grand Master and a real gentleman. Still head and shoulders above the vast majority of EPL players. Vastly adaptable, he can play anywhere, though we've yet to see him in goal.

Andy Monroe born 2 August 1982
The defenceman arrived in Peterborough after four seasons in Hull and found English Premier League hockey to his liking, winning the fans over and collecting a triple of trophies on awards night.

Stephen Wall born 2 December 1981
Stellar performances by the Geordie keeper kept his side in many games, especially in the first half of the season when they suffered a string of injuries and struggled to cope with the BNL's offence.

MOST PROMISING PLAYERS

James Ferrara/Craig Peacock
Peterborough's junior programme, that produced the likes of **David Clarke** and **James Morgan**, is still creating exciting young players and these two (Craig is the son of former import, Tim) are both ones to watch.

FACT FILE 2004-05

English Premier League:	Runners-up
Playoffs:	Finalists
BNL Winter Cup:	Ninth

HISTORY

Founded: 2002. The previous team at Peterborough was the **Pirates** 1982-2002.
Leagues: **Phantoms** English Premier Lge 2002-05. **Pirates** British National Lge 1997-2002; Premier Lge 1996-97; British Lge, Div One 1995-96, 1986-87, 1982-85; British Lge, Premier Div 1987-95, 1985-86.
Honours: **Phantoms** English Premier Lge 2002-03; Premier Cup 2003-04, 2002-03; **Pirates** British Lge, Div. One playoffs 1987-88; British Lge, Div. One 1986-87, 1984-85; Christmas Cup 1999.

ROMFORD RAIDERS

PLAYER	ALL COMPETITIONS					ENGLISH PREMIER LEAGUE					PLAYOFFS				
Scorers	GP	G	A	Pts	Pim	GP	G	A	Pts	Pim	GP	G	A	Pts	Pim
Andrew Power (I)	52	63	79	142	275	27	32	46	78	145	8	10	12	22	88
Kyle Amyotte (I)	42	60	53	113	58	22	31	29	60	48	8	8	14	22	0
Danny Marshall	54	34	68	102	50	29	19	36	55	34	8	9	11	20	2
Lee Cowmeadow	51	23	37	60	26	27	13	23	36	22	8	4	5	9	0
Craig Britton	53	13	31	44	124	30	11	14	25	84	8	2	4	6	6
Richard Whiting	53	8	26	34	44	29	5	12	17	30	7	1	5	6	4
Andrius Kaminskas (I)	41	17	14	31	233	22	6	7	13	107	8	5	5	10	63
Mike Marostega (I)	29	8	12	20	72	16	5	8	13	64	8	2	3	5	2
Mike Galati (I)	9	12	5	17	4	4	6	3	9	2					
Mark Williams 1	36	3	13	16	268	19	2	8	10	150	8	0	2	2	80
Tom Long	55	5	9	14	92	30	2	5	7	62	8	2	1	3	14
Tyrone Miller	38	2	11	13	38	19	2	7	9	32	6	0	0	0	2
Grant Taylor	54	6	4	10	64	31	2	1	3	50	8	1	0	1	0
Robert Jenner	56	5	4	9	48	31	1	2	3	46	8	0	0	0	0
Ben Pitchley	46	1	8	9	36	26	1	4	5	26	8	0	1	1	8
Steve Birch (I)	11	2	6	8	44	6	2	4	6	16					
Fraser Hendry	34	2	6	8	4	20	2	1	3	0	8	0	2	2	0
Antti Makikyro (I)	25	0	3	3	8	17	0	2	2	8					
Bernie Bradford	46	0	3	3	14	24	0	2	2	4	8	0	1	1	2
Aaron Atkin	7	2	0	2	0	5	2	0	2	0					
Ben Smith	34	1	1	2	55	19	0	1	1	43	6	0	0	0	0
Dave Fielder 2	8	0	2	2	4	4	0	2	2	2					
Andy Moffatt (N)	51	0	2	2	18	29	0	1	1	12	8	0	0	0	2
Scott Beeson	3	1	0	1	0	2	0	0	0	0					
Thomas Spinks	28	0	1	1	6	14	0	0	0	2					
Bench Penalties					14					8					2
TEAM TOTALS	56	268	398	666	1599	31	144	218	362	997	8	44	66	110	281
Netminders	GPI	Mins	SOG	GA	Sv%	GPI	Mins	SOG	GA	Sv%	GPI	Mins	SOG	GA	Sv%
Andy Moffatt	51	3115	1925	179	90.7	29	1704	1061	103	90.3	8	480	326	30	90.8
Alan Blyth	9	245	143	15	89.5	6	156	77	10	87.0					
TEAM TOTALS	56	3360	2068	194	90.6	31	1860	1138	113	90.1	8	480	326	30	90.8

Also played for: 1 Peterborough Phantoms; 2 Solihull Kings.

Shutouts (league & playoffs):   Moffat - league: 16 Jan v Wightlink Raiders (30 saves).

All Competitions = league, playoffs and Premier Cup

A cup for Ollie

MICK CAHILL

The smile returned to Romford as Raiders overcame an injury-plagued start and secured a respectable league position, a Playoff Finals place and silverware in the English Premier Cup.

But it nearly didn't happen. **Ollie Oliver**, long-time Chelmsford boss but out of favour at the Riverside, stepped in at the last minute when it looked as if Raiders' future was doomed.

With former Chieftains' manager **Nolan Smith** and coach **Dean Birrell** on board, a team was built virtually overnight.

Although it resembled a Chelmsford reunion - top scorers **Andrew Power**, **Kyle Amyotte** and **Lee Cowmeadow**, goalies **Andy Moffat** and **Alan Blyth**, Brit **Richard Whiting** and Finn **Antti Makikyro** all moved west - Raiders' regulars **Danny Marshall**, **Ben Pitchley**, **Grant Taylor**, **Tyrone Miller**, **Tom Spinks** and **Rob Jenner** provided some familiar faces.

Canadian **Steve Birch** returned to this country, albeit briefly, and Birrell made a smart move in capturing Peterborough's **Craig Britton** and youngsters **Bernie Bradford** and **Grant Hendry**, and Slough's **Tom Long**.

Raiders won their two openers but then the injury hoodoo struck. Hotshot Amyotte suffered terrible facial damage at Slough and was sidelined for two months.

The following Saturday, Hendry was in a Telford hospital with a shattered jaw and a day later, Birch left the game with a hip strain.

'Birchy' was out until November and then out for good as he quit Raiders for Geleen in Holland along with Canadian centre **Mike Galati**, who had been drafted in to prop up the offence.

When the crocks returned, Raiders found a consistency that threatened any team. The blueline was solid, boosted by Canadian **Mike Marostega**, Peterborough's **Mark Williams** and a rejuvenated Pitchley. Power headed the league's scoring race and skipper Marshall finished as the league's top Brit.

With crowd-pleasing Lithuanian **Andrus Kaminskas** on board and Moffat starring in goal, Romford took points in every opposition rink except the Isle of Wight. Only a single goal semi-final defeat by Phantoms denied Raiders the opportunity to take on Lightning in the playoff championship final.

Apart from the locally important Essex Cup victory over neighbours Chelmsford, the highlight was a weekend of full-blooded cup final hockey. Swindon's Link Centre and Rom Valley Way were packed to the rafters as Raiders emerged with the trophy.

PLAYER AWARDS

Players' Player	Andy Moffat
Coach's Player	Andy Moffat
Internet Player of the Year	Danny Marshall
Supporters' Player of the Year	Andrew Power
Best Defenceman	Craig Britton
Best Forward	Andrius Kaminskas

LEADING PLAYERS

Craig Britton *born 24 September 1976*
Model professional who quickly became a firm favourite. Good in the dressing room, with the fans and most importantly, a quality blueliner on the ice.

Andy Moffat *born 9 May 1982*
The GB junior international goalie hardly had an off-day throughout the season. Despite arriving from Chelmsford, the Romford crowd soon took the Fifer to their hearts as his outstanding contribution often tipped the balance. Double awards winner.

Ben Pitchley *born 24 April 1973*
In his final campaign, the assistant coach rolled back the years to perform as well as he ever has. Has a talented son in the club's junior programme who may one day fill dad's big skates.

FACT FILE 2004-05

English Premier League:	Fourth
Playoffs:	Third
Premier Cup:	Champions

HISTORY

Founded: 1987. (Withdrew from British League, Div One midway through 1994-95 due to lack of finance.)

Leagues: English (Premier) League 1995-2005, 1989-90; British League, Div One 1990-94 and 1988-89; British League, Div Two 1987-88.

Honours: English Premier Cup 2004-05, 2001-02; English National League, Premier Div playoffs 2000-01; British League, Div Two 1987-88.

ROMFORD RAIDERS *left to right; back row:* Kyle Amyotte, Craig Britton, Andrius Kaminskas, Andrew Power, Tom Long, Ben Pitchley, Richard Whiting, Grant Taylor, Mike Marostega, Dean Birrell (coach), Nolan Smith (manager); Lee Cowmeadow, Antti Makikyro; *front row (kneeling):* Bernie Bradford, Ben Smith, Fraser Hendry, Alan Blyth, Danny Marshall, Andy Moffat; *(seated)* Mark Williams.

Photo: John Scott

SHEFFIELD STEELERS

PLAYER	ALL COMPETITIONS					ELITE LEAGUE					PLAYOFFS				
Scorers	GP	G	A	Pts	Pim	GP	G	A	Pts	Pim	GP	G	A	Pts	Pim
Erik Anderson (l)	61	25	39	64	26	49	20	29	49	16	10	5	10	15	6
Jeff Christian (l)	55	22	32	54	139	43	17	24	41	137	10	5	8	13	0
Mike Peron (l)	56	22	24	46	177	47	16	18	34	171	8	6	6	12	4
Gerad Adams (l)	59	17	17	34	94	47	14	17	31	86	10	2	0	2	8
Dion Darling (l)	62	10	21	31	98	50	10	13	23	88	10	0	7	7	8
Daryl Andrews (l)	59	9	15	24	38	47	6	12	18	36	10	3	3	6	2
Ron Shudra	62	6	17	23	20	50	4	15	19	20	10	1	2	3	0
Mark Dutiaume (l)	36	8	14	22	28	26	6	11	17	22	8	1	1	2	4
Dave Cousineau (l)	35	4	16	20	48	23	2	10	12	18	10	2	5	7	30
Joe Ciccarello (l) 1	20	8	9	17	22	20	8	9	17	22					
Marc Lefebvre (l)	61	7	3	10	50	49	7	2	9	50	10	0	1	1	0
Paul Sample	62	4	5	9	36	50	4	5	9	34	10	0	0	0	0
Ben Bliss	59	4	3	7	4	47	4	1	5	4	10	0	2	2	0
Les Millie	17	1	1	2	14	12	0	1	1	14	5	1	0	1	0
Brent Bobyck	9	0	2	2	8	9	0	2	2	8					
Ryan Lake	10	0	1	1	10	10	0	1	1	10					
Gavin Farrand	45	0	1	1	16	43	0	1	1	16					
Dwight Parrish (l) 4	3	0	0	0	4	3	0	0	0	4					
Steve Duncombe	42	0	0	0	4	33	0	0	0	2	7	0	0	0	0
Jayme Platt (N) (l)	58	0	0	0	36	49	0	0	0	36	7	0	0	0	0
Bench Penalties					26					0					26
TEAM TOTALS	62	147	220	367	898	50	118	171	289	794	10	26	45	71	88
Netminders	GPI	Mins	SOG	GA	Sv%	GPI	Mins	SOG	GA	Sv%	GPI	Mins	SOG	GA	Sv%
Davey Lawrence	7	259	120	9	92.5	4	105	49	6	87.8	3	154	71	3	95.8
Jayme Platt (l)	57	3392	1429	110	92.3	49	2947	1223	97	92.1	6	325	166	8	95.2
Stevie Lyle 4	2	120	58	7	87.9						2	120	58	7	87.9
Empty Net Goals			9	9				7	7				2	2	
TEAM TOTALS	62	3771	1616	135	91.6	50	3052	1279	110	91.4	10	599	297	20	93.3

Also appeared: Danny Wood, Greg Wood, Mark Florence 3, Michael Bowman 2, Neil Abel, Paul Jones (N), Ryan Johnson, Simon Butterworth, Steve Fone (N).

Also played for: 1 London Racers; 2 Chelmsford Chieftains, Peterborough Phantoms; 3 Hull Stingrays; 4 Bracknell Bees.

Shutouts: Platt (8) - league: 30 Oct v Newcastle Vipers (17 saves), 7 Nov v Belfast Giants (29) 5 Feb at Nottingham Panthers (29), 16 Feb v Guildford Flames (18), 20 Feb v Basingstoke Bison (19), 26 Feb at Belfast Giants (25), 5 March v Nottingham Panthers (31); playoffs: 17 March v Belfast Giants (25 saves).
Lawrence - playoffs: 3 Apr at Cardiff Devils (33 saves)

All Competitions = league, playoffs and Challenge Cup playoffs
Elite League includes Challenge Cup (excluding playoffs) and Crossover Games

SHEFFIELD STEELERS *left to right, back row:* Paul Jones, Ben Bliss, Brent Bobyck, Erik Anderson, Dave Cousineau, Daryl Andrews, Steve Duncombe, Jeff Christian, Mark Dutiaume, Marc Lefebvre, Gavin Farrand, Paul Sample, Simon Butterworth, Andy Akers (equipment); *front row:* Jayme Platt, Ron Shudra, Mike Peron, Rob Stewart (coach), Dion Darling, Gerad Adams, Davey Lawrence.
Photo: Roger Cook.

Three coaches, no trophies

SHARON HODKIN

The departure of Sheffield's most successful coach, **Mike Blaisdell**, just weeks before the start of the new season launched a difficult and disappointing year for Steelers.

Blaisdell returned to Canada for personal reasons (he later took the job of assistant coach of the Regina Pats in the Western Hockey League) and was replaced by former Belfast coach, **Rob Stewart**.

But Stewart, signed too late to recruit his type of team, lasted only months in what turned out to be Sheffield's first trophy-less season since 1998.

Steelers instead kept faith with much the same team that had brought them league and playoff glory in 2003-04, including captain **Dion Darling** and forwards **Mike Peron** and **Erik Anderson**.

Among only five newcomers was netminder **Jayme Platt**, who had iced the previous year in Manchester. A few games in, Stewart recruited **Jeff Christian** from the German DEL.

November brought rumours of a take-over with owner **Norton Lea** making no secret of his desire to sell the club. However, after weeks of negotiations the deal broke down. On the ice, the team's stuttering season was not getting better as they languished in mid-table mediocrity thanks in part to the forwards' inability to find the net.

Top scorer **Mark Dutiaume** returned from Italy in December but he could not stop the rot, and Steelers' Challenge Cup ambitions ended at the semi-final stage with a 5-3 aggregate loss to Cardiff Devils.

By the end of January, amid rumours of dressing room unrest and fans' discontent, the club finally lost patience with Stewart who was sacked after successive defeats to Cardiff.

The man chosen to lead the club into the playoffs was Glaswegian **Paul Heavey** who had performed a similar feat with Manchester the previous season. He arrived too late to change the league position and the team finished fifth.

After the tough league campaign, Steelers were predicted to miss out on the playoff finals but they defied the form book, partly thanks to Belfast's self-destruction, to reach Nottingham and a semi-final showdown with Coventry.

Their championship hopes ended there with a 3-0 loss to the eventual winners after failing to beat **Jody Lehman** in 41 attempts.

Though they bounced back to take the bronze medal, it was scant consolation for Sheffield's fans who expect success.

PLAYER AWARDS

Player of the Year	**Gerad Adams**
Players' Player	**Erik Anderson**
Best Away Player	**Gerad Adams**
Coach's Player	**Mike Peron/Jayme Platt** (tie)

LEADING PLAYERS

Gerad Adams *born 3 May 1978*
Canadian minor leaguer who joined Steelers in 2003-04 as a defenceman but was converted to a forward under former coach **Mike Blaisdell**. First came to Britain in 2001-02 and played for the BNL's Edinburgh Capitals and Superleague's London Knights.

Erik Anderson *born 6 March 1978*
The American forward was invited back to Sheffield after scoring 70 points in his successful first season with the club.

MOST PROMISING PLAYER

Davey Lawrence *born 6 February 1985*
The Barnsley-born netminder has spent his career with the Steelers and Scimitars and impressed in his limited appearances with Steelers. Has been selected for the GB under-18 and under-20 sides.

FACT FILE 2004-05

Elite League	Fifth
Playoffs	Third
Challenge Cup	Semi-finalists

HISTORY

Founded: 1991. Franchise purchased in August 2001 by **Norton Lea**. In May 2002, Lea set up a company, South Yorkshire Franchise Ice Hockey Club Ltd, to own both the team and the franchise.

Leagues: Elite League 2003-05 Superleague 1996-2003; British League, Premier Div 1993-96; British League, Div One 1992-93; English League 1991-92.

Honours: Elite League & playoffs 2003-04; Superleague Playoff Champions 2001-02, 2000-01 & 1996-97; Superleague 2002-03, 2000-01; Challenge Cup 2002-03, 2000-01, 1999-2000 & 1998-99; British League and Championship 1995-96 & 1994-95; B&H Autumn Cup 2000-01, 1995-96.

SLOUGH JETS

PLAYER	ALL COMPETITIONS					ENGLISH PREMIER LEAGUE					PLAYOFFS				
Scorers	GP	G	A	Pts	Pim	GP	G	A	Pts	Pim	GP	G	A	Pts	Pim
Zoran Kozic	48	34	32	66	42	26	19	19	38	22	8	6	5	11	4
Adam Bicknell	51	13	31	44	106	29	8	17	25	50	8	0	4	4	16
Matt Foord 1	45	22	21	43	80	25	10	13	23	50	6	6	0	6	6
Matt Towalski	54	17	22	39	94	31	8	18	26	68	8	2	0	2	8
Nick Burton	48	16	20	36	52	26	12	8	20	28	8	1	4	5	8
Nicky Chinn 4	31	10	20	30	202	14	3	10	13	121	3	1	2	3	14
Terry Miles	48	14	14	28	67	29	9	8	17	57	7	2	0	2	8
Warren Rost	53	13	14	27	78	30	8	9	17	58	8	1	2	3	4
Nicky Watt	45	15	9	24	155	25	9	5	14	76	8	4	2	6	16
Dusan Halloun (I) 1	26	7	15	22	40	18	6	11	17	28	8	1	4	5	12
Norman Pinnington	19	6	13	19	102	11	2	6	8	66	8	4	7	11	36
Adam Greener	42	9	6	15		22	7	5	12	68	7	1	0	1	37
Scott Moody 5	22	1	12	13	62	14	0	7	7	42	8	1	5	6	20
Brian McLaughlin (I) 2	23	1	12	13	16	14	0	7	7	14	1	0	0	0	0
Stewart Tait	47	4	7	11	101	27	3	6	9	69	8	0	0	0	4
Mike Plenty	54	4	5	9	18	31	1	4	5	8	8	1	0	1	0
Jason Reilly 4	10	2	6	8	16	6	2	4	6	2					
Graham Bellamy	54	2	5	7	4	31	2	3	5	2	8	0	0	0	0
Brent Goldie (I)	5	3	2	5	8	2	3	1	4	4					
Richard Hargreaves 1	3	2	3	5	0	2	2	2	4	0					
Tom Smith	32	1	4	5	4	18	1	3	4	2	8	0	1	1	2
David Poulton	9	1	2	3	2	6	1	1	2	0					
Daniel Marashi	1	1	0	1	0										
James Wiggins 4	4	1	0	1	4	2	0	0	0	4					
Chris Babbage	9	1	0	1	0	4	1	0	1	0					
Darren Cotton 3	1	0	1	1	0										
James Day	12	0	1	1	4	6	0	1	1	2					
Daniel Smith	1	0	0	0	2										
Adam Gray 2	4	0	0	0	4	4	0	0	0	4					
Adam Dobson (N) 1	21	0	0	0	2	4	0	0	0	2	1	0	0	0	0
Bench Penalties										6					0
TEAM TOTALS	54	200	277	477	1265	31	122	168	290	857	8	31	36	67	195
Netminders	GPI	Mins	SOG	GA	Sv%	GPI	Mins	SOG	GA	Sv%	GPI	Mins	SOG	GA	Sv%
Tom Wills 1	49	2772	1477	153	89.6	27	1575	842	92	89.1	7	418	222	15	93.2
Adam Dobson 1	7	420	190	23	87.9	4	240	106	12	88.7	1	60	39	6	84.6
Will Sanderson	1	24	16	2	87.5	1	24	16	2	87.5					
Michael Will	1	20	13	2	84.6	1	20	13	2	84.6					
Empty Net Goals		4	0	0			1	0	0			2	0	0	
TEAM TOTALS	54	3240	1696	180	89.4	31	1860	977	108	88.9	8	480	261	21	91.9

Also appeared: Mike Gray (N), Kevin McGurk (N).

Also played for: 1 London Racers; 2 Chelmsford Chieftains; 3 London Racers, Peterboro' Phantoms; 4 Guildford Flames; 5 Newcastle Vipers.

Shutouts: Wills (2) - league: 20 Nov v Solihull Kings (7 saves);
playoffs: 10 April at Chelmsford Chieftains (24).

All Competitions = league, playoffs and Premier Cup

Saving the best 'til last

DICK BELLAMY

Reaching the playoff semi-finals of the English Premier League was the highlight of a very mixed season for the Jets.

An unsettled squad right up to the signing deadline was the main cause with a big turnover of players during the summer and the early part of the season.

Player-coach **Warren Rost** built his squad around forward **Zoran Kozic**, who had joined Jets from Haringey late in season 2003-04, but the former Yugoslav international was a disappointment as he was frequently marked out of games.

Kozic's Canadian team-mate, **Tom Wills**, the oldest player on the squad, relished his position as starting goalie and, though unorthodox, he turned in some great performances.

One of Rost's shrewdest moves was to persuade ex-Jets defenceman **Rob Coutts** to return to the team as bench coach, when his work commitments allowed, freeing Rost to concentrate on playing.

Welsh forward **Nicky Chinn** played, controversially, when he wasn't with the British National League's Guildford Flames, and Rost also did a 'two-way deal' with London Racers of the Elite League

This gained them **Nick Burton** and Czech **Dusan Halloun** but lost them local forward **Matt Foord** for some games and back-up netminder **Adam Dobson** for much of the schedule.

After failing to reach the Premier Cup semis, Jets recovered and were topping the league table by mid-December despite stumbling to a 2-1 defeat at Solihull Kings, the league stragglers.

But after some poor results in the New Year, they slipped back to fifth while Rost took some heat for missing a crucial weekend by playing in a 'pond hockey' tournament in Canada and taking Burton and Kozic with him.

Jets' final league placing of sixth was also controversial as it came on the last weekend of the season with a 5-2 loss at lowly Telford.

However, as they had 12 months earlier, they came good in the playoffs. Everybody raised their game and after two one-goal defeats on the first weekend, they ran up four impressive wins, including a 3-0 shutout of favoured Chelmsford.

Their semi-final loss to Milton Keynes, following some questionable refereeing, was nevertheless the best game of the finals weekend and Rost has to be congratulated for getting Jets that far on a limited budget.

PLAYER AWARDS

Player of the Year	**Tom Wills**
Players' Player	**Adam Greener**
Coach's Player	**Adam Greener**
Captain's Award	**Nicky Watt**
Best British Player	**Adam Greener**

LEADING PLAYERS

Nick Burton *born 19 June 1979*
An investment banker who played in Finland before coming to England at the age of 20, he is at ease both as a forward and on defence. His major contribution to Jets came during the playoffs where he was outstanding on defence.

Matt Foord *born 9 September 1981*
His two consecutive hat-tricks in the playoffs showed how much the forward from High Wycombe learned during his spell 'on loan' to London Racers, his first time away from the Jets.

Adam Greener *born 2 October 1981*
The recipient of three club honours, the Hampshire-born defenceman showed maturity and leadership on and off the ice and was an inspiration to the team's younger members.

FACT FILE 2004-05

English Premier League	Sixth
Playoffs:	Semi-finalists
Premier Cup	3rd in qr-final grp.

HISTORY

Founded: 1986.

Leagues: English Premier Lge 2002-05; British National Lge 1997-2002; Premier Lge 1996-97; British Lge, Premier Div 1995-96; British Lge, Div One 1986-95.

Honours: British National League 1998-99; *Benson and Hedges* Plate 1997-98; British League, Div One 1994-95 (and Playoffs), 1993-94 (south), 1989-90.

SLOUGH JETS *left to right, back row:* Rob Coutts (bench coach), Steve Ranson (equipment), Brian McLaughlin, Dusan Halloun *(partly obscured)*, Norman Pinnington, Matt Towalski, Graham Bellamy, Adam Greener, Warren Rost, Nicky Watt, Nicky Chinn; *middle row:* Tom Smith, Stewart Tait, Michael Plenty, Joe Gibson (equipment); *front row (kneeling):* Tom Wills, Matt Foord, Scott Moody, Terry Miles, Adam Bicknell, Zoran Kozic, Michael Will; *in front (on ice):* Nick Burton.

SOLIHULL KINGS

PLAYER	ALL COMPETITIONS					ENGLISH PREMIER LEAGUE				
Scorers	GP	G	A	Pts	Pim	GP	G	A	Pts	Pim
Miika Kaski (I)	37	20	25	45	6	25	13	21	34	4
Neil Adams 4	41	12	26	38	50	30	10	14	24	24
Jereon Kustermans (I)	46	13	8	21	72	32	12	7	19	52
Rhys McWilliams 1	45	6	11	17	91	31	3	6	9	69
Andrew Howarth	18	8	8	16	40	10	2	5	7	20
Joel Pickering	28	3	10	13	119	20	1	6	7	78
Steve Chartrand	7	6	4	10	2	5	4	3	7	2
Michael Smith	26	2	7	9	66	17	1	3	4	36
Andrew Ayers	33	5	3	8	30	20	4	2	6	8
Dean Mills	24	4	4	8	50	20	4	4	8	46
Stephen Rowlands	27	4	4	8	72	20	3	3	6	39
Richard Taylor	45	1	7	8	97	31	0	6	6	69
Jake Armstrong 2	8	1	6	7	24	4	1	1	2	16
Jon Bell	39	0	6	6	28	29	0	4	4	18
Tom Parker	42	1	4	5	20	28	0	4	4	16
Joe Wightman	10	2	2	4	6	4	0	1	1	4
Jason Price	12	1	3	4	14	6	1	1	2	4
Dave Fielder 3	13	1	3	4	30	13	1	3	4	30
Adam Andrews	20	1	1	2	28	15	1	1	2	20
Toni Scialdone	33	1	1	2	6	24	1	1	2	6
Markus Koivisto (I)	5	1	0	1	2	2	0	0	0	2
Phil Knight	23	1	0	1	8	20	1	0	1	8
Robert Dowd	1	0	1	1	0	1	0	1	1	0
Marcus Kuris (N) (I)	1	0	0	0	6					
Stuart Coleman	7	0	0	0	2	4	0	0	0	2
Matt Darnell	13	0	0	0	2	7	0	0	0	2
Alan Levers (N) 1	43	0	0	0	38	30	0	0	0	36
Bench Penalties					10					8
TEAM TOTALS	46	94	144	238	919	32	63	97	160	619
Netminders	GPI	Mins	SOG	GA	Sv%	GPI	Mins	SOG	GA	Sv%
Marcus Kuris (I)	1	45	40	5	87.5					
Alan Levers 1	43	2346	1903	265	86.1	30	1621	1402	200	85.7
Elliot Folley	1	20	13	2	84.6	1	20	13	2	84.6
Dan Page	11	348	256	51	80.1	9	279	204	41	79.9
Empty Net Goals		1	1	1			0	0	0	
TEAM TOTALS	46	2760	2213	324	85.3	32	1920	1619	243	85.0

Also appeared: Barry Evans, Ryan Selwood, Nick Whyatt.

Also played for: 1 Nottingham Panthers; 2 Peterborough Phantoms; 3 Romford Raiders; 4 Guildford Flames.

Shutouts: None

All Competitions = league and Premier Cup

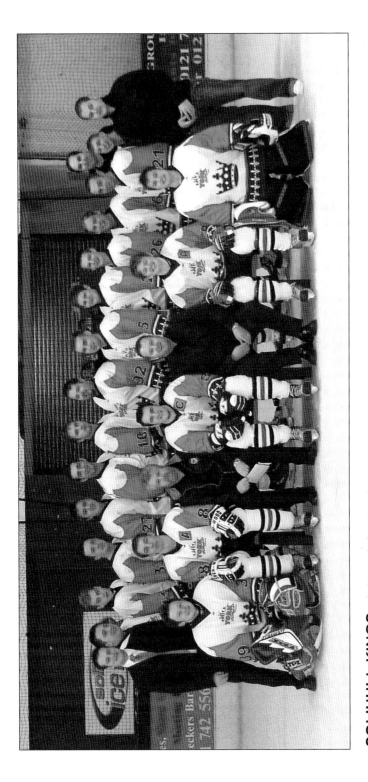

SOLIHULL KINGS *left to right, back row:* Alan Levers, Richard Taylor, Ryan Selwood, Joel Pickering, Phil Knight, Stephen Rowlands, Neil Adams, Dave Fielder, Jon Bell, Toni Scialdone, Tom Parker, Dean Mills, Andy Ayers, Tim Speakman (equipment), Russell Williams (equipment), Adam Andrews; *front row:* Dan Page, Miika Kaski, Bob McWilliams (manager), Jerry Kustermans, Jon Rodway (coach), Rhys McWilliams, Elliot Folley.

Chartrand brings two wins

ELAINE WITTERIDGE

Coach **Jon Rodway** was given another chance to bring some respectability to the Kings after their last place finish in 2003-04. He made several changes to the squad but they won only two league games and he was sacked late in the season.

Rodway kept faith with locally developed young players, adding **Jake Armstrong**, **Rhys McWillliams** and **Stuart Coleman** who had been playing in Peterborough, and defencemen **Tom Parker** from Telford and **Jon Bell** from Nottingham.

Netminding had previously been a problem but this was solved with the signing of GB under-20 international, **Alan Levers**, who had been back-up at the Elite League's Coventry Blaze.

The Kings had run with only two imports the previous year but Rodway brought in three this time - Belgian international defenceman, **Jeroen Kustermans**, and Finns, **Markus Koivisto**, a utility player, and forward **Miika Kaski**.

But in the first two months Kings recorded only one win, in a cup game at Blackburn.

In an attempt to turn things around Rodway made more personnel changes while Armstrong asked to be transferred back to Peterborough.

Steve Chartrand's return brought some success. Though he only played home games, he was instrumental in Kings' only two home wins against Slough and *Wightlink* before a knee problem curtailed his comeback.

The losses resumed, eventually putting the Kings out of the playoff race and leaving them rooted back at the bottom of the league table.

At the beginning of February Rodway was released as coach and former Solihull, Nottingham and GB goalie, **Dave Graham**, agreed to return to the club for the remainder of the season with a view to a permanent position.

Graham, who broke into hockey at Hobs Moat Road 20 years ago, has followed his successful playing career by becoming a level three coach working with the England under-14's and various junior sides.

He was confident that he could transform the fortunes of the young Kings, who were renamed the Barons at the end of the season.

"In the remaining half-a-dozen games, I'm concentrating on getting my team to start enjoying their hockey again," he said. "And I'll be using the remainder of the season to evaluate the players I have and what I need for next season."

PLAYER AWARDS

Most Valuable Player	**Alan Levers**
Players' Player	**Alan Levers**
Most Improved Player	**Tom Parker**

LEADING PLAYERS

Alan Levers *born 30 March 1984*

The under-20 international joined to get more ice time after spending two seasons with Coventry Blaze. Faced over 2,000 shots during the season, ending with an 88.29 save percentage to earn his end-of-season awards.

Rhys McWilliams *born 29 November 1985*

The young forward, who has come through Solihull's junior system, played in the BNL with the MK Kings before spending a season at Peterborough Phantoms. He was signed by Kings on a two-way contract with the Elite League's Nottingham Panthers.

Tom Parker *born 28 September 1988*

The fearless young defenceman got regular shifts and improved with every game. He was part of the victorious England under-16 team in Albany, New York in 2003.

FACT FILE 2004-05

English Premier League:	Ninth
Playoffs:	Did not qualify
Premier Cup:	Fifth in group.

HISTORY

Founded: 2003. The original Solihull team were the *Barons* who were formed in 1965, disbanded in 1996, and reformed again for two seasons in 2000-02. The *Blaze* played in Solihull from 1996 before moving to Coventry in 2000. *MK Kings* played in season 2002-03.

Leagues: *Kings* English Premier League 2003-05; *MK Kings* British National League 2002-03; *Barons* English Premier League 2000-02, British Lge, Div. One/Two 1993-96 & 1982-86; English Lge 1991-93; British Lge, Premier Div. 1986-91; Inter-City Lge 1978-82; Southern Lge 1972-78; *Blaze* British National League 1999-2000, English Premier League 1996-97.

Honours: *Blaze* English Lge, Premier Div 1998-99, 1997-98; *Barons* English League 1992-93, British Lge, Div One 1985-86, Div Two 1983-84, Southern League 1977-78.

SWINDON WILDCATS

PLAYER	ALL COMPETITIONS					ENGLISH PREMIER LEAGUE					PLAYOFFS				
Scorers	GP	G	A	Pts	Pim	GP	G	A	Pts	Pim	GP	G	A	Pts	Pim
Brock Harrison (I)	54	41	66	107	104	31	17	40	57	70	6	3	5	8	10
Justyn Schollar (I)	54	36	51	87	32	31	20	32	52	63	6	3	2	5	16
Ken Forshee	54	22	33	55	32	32	10	11	21	12	6	1	5	6	6
Gareth Endicott	51	27	9	36	125	31	10	4	14	91	6	2	0	2	12
Brant Becker (I)	23	21	14	35	46	16	18	12	30	38	5	2	2	4	4
Lee Brathwaite	42	8	21	29	156	24	4	10	14	26	5	0	2	2	28
Wayne Fiddes	53	10	17	27	40	32	10	10	20	34	6	0	2	2	0
Mike Smith	54	12	12	24	63	31	5	2	7	55	6	1	1	2	2
Michael Hargreaves	53	8	14	22	114	30	3	5	8	50	6	2	2	4	18
Alan Armour	47	4	13	17	48	29	2	4	6	28	4	0	0	0	10
Andrew Shurmer	50	3	12	15	51	27	1	8	9	12	6	0	0	0	2
Sheldon Rafuse (I)	19	5	9	14	62	11	2	1	3	50					
Gareth Owen 1	22	5	7	12	26	13	0	1	1	26					
Shane Moore	38	3	7	10	153	25	1	5	6	92	2	0	0	0	4
Drew Chapman	28	3	6	9	76	16	2	3	5	52	3	0	0	0	6
James Manson	19	1	6	7	26	11	0	4	4	16	6	1	2	3	10
Robin Davison	8	0	7	7	42	5	0	4	4	36					
Shaun Littlewood 2	54	1	4	5	16	31	0	2	2	12	6	0	0	0	0
Ian Clark	53	0	4	4	125	31	0	1	1	93	5	0	1	1	6
Graham Newell 2	43	1	2	3	8	24	0	1	1	2	4	0	0	0	0
Chris Douglas (N)	53	0	3	3	2	30	0	1	1	2	6	0	0	0	0
Tom Mills	23	1	1	2	0	12	0	0	0	0	2	0	0	0	0
Greg Martyn	35	1	0	1	0	22	1	0	1	0	3	0	0	0	0
Dean Mills	19	0	1	1	6	11	0	0	0	4					
Jonathan Boxill	20	0	1	1	0	10	0	0	0	0	2	0	0	0	0
Andy Morton Holmes	9	0	0	0	2										
Bench Penalties					18					14					2
TEAM TOTALS	55	213	320	533	1432	32	106	161	267	878	6	15	24	39	136
Netminders	GPI	Mins	SOG	GA	Sv%	GPI	Mins	SOG	GA	Sv%	GPI	Mins	SOG	GA	Sv%
Joe Dollin	11	313	176	11	93.7	5	150	117	9	92.3	1	18	7	0	100.0
Chris Douglas	52	2926	1722	147	91.5	30	1709	1052	86	91.8	6	342	209	29	86.1
Dave Clancy	1	55	32	6	81.3	1	55	32	6	81.3					
Empty Net Goals		1	1	1			1	1	1			0	0	0	
TEAM TOTALS	55	3295	1931	165	91.5	32	1915	1202	102	91.5	6	360	216	29	86.6

Also appeared: James Skaife (N), Jamie Stephenson (N).

Also played for: 1 Telford Wild Foxes; 2 Edinburgh Capitals.

Shutouts (league &: playoffs): Douglas (2) - league: 11 Dec v Solihull Kings (26 saves), 6 March at Solihull Kings (35).

All Competitions = league, playoffs and Premier Cup

Building with a Brock

DAVE LITTLEWOOD

After 18 years and various team names, Swindon's fortunes were revived - along with their old Wildcats' tag - as they reached the final of the Premier Cup after a lacklustre league and playoff campaign.

With *npower* returning as the club's main sponsor, coach **Daryl Lipsey** was able to retain the services of import **Ken Forshee** and add three more from his home town of North Battlefield, Saskatchewan - defenceman **Sheldon Rafuse** and forwards **Brock Harrison** and **Justyn Schollar**. Ex-Romford goalie **Chris Douglas** joined after the first weekend.

The only major line-up change came in January when, with Rafuse needing shoulder surgery, Canadian forward **Brant Becker** was signed to fill the vacant import slot.

The season progressed with results differing widely between the league and the Premier Cup. By mid-November 'Cats topped the northern group of the cup. But their slender margin over Telford was wiped out when the EIHA belatedly announced the reversal of their 4-2 home win over Blackburn for icing an ineligible player.

This set up a crucial four-pointer at Telford in November when Swindon were missing six key players. However, they produced a spirited display, held on for a 2-2 draw and went on to qualify for the two-legged final against Romford Raiders for the first time since 2001.

In a fast and furious first leg in front of nearly a thousand fans in the Link Centre - the highest since the days of the IceLords - Wildcats fell to two late third period goals. Though Harrison and Becker put them 2-0 up by 27.43 of the second leg, Raiders battled back to tie the game 3-3, enough to lift the trophy on aggregate.

In contrast, Swindon's league campaign spluttered, with Saturday home wins commonly followed by Sunday away defeats.

From December to early January 'Cats enjoyed an eight-game unbeaten run which included excellent wins at Romford and Peterborough. Then with a top three place in sight, three consecutive defeats followed and they had to settle for fifth.

Their playoff hopes were dealt a blow when they lost 6-2 to Wild Foxes in their opening home game. It was still possible for them to reach the finals if they won their final two games but instead they fell 4-1 at home to Romford.

"There are plenty of positives to take from the season," said an upbeat Lipsey. "We've begun to build up our fan base and we're putting the Wildcats back on the sporting map in Swindon."

PLAYER AWARDS

Player of the Year	**Chris Douglas**
Players' Player	**Wayne Fiddes**
Supporters' Player	**Brock Harrison**
Best Forward	**Justyn Schollar**
Best Defenceman	**Chris Douglas**
Most Improved Player	**Andrew Shurmer**
Best British Player	**Gareth Endicott**
Promotion of the Sport	**Brock Harrison**

LEADING PLAYERS

Chris Douglas *born 25 August 1979*

The netminding son of former Romford coach, Erskine, topped the league stats with a 91.46 save percentage. Perhaps his most notable achievement came in the cup final where he saved 87 of 92 shots over the two games.

Justyn Schollar *born 19 July 1982*

A superb playmaker, he was among the league's top scorers with 36 goals and 51 assists from 54 games. Came from the hockey programme at Red Deer College in Alberta.

MOST PROMISING PLAYER

Shane Moore *born 4 January 1987*

The rapidly improving junior from Swindon's highly rated youth system had an impressive season on the blueline. He represented Britain at under-18 and under-20 level, as well as playing a number of games on a two-way arrangement with the Elite League's Basingstoke Bison.

FACT FILE 2004-05

English Premier League: Fifth
Playoffs: 4th in qr-final grp.
Premier Cup: Finalists

HISTORY

Founded: 2001 as Lynx. Changed name to Wildcats in 2004. Previous clubs in the Link Centre were *Phoenix* 2000-01, *Chill* 1997-2000, *IceLords* 1996-97 and *Wildcats* 1986-96.

Leagues: *Wildcats* - English Premier League 2004-05 and British League, Div One 1986-96; *Lynx* and *Phoenix* - English (Premier) League 2000-04; *Chill* - English League 1997-2000; *IceLords* - Premier League 1996-97;

SWINDON WILDCATS *left to right, back row:* Greg Martyn, Shane Moore, Tom Mills, Jonathan Boxill, Graham Newell, Dean Mills; *middle row:* Paul Avis (physio), Ian Smith (equipment), Ian Clark, Justyn Schollar, Andrew Shurmer, Drew Chapman, Shaun Littlewood, Lee Brathwaite, Gareth Owen, Mike Smith, Andrew Morton-Holmes, Tim Pickett (equipment), Ray Taylor (asst. coach); *front row:* Simon Anderson (asst. coach), Jamie Stephenson, Mike Hargreaves, Brock Harrison, Ken Forshee, Chris Douglas, Wayne Fiddes, Gareth Endicott, Alan Armour, Joe Dollin, Daryl Lipsey (coach); *inset:* James Manson, Brant Becker, Willie the Wildcat, Sheldon Rafuse.

TELFORD WILD FOXES

PLAYER	ALL COMPETITIONS					ENGLISH PREMIER LEAGUE					PLAYOFFS				
Scorers	GP	G	A	Pts	Pim	GP	G	A	Pts	Pim	GP	G	A	Pts	Pim
Claude Dumas	54	71	50	121	56	32	36	30	66	32	6	5	3	8	14
Daniel Mackriel	48	38	41	79	12	29	20	22	42	6	6	1	4	5	4
Joe Miller	49	35	42	77	110	29	16	19	35	53	6	4	4	8	4
Adam Brittle 2	49	15	44	59	20	31	11	32	43	18	5	1	1	2	0
Tom Carlon 2	40	27	24	51	123	26	15	12	27	80	2	0	1	1	0
Tomas Janak (I)	49	13	31	44	80	28	7	10	17	47	5	1	3	4	0
Jared Owen	35	16	25	41	24	18	6	9	15	8	6	4	3	7	2
Peter Rojik (I)	46	6	30	36	106	25	4	15	19	47	6	1	3	4	6
Matt Towe	36	8	15	23	16	25	4	11	15	16					
Jason Parry	51	7	14	21	56	30	1	7	8	46	6	0	0	0	4
Ashley Stanton	50	3	16	19	176	28	3	8	11	119	6	0	1	1	10
Gareth Owen 1	23	10	8	18	28	17	8	5	13	24	6	2	4	6	4
Ryan Stanton	48	7	7	14	34	29	5	5	10	10	5	0	0	0	4
Daniel Croft	51	0	10	10	115	30	0	4	4	54	5	0	1	1	29
Marc Lovell	33	5	4	9	28	22	2	1	3	24	6	1	0	1	2
David James	24	3	6	9	57	13	1	2	3	14					
Stuart Bates	26	0	2	2	4	19	0	2	2	2					
Barry Hollyhead (N)	45	0	1	1	33	29	0	1	1	31	6	0	0	0	2
Daniel Heslop (N)	54	0	1	1	14	32	0	0	0	2	6	0	0	0	10
Gareth Bates	2	0	0	0	2	2	0	0	0	2					
Michael Roden	7	0	0	0	18	4	0	0	0	16					
Rob Perks	38	0	0	0	2	21	0	0	0	0	5	0	0	0	2
Bench Penalties					14					10					2
TEAM TOTALS	54	264	371	635	1128	32	139	195	334	661	6	20	28	48	99
Netminders	GPI	Mins	SOG	GA	Sv%	GPI	Mins	SOG	GA	Sv%	GPI	Mins	SOG	GA	Sv%
Barry Hollyhead	31	1607	1093	113	89.7	22	1148	793	75	90.5	5	266	198	29	85.4
Daniel Heslop	31	1567	915	101	89.0	15	766	495	60	87.9	3	94	58	6	89.7
Daniel Brittle	1	60	19	4	78.9										
Empty Net Goal		1	1	1			1	1	1			0	0	0	
TEAM TOTALS	54	3235	2028	219	89.2	32	1915	1289	136	89.4	6	360	256	35	86.3

Also played for: 1 Swindon Wildcats; 2 Coventry Blaze.

Shutouts (league & playoffs): Barry Hollyhead - 10 Feb at Solihull Kings (31 saves).

All Competitions = league, playoffs and Premier Cup

TELFORD WILD FOXES *left to right, back row:* Dave Candlin (manager), Peter Rojik, Tomas Janak, Joe Miller, Gareth Bates, Ryan Stanton, Tom Carlon, Simon James, Rob Perks, David James, Andy Phillips (equipment); *front row:* Barry Hollyhead, Jared Owen, Adam Brittle, Stuart Bates, Daniel Heslop, Daniel Mackriel, Jason Parry, Matt Towe, Claude Dumas, Daniel Brittle.

Claude their way up

DAVID HALL

When **Claude Dumas** started his first full season in charge of the Wild Foxes, hopes were high that they would have their best campaign yet in the English Premier League.

And they didn't disappoint, almost tripling their number of league victories and only missing out on a Premier Cup semi-final place by the closest of margins.

Player-coach Dumas persuaded netminder **Barry Hollyhead** to return to the club and added Slovakian defenders **Thomas Janak** and **Peter Rojik**. Forward **Marc Lovell**, Wild Foxes' player of the year in season 2002-03, also returned after spending most of last season in Manchester.

Grouped in the cup's first round with Swindon Wildcats, Solihull Kings and National League outfits, Sheffield Scimitars and Blackburn Hawks, the Wild Foxes lost out to the Wiltshire side only on results between the clubs.

All season long they had some exciting battles with the Wildcats. "We were well matched and results pretty much evened themselves out over the season," said Dumas. "They are the type of club that we need to be targeting in the future if we are to make any progress."

NICER TO STAY AT HOME

But it wasn't just about Swindon. The Wild Foxes picked up some other notable scalps, including becoming the first side to get the better of champions-to-be, Milton Keynes Lightning, with a stunning 6-5 away victory in November.

However, home form was the key to Telford's best season since the old Tigers' days. They dropped just one point on their own ice in the cup, and enjoyed a creditable home league record of seven wins, four draws and five defeats.

Alll that from a side that managed just four league wins in the entire 2003-04 campaign.

"We're beginning to get it right," agreed Dumas, who once again showed his class by finishing as runner-up in league scoring. "We're a small club compared to some of the sides we face. I think my players did a fantastic job against teams, most of which had a far bigger budget than ours."

Dumas' talent for getting the best out of his players was reflected in the increase in attendances at games, and gives the club good reasons to look forward again with optimism.

PLAYER AWARDS

Player of the Year	**Daniel Brittle**
Players' Player	**Daniel Brittle**
Most Improved Player	**Matt Towe**

LEADING PLAYERS

Barry Hollyhead *born 4 June 1975*

Returned to the Telford cage for the first time since backstopping the old Tigers in 1997. With the vast experience he had gained at Coventry and Milton Keynes, he proved to be a crucial element in the Wild Foxes' success.

Joe Miller *born 14 March 1985*

First full season with the Shropshire side for the former Cardiff junior who has spent time with the junior Cleveland Barons in North America. The talented young forward was used to the full as he contributed 77 points (35 goals) to the cause and finished third in the club's scoring.

MOST PROMISING PLAYER

Stuart Bates *born 15 April 1987*

Beginning the season on the bench, the 17-year-old was used increasingly as the campaign progressed. A product of the club's successful junior programme, he is tipped to become a star of the future by the coaching staff.

FACT FILE 2004-05

English Premier League: Eighth

Playoffs:	3rd in qr-final grp
Premier Cup:	Second in group

HISTORY

Founded: 2001. Previous teams in Telford were **Royals** 1997-2001 and **Tigers** 1985-97. The **Timberwolves** played six *B&H* Cup games in September 1999.
Leagues: **Wild Foxes** English Premier League 2002-05; English National League South 2001-02; **Royals** English (National) League 1997-2001; **Tigers** Premier League 1996-97, British League, Div One 1985-96.
Honours: None.

WHITLEY WARRIORS

PLAYER	ALL COMPETITIONS					ENGLISH NATIONAL LEAGUE					PLAYOFFS				
Scorers	GP	G	A	Pts	Pim	GP	G	A	Pts	Pim	GP	G	A	Pts	Pim
Paul Graham	28	30	24	54	10	16	18	20	38	4	6	6	2	8	4
Andrew Tindale	24	21	24	45	29	13	16	17	33	2	5	1	4	5	0
Andrew Robinson	27	2	19	21	24	15	2	13	15	14	6	0	1	1	8
Bryan Dunn	16	8	11	19	102	8	6	6	12	82	4	1	2	3	2
Ben Campbell	23	7	10	17	0	13	5	7	12	0	5	0	1	1	0
Ben Buckley	24	11	4	15	59	15	8	2	10	45	3	1	0	1	12
Richard Dunn	25	4	9	13	114	16	3	6	9	74	3	0	0	0	22
Ray Haslam	21	5	7	12	53	10	4	5	9	4	5	1	1	2	35
Paul Sample	16	2	10	12	76	12	2	9	11	74					
Shaun Kippin	27	7	3	10	68	15	6	2	8	24	6	0	1	1	26
Ryan Sample	20	7	2	9	55	10	5	1	6	16	6	1	1	2	35
Ian Emerson	26	5	4	9	14	15	3	4	7	4	6	2	0	2	4
Lee Baxter	5	1	6	7	0	4	1	6	7	0					
Robert Wilson 1	16	1	6	7	113	12	1	4	5	81	1	0	0	0	4
Jeremy Lundin	22	2	3	5	30	11	1	1	2	6	6	0	1	1	18
Chris Taylor	21	1	4	5	51	14	1	4	5	43	3	0	0	0	4
Stephen Winn	6	1	2	3	4	5	1	2	3	4					
David Barrett	20	0	3	3	10	10	0	2	2	2	5	0	0	0	2
Scott Taylor	12	2	0	2	35	9	1	0	1	35					
Andrew Wile	6	1	1	2	2	4	1	1	2	2					
Paul Ellis	14	1	1	2	35	8	1	1	2	33	3	0	0	0	2
Jonathan Hester	22	1	1	2	4	13	1	1	2	0	5	0	0	0	4
Rory Dunn (N)	23	0	1	1	10	14	0	0	0	10	4	0	0	0	0
Stephen Hoult (N)	28	0	1	1	4	16	0	0	0	4	6	0	1	1	0
Phillip Atherton	1	0	0	0	2	1	0	0	0	2					
Adrian Huggins	7	0	0	0	2	6	0	0	0	2					
Bench Penalties					8					8					0
TEAM TOTALS	28	120	156	276	914	16	87	114	201	575	6	13	15	28	182
Netminders	GPI	Mins	SOG	GA	Sv%	GPI	Mins	SOG	GA	Sv%	GPI	Mins	SOG	GA	Sv%
Rory Dunn	23	461	258	42	83.7	14	250	122	20	83.6	4	80	49	6	87.8
Stephen Hoult	28	1214	794	98	87.6	16	705	475	53	88.8	6	280	173	28	83.8
Liam McAllister	1	4	7	1	85.7	1	4	7	1	85.7					
Empty Net Goals		1	1	1			1	1	1						
TEAM TOTALS	28	1680	1060	142	86.6	16	960	605	75	87.6	6	360	222	34	84.7

Also appeared: Michael Christie, John Shreeve, Jamie Tinsley, Andrew Wood, Gary Wood, Peter Zajac.

Also played for: 1 Newcastle Vipers

Shutouts (league & playoffs): None.

All Competitions = league, playoffs and English Cup

The young ones

DAVID HALL

Warriors started the campaign with arguably the youngest squad in the club's long history, but it didn't stop them finishing with a deserved place in the top four of the English National League.

"We targeted a playoff place at the start of the season and we got there by sheer hard work," said coach **Gary Wood**. "With an average age around 21 and only one player over 25, we were certainly the youngest side in the ENL North. But these players hardly seemed to know the meaning of defeat."

Their games against Blackburn Hawks must have been among the most entertaining anywhere in the country last season, with four of the six matches ending in draws. Twice the Warriors trailed by three goals in Blackburn with just 10 minutes remaining, yet produced comebacks to grab a point.

Their place in the playoffs was probably clinched with their clinical destruction of north-east rivals, Billingham Bombers, who were dispatched 7-1 at Hillheads. It was easily Warriors' best performance of the season.

Grand slam winners, Sheffield Scimitars, were the only side that the young Warriors couldn't get to grips with, the Yorkshiremen having too much experience. But when Warriors went there in the playoffs with just 10 skaters and lost 5-0, they earned a standing ovation from the iceSheffield crowd for their brave display.

"That night summed up our season," said Wood. "We gave Sheffield a good game but we just didn't have enough [players] to worry them. Outside of matches with Scimitars, we were as good as anyone on our night.

"We made a few mistakes along the way," he admitted. "We led Nottingham Lions at home with less than 10 minutes remaining but failed to close out the game, and it was a similar story when Flintshire visited.

"But the experience we gained this season will definitely help the players in the future and I don't see any reason why the Warriors can't get better from here."

Certainly the future is bright with the exciting crop of young talent coming through the ranks. But unless a bridge is created in north-east England between Elite League hockey and the English National League, those good young players at Whitley - as well as at Sunderland and Billingham - will have to find employment outside the region if they want to progress.

PLAYER AWARDS
Hillheads Player of the Year   **Ben Campbell**

LEADING PLAYERS
Ben Campbell *born 16 May 1987*
With good hands and a turn of speed that caught opponents by surprise, the forward became the youngest player ever to collect the Hillheads trophy. Only 18, he looks set to have whatever future he wants in the game.

Shaun Kippin *born 22 April 1987*
No respecter of reputations, he was a vital member of the squad, chipping in some crucial goals. With his all-action style, he has made considerable progress over the last 12 months.

Jeremy Lundin *born 9 February 1988*
America-born defender who joined Whitley from Sunderland, he scored in his opening game and went on to became one of the team's leading blueliners.

FACT FILE 2004-05
English National League:	Fourth in North
Playoffs:	Fourth in North
English Cup:	Third in North

HISTORY
Founded: 1956. Known as Newcastle Warriors in 1995-96, playing part of the season in Newcastle's *Telewest* Arena.
Leagues: English (National) League 1997-2005; Northern Premier League 1996-97; British League, Premier Division 1982-96; Northern League 1966-82.
Honours: English National League playoff champions 2000-02; English National League North and English Cup 2001-02; English League, Div One playoffs 1999-2000; Scottish Cup 1992; Northern League 1973-75; Icy Smith Cup 1972-73 & 1973-74.

WHITLEY WARRIORS *left to right, back row:* Jonathan Hesler, Ben Campbell, Andrew Wile, Ian Emerson, Michael Christie, Bryan Dunn; *middle row:* Shaun Kippin, Paul Graham, John Shreeve, Rob Wilson, Andrew Robinson, Richard Dunn, Paul Sample; *front row:* Ray Haslam, Liam McAllister, Andrew Tindale, Stephen Hoult, Chris Taylor.

WIGHTLINK RAIDERS

PLAYER	ALL COMPETITIONS					ENGLISH PREMIER LEAGUE					PLAYOFFS				
Scorers	GP	G	A	Pts	Pim	GP	G	A	Pts	Pim	GP	G	A	Pts	Pim
Jason Coles	49	55	33	88	117	29	36	16	52	85	6	4	6	10	16
Rob Lamey	51	31	44	75	40	31	15	27	42	28	5	7	2	9	2
Chris Crombie (I)	51	23	50	73	90	31	14	30	44	64	6	2	3	5	18
Scott Carter	50	10	25	35	20	30	4	15	19	12	6	3	2	5	4
Andy Pickles	49	10	24	34	109	29	4	15	19	89	5	0	1	1	2
Dominic Hopkins 2	30	9	14	23	18	22	8	6	14	14	4	0	6	6	2
Matt Cote	48	6	17	23	36	30	4	12	16	24	6	0	0	0	4
Simon Beere	45	10	7	17	8	29	9	7	16	4	1	0	0	0	0
Joe Baird	52	4	13	17	112	31	4	11	15	58	6	0	0	0	24
Steve Gannaway	48	4	12	16	34	31	2	9	11	16	6	0	1	1	2
Daniel Giden	52	7	6	13	2	31	5	4	9	2	6	0	1	1	0
Andrew Robinson 3	51	5	6	11	107	30	4	5	9	67	6	0	0	0	4
Anthony Blaize	50	4	5	9	44	31	3	4	7	20	4	0	0	0	0
Tom Boney	44	4	3	7	8	26	4	3	7	4	6	0	0	0	0
Damon Larter	45	1	3	4	16	26	0	1	1	2	6	0	0	0	4
Adam Hyman	16	1	1	2	14	6	1	0	1	2					
Neil Leary	36	0	2	2	30	20	0	2	2	8	5	0	0	0	0
Ashley Skinns 1	51	0	1	1	63	31	0	1	1	59	6	0	0	0	0
Steve Gossett	3	0	0	0	27	1	0	0	0	27	1	0	0	0	0
Joe Reynolds	13	0	0	0	6	6	0	0	0	2					
Toby Cooley (N)	49	0	0	0	6	30	0	0	0	6	6	0	0	0	0
Bench Penalties					8					4					0
	52	184	266	450	915	31	117	168	285	597	6	16	22	38	82
Netminders	GPI	Mins	SOG	GA	Sv%	GPI	Mins	SOG	GA	Sv%	GPI	Mins	SOG	GA	Sv%
Toby Cooley	36	2162	1158	125	89.2	22	1380	738	71	90.4	5	276	171	29	83.0
David Hurst	17	954	525	57	89.1	8	479	262	30	88.6	2	83	54	5	90.7
Empty Net Goals		4	2	2			1	1	1			1	1	1	
TEAM TOTALS	52	3120	1685	184	89.1	31	1860	1001	102	89.8	6	360	226	35	84.5

Also appeared: Richard Gutteridge, James Spencer (N).

Also played for: 1 Basingstoke Bison, Edinburgh Capitals; 2 Basingstoke Bison; 3 Edinburgh Capitals.

Shutouts (league & playoffs): Hurst - league: 24 Oct at Chelmsford Chieftains (24 saves).

All Competitions = league, playoffs and Premier Cup

***WIGHTLINK* RAIDERS** *left to right*, *back row*: Neil Leary, Steve Gossett, Anthony Blaize, Damon Larter, Simon Beere, Dominic Hopkins, Daniel Giden, Andy Robinson, Ashley Skinns, Tom Bone; *front row*: Toby Cooley, Rob Lamey, Chris Crombie, Jason Coles, Steve Gannaway, Andy Pickles, Joe Baird, Scott Carter, David Hurst.

Beere helped

CLARE WALL

It was a topsy-turvy season as Raiders enjoyed a short spell at the top of the English Premier League only to collapse in the Playoffs.

Player-coaches **Andy Pickles** and **Jason Coles** returned and constructed a team with a good blend of youth and experience. Veteran **Matt Coté** stayed to lead the defence while youth was provided by **Simon Beere** with his bullet-like slapshots, **Andy Robinson's** aggressive attack and **Damon Larter's** defensive prowess.

Also back in the squad were **Rob Lamey** and import **Chris Crombie**; together with Coles, they headed the team's goal scoring.

Other Raiders' veterans, **Scott Carter** and **Steve Gannaway**, also enjoyed good form and Gannaway's testimonial game - marking his tenth season with the club - will be remembered for many years by his fans.

Toby Cooley and **Dave Hurst** continued to impress in the nets, with Cooley at one point registering three shutouts in a row, greatly improving his save percentage. The third line of **Tom Boney**, **Neil Leary** and **Ashley Skinns** gave their all and enjoyed some success in frustrating the opposition's top lines.

Though Raiders failed to make it through the group stages of the Premier Cup, their hard work and determination paid off in the league and helped them win many of their games. Not for Raiders the flair displayed by sides such as Milton Keynes, but they had a strong work ethic.

Most of their best results came in the first half of the season, with wins over Peterborough Phantoms and an historic 3-1 victory at Milton Keynes - the first time Raiders had taken two points from the league champions away from Ryde Arena.

Complacency set in during games against the minnows, however, as they lost three times to up-and-coming Telford Wild Foxes and Solihull Kings. And old rivals Romford Raiders and Chelmsford Chieftains continued to be a thorn in Raiders' side. They lost to the Essex lads no less than seven times.

But some big wins against the big clubs lifted Raiders to the league summit, albeit for only a brief period, a first for the club. They finally finished third, tied on points with runners-up Phantoms and a great improvement on their sixth place in 2004.

Any hopes the Raiders had of extending their league form into the playoffs were dashed when a virus spread through the side and they finished their season with defeats in all four of their playoff games.

PLAYER AWARDS

Player of the Year	**Scott Carter**
Players' Player	**Rob Lamey**
British Player of the Year	**Rob Lamey**
Best Forward	**Jason Coles**
Best Defenceman	**Matt Coté**

LEADING PLAYERS

Scott Carter

The amiable Canadian continued to be a fan favourite with his super-charged style of play. By far the best skater in the league, he skated fast on attack and hit hard on defence.

Matt Coté *born 19 January 1966*

In his last season, he left with the respect of every player and fan on the Island. His die-hard attitude to preventing goals inspired many of the newer players while drawing admiration from fans everywhere.

MOST PROMISING PLAYER

Simon Beere

The 24-year-old defenceman from Basingstoke Buffalo made a huge impact on his new team. With a slapshot unrivalled in the league he scored many goals from the blue line. His ability to read the game and his team spirit gained him much respect.

FACT FILE 2004-05

English Premier League:	Third
Playoffs:	4th in qr-final grp.
Premier Cup:	Fourth in group

HISTORY

Founded: 1992. The first club on the Island in 1991-92 was Solent Vikings. *Wightlink Ferries* have sponsored the club in most years except 1999-2003 when the team was known as Isle of Wight Raiders.
Leagues: English (Premier) League 1991-2005.
Honours: English Premier Cup 2001; English League 1993-97.

GOAL!

Ashley Tait, *far right*, beats Nottingham Panthers' netminder, **Ladislav Kudrna**, with the winning goal for Coventry Blaze in the 2005 Elite League playoff final at Nottingham's National Ice Centre.

Photo: Dave Page

Britain's top leagues - a history

Although ice hockey has been played in this country since the early years of the 20th century, it first became prominent in the 1930s with the opening of large indoor arenas at Wembley, Harringay and Earls Court (Empress Hall). Teams were staffed almost entirely by Canadian professionals, several of whom went on to compete in the National Hockey League.

The 13 seasons either side of World War Two (1935-54) are often referred to as the sport's golden era. As well as the national team's successes, there were two professional leagues, the English National League and the Scottish National League which drew large crowds to arenas in London, Brighton, Nottingham and Scotland.

The two leagues merged in 1954 into a British National League but rising wages and falling crowds caused it to fold in 1960. With no new rinks being built, the sport went into a decline.

It only began to achieve wide popularity again in 1982 when the British League was re-formed with teams composed mostly of home-grown players and a strict limit (usually three) on imported professionals. This is generally seen as the start of the game's modern era.

With a new generation of fans, the Whitbread Company agreed to sponsor the league under the *Heineken* banner. The (*Heineken*) British Championships, 1983-1996, were televised and drew capacity crowds to Wembley Arena.

The (*Heineken*) British League, which ran for the same 13 seasons, was split into two divisions - Premier Division and Division One - with promotion and relegation.

This success, coupled with the promise of more arenas like the new ones in Sheffield and Manchester, prompted a revival of the professional game. The Superleague, which was formed in 1996, reverted to a heavy reliance on overseas players and although at first the crowds continued to increase, many clubs eventually found the league too expensive and it collapsed in 2003.

The current Elite League was created from the surviving Superleague sides and has gradually absorbed several of the second tier British National League (1997-2005) teams.

- For a list of all league winners, see our exclusive *Roll of Honour* at the back of the *Annual*. For a history of the GB national team, see *World Championships* elsewhere in the book.

LEAGUE ORGANISATION

Senior ice hockey in 2004-05 was run by three separate organisations, the first two under licence from the governing body, Ice Hockey UK.

The **Elite Ice Hockey League Ltd** (EIHL), a limited liability company, was run by its member clubs with each having one seat on the league's board of directors.

There were no restrictions on the origin of the players. The salary cap for each club was £7,000 per week, making £210,000 for a 30-week season. Team rosters were limited to 20 skaters plus two netminders with a maximum of 12 professional players. Two players had to be eligible to play for the GB under-20 team.

Each team was restricted to five work permit holders.

The **British National Ice Hockey League** Ltd (BNL), also a limited liability company, was run on similar lines to the Elite League, with each member club having a director on the board.

The clubs agreed that at least 50 per cent of each team's players on the ice should be British trained and eligible to play for the GB national team but clubs could sign as many International Transfer Card (ITC) holders as they wished.

The league imposed a wages' ceiling of £4,500 a week per club (over 30 weeks this amounted to £135,000), though this could be increased up to £6,750 (£202,500) provided the club paid a 20 per cent 'luxury tax' to the league. The 'tax' was designed to help support and promote the smaller fan-based clubs and help them build upwards.

The league's policy on work permit players was to employ as few as possible.

The English Ice Hockey Association (EIHA), a company limited by guarantee, ran the **English Leagues** which comprised clubs with a wide range of financial resources.

Each **Premier League** team could dress a maximum of four ITC holders per game but have only three in play at any one time. The other players must have completed two years at under-19 level under the auspices of the EIHA. **National League** teams were allowed only one ITC-holding player or player-coach on the ice at any one time but could dress two.

All players had to be registered with the EIHA at a fee of £125 per player in the Premier League and £85 in the National League.

Players requiring a work permit were not allowed to play in the English leagues; there was no wage cap.

IMPORTS

International Transfer Card (ITC) Holders

A signed International Transfer Card (ITC) is required by any player who played for another country governed by the International Ice Hockey Federation (IIHF) during his last playing season.

There are two types of ITC - 'limited' for one season, and 'unlimited' for players who intend to remain in this country. The latter are often dual national British-Canadians who are technically not imports.

Ice Hockey UK keeps records only of players needing 'limited' cards. These players are indicated by the letter 'I' appearing against their name in the *Annual's* club pages. It is left to the clubs to decide how many of these players they wish to employ.

For season 2004-05 Ice Hockey UK issued 184 'limited' ITCs to the three leagues - 87 to the Elite (average 12.4 per team), 68 to the BNL (average 9.7), and 29 to the English Premier League (average 3.2).

■ For season 2004-05 the Elite League sides went with a maximum of 11 ITC holders per team at any one time, as recommended by the world governing body, the IIHF.

Work Permit Holders

In addition to an ITC, work permits are required by players originating from outside the European Union who do not qualify for an EU passport.

The government body, Work Permits UK, issues work permits only to 'established sports people whose employment will not displace or exclude resident workers.

'The overseas person should be internationally established at the highest level in their sport, and their employment should contribute to the development of the sport in this country'.

Each year the sport's representatives - in 2004-05: Ice Hockey UK, the Elite League, the British National League and the Ice Hockey Players Association - meet to agree the criteria for work permit holders in ice hockey.

For season 2004-05 the criteria were that players from North America must have played in a league at ECHL level or above; Europeans had to have played on a team from a country which competed in the World Championships (elite group) in the previous season.

❑ For more on this topic, turn to our *Review of the Year, Diary of the Season* and go to www.icehockeyuk.co.uk.

ELITE LEAGUE

FINAL STANDINGS

	GP	W	L	OL	D	GF	GA	Pts	Pct.
(*-3) **Coventry Blaze** COV	50	33	6	5	6	181	104	77	77
(2-4) **Belfast Giants** BEL	50	31	10	2	7	170	104	71	71
(*-5) **Cardiff Devils** CAR	50	30	15	1	4	152	121	65	65
(3-2) **Nottingham Panthers** NOT	50	25	14	6	5	136	101	61	61
(1-1) **Sheffield Steelers** SHE	50	25	17	3	5	118	110	58	58
(7-1) **London Racers** LON	50	19	19	3	9	116	124	50	50
(*-7) **Basingstoke Bison** BAS	50	15	28	2	5	128	178	37	37

Includes Crossover Games with British National League teams.
Figures in brackets are the last two seasons' positions (Superleague position in 2002-03).
* spent season in British National League.
Scoring system*: two points for a win (W), one point for a draw (D) or overtime loss (OL).*
Pct. *= percentage of points gained to points available*

LEADING SCORERS

	GP	G	A	Pts	Pim
Tony Hand BEL	50	19	49	68	60
Vezio Sacratini CAR	50	23	43	66	68
Dan Carlson COV	50	22	42	64	48
Jon Cullen CAR	46	26	34	60	32
Shawn Maltby BAS	47	22	37	59	60
Adam Calder COV	44	32	26	58	183
Doug Sheppard BAS	50	27	30	57	28
George Awada BEL	50	32	23	55	40
Curtis Huppe BEL	48	24	30	54	42
Curt Bowen BEL	50	24	36	50	70

ELITE LEAGUE AWARDS

PLAYER OF THE YEAR
Neal Martin, Coventry

ALL-STARS

Netminder:	**Jody Lehman**, Coventry
Defence:	**Neal Martin**, **Wade Belak** Coventry
Forwards:	**Adam Calder**, Coventry
	Tony Hand, Belfast
	Jon Cullen, Cardiff

Selected by fans on league's website
*Sponsored by **Cardtraders.co.uk***

LEADING NETMINDERS

	GPI	Mins	SoG	GA	Sav%
Sylvain Daigle LON	30	1836	1036	70	93.24
Jody Lehman COV	48	2870	1315	89	93.23
Curtis Cruickshank NOT	48	2867	1279	97	92.41
Martin Klempa BEL	47	2810	1206	92	92.37
Jason Cugnet CAR	49	2859	1361	106	92.21
Jayme Platt SHE	49	2947	1223	97	92.07

Qualification: 1,000 minutes

PAST WINNERS

Elite League
2003-04 Sheffield Steelers
Superleague
2002-03 Sheffield Steelers
2001-02 Belfast Giants
2000-01 Sheffield Steelers
1999-00 Bracknell Bees
1998-99 Manchester Storm
1997-98 Ayr Scottish Eagles
1996-97 Cardiff Devils

LEADING BRITISH SCORERS

	GP	G	A	Pts	Pim
Tony Hand BEL	50	19	49	68	60
Ashley Tait COV	50	28	20	48	50
David Clarke NOT	50	27	19	46	24
Russ Cowley COV	45	8	14	22	16
Jonathan Phillips CAR	43	6	15	21	44
Marc Levers BEL	48	10	8	18	46
Matt Myers NOT	49	3	15	18	75
Tom Watkins COV	48	7	8	15	20
Tony Redmond BAS	42	2	11	13	20
Paul Moran NOT	40	5	6	11	30

FAIR PLAY

Team Penalties	GP	Pim	Ave
Nottingham Panthers	50	559	11.2
Cardiff Devils	50	712	14.2
Sheffield Steelers	50	794	15.9
Basingstoke Bison	50	827	16.5
Belfast Giants	50	867	17.3
London Racers	49	1152	23.5
Coventry Blaze	50	1237	24.7

SIN-BIN

Most Penalised Players	GP	Pim	Ave
Andre Payette COV	46	369	8.02
Scott Nichol LON	16	88	5.50
Mel Angelstadt BEL	49	253	5.16
Wade Belak COV	30	129	4.30
Adam Calder COV	44	183	4.16

SCORING RECORDS

INDIVIDUAL - HAT-TRICKS

3 - **Chris McNamara** COV, **Doug Sheppard** BAS,

2- **David Clarke** NOT, **Curtis Huppe** BEL, **Frederick Nasvall** BEL,

1 - **Adam Calder** COV, **Dan Carlson** COV, **Jon Cullen** CAR, **Marek Ivan** NOT, **Konstantin Kalmikov** NOT, **Dennis Ladouceur** LON, **Shawn Maltby** BAS, **Steve Moria** LON, **Scott Nichol** LON, **Andre Payette** COV.

LONGEST POINTS SCORING STREAK

13 games - **Tony Hand** BEL.

Figures compiled by Powerplay magazine.

MOST GAMES PLAYED

64 - **Jeff Burgoyne** CAR, **Kirk DeWaele** CAR, **Nathan Rempel** CAR, **Vezio Sacratini** CAR, **Graham Schlender** COV, **Ashley Tait** COV; 62 - **Calle Carlsson**, **David Clarke**, **Scott Ricci**, all NOT.

TEAM

Biggest victory margin *(excluding Crossover Games)* - 8 goals: Coventry beat Basingstoke 9-1 on 14 November 2004.

OVERTIME GAME WINNING GOALS

See Results Chart on next page

1	COV Michel Vrabel pp (unassisted)	62.09
2	BEL George Awada (unassisted)	64.50
3	SHE Daryl Andrews (Anderson, Christian)	
		63.48
4	LON Mark Thomas (Nichol, Maxwell)	60.32
5	BEL Frederik Nasval (Bowen, Gavalier)	60.24
6	SHE Gerad Adams (Dutiaume) sh	64.42
7	SHE Ron Shudra (Peron, Andrews) sh	61.22
8	LON Dennis Maxwell (Moria)	63.14
9	CAR Dave Matsos (Sacratini, Rempel)	62.57
10	SHE Jeff Christian (unassisted)	64.41
11	SHE Erik Anderson (Adams, Darling)	60.32
12	SHE Mike Peron (Darling, Cousineau)	64.59
13	SHE Ron Shudra (Christian, Dutiaume)	61.44
14	CAR Nathan Rempel (Sacratini, Burgoyne)	
		62.59
15	CAR Jeff Burgoyne (Sacratini)	64.59
16	CAR Jon Cullen (Matsos, Sacratini) pp	
		60.42
17	COV Adam Calder (Carlson)	63.14
18	COV Joel Poirier	64.43

OFFICIAL WEBSITE
www.eliteleague.co.uk

THE ELITE LEAGUE COACHES

Left to right: **TONY HAND** (Belfast), **PAUL HEAVEY** (Sheffield), **PAUL THOMPSON** (Coventry), **MARK BERNARD** (Basingstoke), **PAUL ADEY** (Nottingham), **DENNIS MAXWELL** (London); *missing*: **DAVE WHISTLE** (Cardiff).   *Photo*: Diane Davey

Blaze, not 'Blaiser'

The second season of the Elite League brought a changing of the guard with two of the sport's newer clubs, *Coventry Blaze* and *Belfast Giants*, leading the table ahead of their more established rivals.

Blaze's success was unexpected as they were playing in only their second season at the top level. But coach **Paul Thompson** recruited well with four of his squad making the league's All-Star team, including Toronto Maple Leaf defenceman **Wade Belak**.

Legendary Scottish forward **Tony Hand** did a fine coaching job with Giants in his first season in the league. He turned former Manchester forward **George Awada** into the league's joint top goalscorer and discovered a hot goalie in shutout king, **Martin Klempa**.

Many fans were delighted to see *Cardiff Devils* back among the leading teams after a few seasons in the wilderness. Again, good coaching was the key with **Dave Whistle** returning and forwards **Jon Cullen** and **Vezio Sacratini** gaining All-Star honours.

Nottingham Panthers endured their most unlucky season for injuries in years so that their fourth place finish could easily have been higher, but skipper **Calle Carlsson** enjoyed a career season.

One has a sneaking suspicion that simply finishing higher than their bitter rivals up the road in Sheffield - for the first time since 1998-99 - will have been some compensation for Panthers.

Life for the *Steelers* without their Hall of Fame coach **Mike Blaisdell**, who suddenly returned to Canada late in summer 2004, made recruitment difficult for his successor, former Belfast coach, **Rob Stewart**. When Stewart was sacked towards the end of the season, the move again came too late for **Paul Heavey** to turn the ship around.

Against the odds - a tight budget and crowds of barely 500 watching their games in their small East London home - *London Racers* moved up to sixth place from last in 2003-04 and played .500 hockey. Coach **Dennis Maxwell**'s ace signing was goalie **Sylvain Daigle** who led the league's save percentages. It was just a shame that the French-Canadian quit unhappily at Christmas.

Former Superleague netminder **Mark Bernard** returned to the UK as coach of the *Basingstoke Bison*, another small budget side. But Bernie found the league tougher than he perhaps expected and, despite having two exciting forwards in **Doug Sheppard** and **Shawn Maltby** (brother of Detroit's Kirk), Bison dropped into the cellar.

ELITE LEAGUE
RESULTS CHART

	BAS	BEL	CAR	COV	LON	NOT	SHE
Bison		3-3ot 20/11	1-1ot 2/10	4-4ot 11/9 CC	3-3ot 16/10	0-3 7/11	2-3ot (6) 4/12 CC
	**	3-2 9/1	3-5 27/11	2-5 30/10	2-4 13/11	1-3 11/12	2-4 3/1
		4-2 5/2	1-6 26/12	2-6 19/2	0-3 18/12	0-3 29/1	5-3 12/3
Giants	0-2 9/10		2-3 18/9 CC	2-0 2/10	5-0 25/9	2-4 13/11	3-2 16/10
	3-0 14/1	**	5-2 3/3	6-6ot 11/3	2-1 6/11	4-1 30/12	6-4 8/1
	6-0 11/2		5-2 4/3	5-6ot (18) 12/3	2-2ot 19/11	3-1 15/1	0-2 26/2
Devils	4-3 3/10	5-0 24/10 CC		2-6 25/9	1-0 30/10 CC	3-2 12/9 CC	6-1 13/11
	5-2 21/11	1-2ot (5) 28/11	**	1-3 6/11	5-0 4/12	0-2 23/12	2-2ot 11/12
	3-2 13/3	2-2ot 3/2		1-7 8/1	3-2ot (16) 26/2	3-2ot (14) 23/1	2-0 30/1
Blaze	3-2 17/10 CC	3-3ot 12/9	2-4 31/10		2-3 7/11	3-2ot (1) 19/9	2-1 24/10 CC
	9-1 14/11	3-1 10/10	4-0 16/1	**	2-2ot 19/12	1-1ot 9/1	2-3ot (7) 5/12
	6-3 23/1	2-1 20/2	4-2 5/2		5-1 6/3	3-1 13/2	2-3ot (12) 27/12
Racers	4-2 17/9	2-3ot (2) 15/10 CC	0-4 24/9 CC	0-2 21/11		4-5 10/10 CC	4-0 1/10
	1-1ot 17/12	0-3 3/12	2-2ot 27/2	1-4 28/1	**	1-2 14/1	2-1ot (4) 12/11
	3-4 29/12	1-3 6/2	5-2 8/3	2-3ot (17) 1/3		4-3 29/10	2-2ot 13/3
Panthers	4-1 6/11	1-2 26/10 CC	4-1 23/10 CC	2-2ot 28/12	3-3ot 18/9 CC		3-1 31/10
	3-5 8/1	4-4ot 2/1	4-1 20/11	1-2 22/1	1-2ot (8) 12/12	**	1-2ot (11) 26/12
	3-0 16/2	1-2 19/2	2-0 12/3	0-3 26/2	4-1 11/2		0-1 5/2
Steelers	3-2 12/9 CC	0-3 11/9	5-1 9/10	3-2ot (3) 23/10 CC	2-1 2/10	3-3ot 25/9	
	3-1 26/11	1-0 7/11	1-2ot (9) 12/12	4-3ot (13) 15/1	2-2ot 8/12	3-2ot (10) 19/12	**
	4-0 20/2	3-6 6/3	2-3ot (15) 29/1	1-2 2/2	1-2 22/1	3-0 5/3	
	BAS	**BEL**	**CAR**	**COV**	**LON**	**NOT**	**SHE**

Second figure is date of game
CC - *also played for Challenge Cup.*
Excludes Crossover Games. See separate table.

BELIEVE IT OR NOT

This wasn't a vintage season for Sheffield Steelers but they set a couple of unusual, not to say bizarre records. Between 30 January and 5 March - a run of eight games including two Crossover Games - all bar one of their contests ended in a shutout, with Steelers winning four of them, the last three in a row. In the middle of the streak, Steelers tied 0-0 with Guildford Flames. Goalie **Jayme Platt** played in all eight games, having five whitewashes in seven outings, four of them consecutively.

Earlier, between 4 and 27 December, Steelers were involved in eight consecutive games that went into overtime, winning five of them. All the other Elite League sides featured in the games apart from Belfast Giants.

PLAYOFFS

The league's top six teams were split into two groups for the playoffs: group A contained the teams finishing first, fourth and sixth and group B the teams who came second, third and fifth.

Each team played the others in their group four times (twice at home and twice away) with the top two teams in each group qualifying for the finals weekend in Nottingham.

In the semi-finals the winner of group A played the runner-up in group B. The first semi-final comprised the group winners that finished higher in the league table.

QUALIFYING ROUND STANDINGS

Group A	GP	W	L	D	GF	GA	Pts
Coventry Blaze	8	5	1	2	29	15	12
Nott'ham Panthers	8	3	3	2	21	29	8
London Racers	8	2	6	0	19	25	4
Group B							
Cardiff Devils	8	4	1	3	18	12	11
Sheffield Steelers	8	3	1	4	22	15	10
Belfast Giants	8	0	5	3	14	27	3

QUALIFYING ROUND RESULTS

Group A	COV	LON	NOT
Coventry Blaze	-	5-2	7-1
	-	2-0	3-3
London Racers	2-3	-	4-2
	1-4	-	7-3
Nottingham Panthers	1-1	2-1	-
	5-4	4-2	-
Group B	BEL	CAR	SHE
Belfast Giants	-	3-3	5-5
	-	1-4	2-2
Cardiff Devils	2-1	-	4-2
	3-0	-	0-3
Sheffield Steelers	4-0	1-1	-
	4-2	1-1	-

LEADING PLAYOFF NETMINDERS

	GPI	Mins	SoG	GA	Sv%
Jody Lehman COV	9	538	288	11	96.2
Jayme Platt SHE	6	325	166	8	95.2
Jason Cugnet CAR	8	480	202	11	94.6

SEMI-FINALS

9 April at National Ice Centre, Nottingham

Coventry Blaze-Sheffield Steelers	**3-0**
Cardiff Devils-Nottingham Panthers	**1-3**

THIRD PLACE PLAYOFF

Sheffield Steelers-Cardiff Devils	4-2

FINAL

10 April at National Ice Centre, Nottingham

Coventry Blaze-Nottingham Panthers   2-1ot

Ashley Tait (Lukac) scores winning goal at 63.07.

COVENTRY BLAZE win Elite League Playoff Championship

THE FINAL FOUR

CARDIFF DEVILS

Jason Cugnet, Mike Brabon; Jeff Burgoyne, Rob Davison, Jason Stone, Kirk DeWaele, Jason Becker; Phil Manny, Nathan Rempel, Russ Romaniuk, Phil Hill, Jonathan Phillips, Dave Matsos, Jon Cullen, Vezio Sacratini (capt), Neil Francis, Warren Tait, John Craighead.
Manager/Coach: Dave Whistle.

COVENTRY BLAZE

Jody Lehman, Dan Shea; Wade Belak, Doug Schueller, Neal Martin, Jozef Lukac, James Pease; Andre Payette, Graham Schlender, Russ Cowley, Tom Watkins, Ashley Tait (capt), Adam Calder, Dan Carlson, Chris McNamara, Joel Poirier, Nathaniel Williams.
Manager/Coach: Paul Thompson.

NOTTINGHAM PANTHERS

Ladislav Kudrna, Geoff Woolhouse; Scott Ricci, Ian Moran, Nick Boynton, Calle Carlsson (capt); David Clarke, Matt Myers, Jason Buckman, Rhys McWilliams, Konstantin Kalmikov, Steve McKenna, Lewis Buckman, Paul Moran, Marek Ivan, Mikhail Nemirovsky.
Coach: Paul Adey.   Manager: Gary Moran.

SHEFFIELD STEELERS

Jayme Platt, Davey Lawrence; Daryl Andrews, Steve Duncombe, David Cousineau, Ron Shudra; Gerad Adams, Marc Lefebvre, Simon Butterworth, Mike Peron, Erik Anderson, Les Millie, Ben Bliss, Dion Darling (capt), Paul Sample, Jeff Christian.
Manager/Coach: Paul Heavey.

LEADING PLAYOFF SCORERS

	GP	G	A	Pts	Pim
Erik Anderson SHE	10	5	10	15	6
Jeff Christian SHE	10	5	8	13	0
David Clarke NOT	10	5	9	14	4
Dan Carlson COV	10	7	5	12	4
Mike Peron SHE	8	6	6	12	4

PLAYOFF HEROES

Left: **LADISLAV KUDRNA**, Nottingham Panthers' goalie took his team all the way to the Elite League playoff final; *right*: **RON SHUDRA**, Coventry Blaze's veteran defenceman scored in the semi-final against his old team, Sheffield Steelers.

Photos: Bob Swann

Two Giants out

The most demanding schedule of playoff games ever played in this country - 24 in 19 days - produced many complaints from fans, let alone the players. The team to suffer most were league runners-up, Belfast Giants.

Tony Hand's squad, one of the playoff favourites, were so demoralised by having to play their final seven games in just 11 days that they failed to win a match in group B.

The group was won by Cardiff Devils whose 'secret weapon' was the regular use of three forward lines by coach **Dave Whistle** while his opponents made do with two. "Cardiff's third line of [Brits] **Neil Francis**, **Warren Tait** and **Phil Manny** has more experience than our British lads," admitted Sheffield Steelers' coach, **Paul Heavey**.

Steelers had a shakey start to the playoffs, collecting only four points in four games. "Some guys didn't play well, the distribution was poor and we didn't shoot enough," moaned Heavey. But the strict Glaswegian whispered gently in a few ears and, with a little help from the schedule, Steelers reached the final weekend for the sixth successive year.

Over in A group, Nottingham Panthers' injury jinx didn't go away just because the league games were finished. Goalie **Curtis Cruickshank** suffered damaged cruciate ligaments in their opening game at Coventry which ended in a disastrous 7-1 defeat with rarely used Brit, **Geoff Woolhouse**, having to take over between the pipes.

But that proved to be a blessing in disguise as coach **Paul Adey** was able to pick up Hull's excellent **Ladislav Kudrna** who went on to win three successive man of the match awards. The team lost only two more games, none to the Blaze.

The little Lee Valley rink (only the Wales National Ice Rink is as small in the top two leagues) was a haven for London Racers who lost all their games on the road but proved to be a tough opponent in E10.

(Unfortunately, not all Racers' fans were able to enjoy the action as team owner **Roger Black** pushed up the ticket prices by a third and the crowds suddenly found other things to do.)

Only the Blaze won twice in Lee Valley, but the second game was played after Racers had been knocked out, and the first was by a single goal, 3-2, when Blaze coach **Paul Thompson**, admitted "they threw the kitchen sink at us".

Panthers lost both their contests amid the hanging flower baskets, but it was the first one - on a Thursday night, 24 March - that will live in Elite League infamy.

NHLer **Eric Cairns** chased referee **Andy Carson** round the ice, sparking off a brawl which ended with the giant forward being suspended for the rest of the year and next. (See *Review of the Season*).

PLAYOFF SEMI-FINALS
National Ice Centre, Nottingham
Saturday 9 April 2005

COVENTRY BLAZE	3	(0-1-2)
SHEFFIELD STEELERS	0	(0-0-0)

Scoring
1-0 COV Shudra (unass.)   30.53
2-0 COV Watkins (Cowley, Schlender)   42.14
3-0 COV Poirier (Schueller)   eng   58.59
Netminding
Lehman COV   13-8-20 41   *save%*   100.00
Platt SHE   11-9- 7 27   *save%*   88.89
Penalty minutes Blaze 0, Steelers 0.
Men of Match: Lehman COV, Lefebvre SHE.
Referee: Nigel Boniface. *Attendance*: 6,500 est.
Linesmen: Andy Dalton, Tom Darnell.

CARDIFF DEVILS	1	(1-0-0)
NOTTINGHAM PANTHERS	3	(1-0-2)

Scoring
1-0 CAR Cullen (Rempel)   18.58
1-1 NOT McKenna (Myers, Carlsson)   19.27
1-2 NOT Clarke (unass.)   44.27
1-3 NOT Kalmikov (Myers)   eng   59.56
Netminding
Cugnet CAR   7-7- 9 23   *save%*   86.96
Kudrna NOT   12-8-11 31   *save%*   96.77
Penalty minutes: Devils 6, Panthers 8.
Goals/powerplays: Devils 0/1, Panthers 0/0.
Men of Match: Burgoyne CAR, McKenna NOT.
Referee: Moray Hanson. *Attendance*: 6,600 est.
Linesmen: Marco Coenen, Mark Drennan.

PLAYOFF FINAL
National Ice Centre, Nottingham
Sunday 10 April 2005

COVENTRY BLAZE	2	(0-1-0-1)
NOTTINGHAM PANTHERS	1	(0-1-0-0)
after overtime		

Scoring
1-0 COV Martin (Carlson, Belak)   20.38
1-1 NOT Boynton (Nemirovsky, Ivan)   21.18
2-1 COV Tait (Lukac)   63.07
Netminding
Lehman COV   5-14-6-0   25   *save%*   96.00
Kudrna NOT   15-15-12-3 45   *save%*   95.55
Penalty minutes: Blaze 8, Panthers 6.
Goals/powerplays: Blaze 0/0, Panthers 0/1.
Men of Match: Martin COV, Kudrna NOT.
Referee: Moray Hanson. *Attendance*: 6,800 est.

Third trophy sent to Coventry

Ashley **Tait**'s dramatic overtime winner gave Coventry Blaze the Elite League's Grand Slam of league, Challenge Cup and playoff titles.

For Blaze and their loyal coach, **Paul Thompson**, it was also the climax of a 10-year partnership, starting in the English League in 1995-96. Blaze's managing director, **Mike Cowley**, said: "I never dreamed we would achieve this in such a short time. To go from the bottom level and win a triple at the top level - that's going to take some time to sink in."

The defeat produced mixed emotions from Panthers who were beaten finalists for the second straight year. "Getting to the finals was an accomplishment in itself, and beating Cardiff in the semi-final was a super-human effort," said their coach **Paul Adey**, who had been under fire from his owner for most of the season over his injury-hit team's disappointing results.

Tait's winner, a slapshot from the right face-off circle after he snared **Jozef Lukac**'s inch-perfect pass from the opposite wing, beat the rock-steady **Ladislav Kudrna**. Ironically, the Czech keeper had been brought in by Adey when Panthers' number one, **Curtis Cruickshank**, joined the lengthy injury list in their first playoff game - against the Blaze.

Sheffield Steelers, the defending title-holders, had their least successful playoff weekend since 2002-03, failing to score against **Jody Lehman** despite pouring 41 shots on his net.

"Losing Dutes [**Mark Dutiaume**] was a big blow," said Steelers' captain **Dion Darling**. The fast skating centreman, who missed last year's final through injury, was away fulfilling his duties as best man at his brother Todd's wedding in Kirkcaldy. Although this had been planned well in advance, it reportedly came as an unwelcome surprise to new coach **Paul Heavey**.

The Devils-Panthers' semi was described as being "like a game seven" by locked-out NHLer **Steve McKenna**, Panthers' man of the match. Ukrainian **Konstantin Kalmikov** scored the winner just four seconds from time.

From the spectator's viewpoint, all three games were great entertainment, hard, fast and intensely competitive. Only 14 minor penalties were handed out in the semis and final and the Blaze-Steelers game remarkably passed off without a single penalty-worthy incident.

If only the league hadn't made that dreadful decision to have a third place playoff...!

• Devils' backer, *Thomson Holidays*, was the Nottingham weekend's main sponsor. *Sky Sports* screened one-hour highlights of the games later the same week which we understand was facilitated by *Thomson*'s financial support.

CHALLENGE CUP

The seven Elite League teams were divided into two groups with the teams in each group playing a round-robin. The results in the first league games played between the sides counted towards the Qualifying Round of the Challenge Cup. (See Results Chart)

The top two teams in each qualifying group went forward to the semi-finals with the first placed team in one group playing the runner-up in the other. Games were played home and away on an aggregate scores basis.

The final was also played over home and away legs, the team finishing higher in the preliminary round receiving choice of home leg.

QUALIFYING ROUND STANDINGS

	GP	W	L	OL	D	GF	GA	Pts
Sheffield Steelers	4	3	1	0	0	10	8	6
Coventry Blaze	4	2	0	1	1	11	10	6
Basingstoke Bison	4	0	2	1	1	10	13	2
Group B								
Cardiff Devils	6	5	1	0	0	17	8	10
Nott'ham Panthers	6	3	2	0	1	19	15	7
Belfast Giants	6	3	3	0	0	14	15	6
London Racers	6	0	4	1	1	9	21	2

Tied teams separated by the number of wins.

SEMI-FINALS

First semi-final, first leg, 18 December 2004
COVENTRY-NOTTINGHAM **2-1** (0-0,2-0,0-1)
Goal scorers: COV Tait 2, NOT Cadotte.
First semi-final, second leg, 19 January 2004
NOTTINGHAM-COVENTRY **3-3** (0-0,2-2,1-1)
Goal scorers: NOT Ivan, Cadotte, Ahlroos; COV Calder, Lukac, Schueller.
COVENTRY BLAZE win 5-4 on aggregate.

Second semi-final, first leg, 12 January 2005
SHEFFIELD-CARDIFF **2-2** (1-0,0-2,1-0)
Goal scorers: SHE Dutiaume, Shudra; CAR Rempel 2.
Second semi-final, second leg, 20 January 2005
CARDIFF-SHEFFIELD **3-1** (1-0,2-1,0-0)
Goal scorers: CAR Matsos, Craighead, Hill; SHE Adams.
CARDIFF DEVILS win 5-3 on aggregate

FINAL

First leg, 16 February 2005
COVENTRY-CARDIFF **6-1** (2-1,3-0,1-0)
Scoring:
1-0 COV Calder (Carlson) sh 08.36
2-0 COV Watkins (Schlender) 10.37
2-1 CAR Davison (W Tait) 17.00
3-1 COV McNamara (A Tait, Poirier) 21.21
4-1 COV Belak (McNamara, Poirier) pp 23.04
5-1 COV A Tait (unass.) 36.24
6-1 COV Poirier (McNamara, A Tait) 55.53
Netminding:
Lehman COV 14-11-11 36 save% 97.22
Cugnet CAR 12-13- 9 34 save% 82.35
Goals/powerplays: Blaze 1/3, Devils 0/4.
Penalty minutes: Blaze 14, Devils 47 (Francis 2+10 hook, Whistle match - abuse of official).
Referee: Simon Kirkham. Attendance: 2,770
Linesmen: Marco Coenen, Tom Darnell.

Second leg, 24 February 2005
CARDIFF-COVENTRY **4-5** (2-1,2-2,0-2)
Scoring:
1-0 CAR Cullen (DeWaele) 05.07
1-1 COV A Tait (Poirier) 06.18
2-1 CAR Matsos (Romaniuk) 11.56
3-1 CAR Rempel (Cullen, Sacratini) pp 29.59
4-1 CAR Sacratini (Matsos) 32.34
4-2 COV Cowley (Schueller) pp 35.10
4-3 COV Watkins (unass.) 36.00
4-4 COV Lukac (unass.) 44.14
4-5 COV McKenzie (unass.) 53.14
Netminding:

For only the third time since the Challenge Cup was created in 1997, neither Nottingham Panthers nor Sheffield Steelers reached the final. Both were knocked out in the semis leaving their conquerors to battle through a stormy 16-goal, two-leg contest with Devils' coach **Dave Whistle** being thrown out in the first game after blowing his top over a disputed penalty to his star player, **Jon Cullen**. 'Whis' wasn't much happier in the fight-filled return, though his men clawed to within two goals, and he had to admit "Blaze have a great team".

Cugnet CAR 5-11-10 26 save% 80.77
Lehman COV 23-16-16 55 save% 92.73
Goals/powerplays: Devils 1/6, Blaze 1/2.
Penalty minutes: Devils 85 (Sacratini 2+10 - ch/behind, Craighead 5+game - rough, Romaniuk 2+10 - ch/head, DeWaele game - 3rd man), Blaze 113 (Payette 5+game - rough, McNamara game - 3rd man, Belak match - fight, Schlender 5+game - rough).
Referee: Nigel Boniface. Attendance: 2,060.
Linesmen: Andy Dalton, Joy Tottman.

COVENTRY BLAZE win Challenge Cup 11-5 on aggregate

COVENTRY BLAZE

As in the Elite League Playoffs, with the addition of **Bari McKenzie**.

BRITISH NATIONAL LEAGUE

FINAL STANDINGS

	GP	W	L	OL	D	GF	GA	Pts	Pct
(*-4) **Bracknell Bees** BRK	38	24	10	2	2	154	89	52	68.4
(8-5) **Newcastle Vipers** NEW	38	18	17	2	1	123	139	39	51.3
(3-2) **Guildford Flames** GUI	38	16	18	2	2	113	112	36	47.4
(9-7) **Hull Stingrays** HUL	38	16	19	2	1	96	121	35	46.1
(2-6) **Dundee Stars** DUN	38	14	24	0	0	117	155	28	36.8
(7-1) **Fife Flyers** FIF	38	12	25	1	0	112	171	25	32.9
(6-3) **Edinburgh Capitals** EDI	38	6	29	2	1	102	189	15	19.7

*Includes Crossover Games with Elite League teams. *Joined from Superleague in 2003-04.*
Figures in brackets are the league positions in each of the last two seasons.
Scoring system: *two points for a win (W), one point for a draw (D) or overtime loss (OL).*
Pct. *= percentage of points gained to points available.*

LEADING SCORERS

	GP	G	A	Pts	Pim
Peter Campbell BRK	38	30	31	61	70
Lukas Smital BRK	35	25	30	55	22
Dino Bauba EDI	35	19	36	55	91
Jonathan Weaver NEW	36	15	32	47	42
Matus Petricko BRK	37	22	24	46	42
Martin Masa BRK	34	19	27	46	20
Marty Johnson EDI	28	18	27	45	45
Martin Cingel EDI	38	16	28	44	42
David Longstaff NEW	33	13	30	43	22
Jozef Kohut GUI	36	21	21	42	40
Matt Beveridge NEW	36	11	30	41	24
Jeff Glowa HUL	37	20	19	39	41
Cory Morgan DUN	31	18	21	39	60

LEADING NETMINDERS

	GPl	Mins	SoG	GA	Sv%
Stevie Lyle BRK	38	2284	1107	76	93.1
Miroslav Bielik GUI	34	2041	1089	92	91.5
Ladislav Kudrna HUL	38	2249	1337	113	91.5
Scott Hay FIF	23	1362	917	88	90.4
Evan Lindsay DUN	32	1874	1185	115	90.3
Qualification: 760 mins					

SIN BIN

Players' Penalties	GP	Pim	Ave
Jason Shmyr DUN	36	201	5.58
Scott Barnes DUN	34	123	3.62
Nicky Chinn GUI	24	86	3.58
Rob Trumbley NEW	29	92	3.17
Pavel Gomenyuk HUL	32	95	2.97

FAIR PLAY

Team Penalties	GP	Pim	Ave
Hull Stingrays	38	394	10.4
Bracknell Bees	38	463	12.2
Edinburgh Capitals	38	466	12.3
Guildford Flames	38	506	13.3
Fife Flyers	38	549	14.4
Newcastle Vipers	37	551	14.9
Dundee Stars	38	696	18.3
LEAGUE TOTALS		3625	13.7

ALL-STAR TEAM

Goal	**Ladislav Kudrna**, Hull.
Defence	**Greg Kuznik**, Fife,
	Pavel Gomenyuk Hull.
Forwards	**Martin Masa, Lukas Smital,**
	Peter Campbell, all Bracknell.
Coach	**Mike Ellis** Bracknell.

Selected by the BNL coaches.

BRITISH NATIONAL LEAGUE

RESULTS CHART

	BRK	DUN	EDI	FIF	GUI	HUL	NEW
Bees	**	5-3 16/1	6-1 8/1	10-1 17/10	4-2 11/12	2-1 26/1	1-2 27/11
		3-1 26/2	13-0 30/12	4-1 21/11	1-4 19/2	4-0 6/2	6-2 2/2
Stars	6-3 22/1	**	5-4 3/2	1-5 31/10	7-2 28/11	5-2 13/11	3-4 26/12
	6-3 27/2		3-4 12/2	3-1 6/1	4-3 9/1	1-4 3/1	3-5 19/2
Capitals	5-3 2/1	2-6 18/12	**	1-2 26/12	0-5 25/9	4-1 9/1	2-3 21/11
	4-4ot 23/1	5-6ot (6) 20/2		7-3 30/1	2-6 6/2	1-4 15/1	7-4 27/2
Flyers	2-4 16/10	7-3 25/9	2-4 1/1	**	0-3 13/11	2-3 6/11	4-1 16/11
	2-4 29/1	5-7 5/2	8-2 19/2		4-3 22/1	5-4 8/1	2-3 22/2
Flames	0-5 26/12	5-2 29/1	3-2 9/2	3-4ot (1) 7/11	**	1-1ot 21/9	5-2 8/1
	1-3 15/1	4-2 13/2	4-3 26/2	9-0 23/1		5-2 9/10	1-2 5/2
Stingrays	5-6ot (2) 7/11	7-4 20/11	5-3 5/2	3-2 2/1	3-2 10/10	**	5-3 29/1
	0-2 9/2	4-2 29/12	7-1 23/2	3-1 16/1	3-4ot (4) 12/2		0-1 26/2
Vipers	1-5 24/10	8-3 7/11	6-5 19/12	11-2 9/1	6-3 28/12	3-4 22/12	**
	6-5ot (3) 10/2	4-2 5/12	5-3 16/1	6-7ot (5) 13./2	6-2 24/1	5-3 16/2	

Second figure is date of game
Excludes Crossover Games. See separate table.

Bees top final league season

Bracknell Bees put together one of the finest teams in their history to win what turned out to be the final British National League competition.

From Welsh goalie **Stevie Lyle** out through young GB international defender **Danny Meyers** up to All Star forwards, Czechs **Martin Masa** and **Lukas Smital** and Canada international **Peter Campbell**, Bees dominated the league under player-coach **Mike Ellis**.

Their most striking achievement was not to lose a home game, in regulation time, to an Elite League side in the Crossover Games. Only Cardiff Devils took both points, and they needed nearly four minutes of overtime to do it.

Against BNL teams, Bees lost only twice in the Hive, the heaviest defeat coming after they had clinched the title.

Newcastle Vipers endured the usual torrid time awaiting the teams that play to small crowds out of the city's vast arena. But their continuing money problems didn't seem to affect **Rob Wilson** and **Clyde Tuyl's** squad - they signed locked-out NHLer **Chris McAllister** a few days before the club went into liquidation - as they stormed to the runners-up place, though a distant 13 points adrift of Bracknell.

Finance was the last of *Guildford Flames'* problems, but **Stan Marple's** team under-achieved, not for the first time. Apart from signing a hot young Slovak goalie **Miroslav** Bielik, 20, Flames did not have enough depth or enough fire-power.

Guildford and Newcastle were almost beaten in the last couple of weeks of the season by the low budget but cleverly coached *Hull Stingrays*. **Rick Strachan**, who was appointed GB coach during the season, also signed a hot goalie, Edinburgh's Czech **Ladislav Kudrna**, and built the team around him.

It's hard to know quite why *Dundee Stars* finished so low in the standings. Maybe **Roger Hunt's** new signings needed time to gel; they certainly took too many penalties. Wait 'til the playoffs!

It was a bad year for all three Scots teams. Defending champs *Fife Flyers* lost influential import forwards **Karry Biette** and **Dreu Volk** to injury, while coach **Mark Morrison** perhaps left it too late before bringing back popular Canadian netminder **Steve Briere**.

Edinburgh Capitals' failure to get off the bottom of the table can be explained in two words - **Tony Hand**. Britain's finest native player, who as player-coach had guided Capitals to third place in 2003-04, spent the season away from his home town across the Irish Sea.

But Caps' miserable season was not the fault of their forwards. Veteran Lithuanian **Dino Bauba**, the ECHL's **Marty Johnston** and the returning **Martin Cingel** scored almost 250 points between them.

PLAYOFFS

The top six league clubs competed in the Playoffs in a double round-robin tournament played over three weeks after the end of the league season.

The top four teams from the first round advanced to the semi-finals which were contested in a best-of-three series with the top team meeting the fourth placed side and second playing third. The winners met in a best-of-five series to determine the Playoff champion.

The team finishing highest in the league table was given the choice of home games in the final and semi-finals.

If any final or semi-final game finished in a tie after 60 minutes, the teams played ten minutes sudden death overtime, followed by five penalty shots and sudden death penalty shots as required to produce a result.

*The winning team was awarded the **John Brady** Bowl, presented in memory of the late manager of the Fife Ice Arena who was influential in creating the league.*

QUARTER-FINAL STANDINGS

	GP	W	L	OL	D	GF	GA	Pts
Bracknell Bees	10	6	2	0	2	35	23	14
Guildford Flames	10	7	3	0	0	30	20	14
Fife Flyers	10	6	3	1	0	34	33	13
Dundee Stars	10	4	4	1	1	36	36	10
Newcastle Vipers	10	3	6	0	1	27	35	7
Hull Stingrays	10	2	6	2	0	21	36	6

Tied teams separated by the results between them.

QUARTER-FINAL RESULTS

	BRK	DUN	FIF	GUI	HUL	NEW
Bees	-	4-3	4-1	0-2	4-3	5-2
Stars	3-3ot	-	5-4ot (3)	4-2	3-6	4-2
Flyers	3-2	5-4ot (1)	-	3-1	2-5	7-3
Flames	2-5	4-2	4-1	-	5-2	4-1
Stingrays	1-5	1-5	2-3ot (4)	1-2ot (2)	-	1-3
Vipers	3-3ot	5-3	6-2	1-4+	1-2	-

Newcastle's home games played at Whitley Bay except +

SEMI-FINALS
best of three games
First semi-final

Game 1 *26 Mar* **Bracknell-Dundee**   **3-3ot**
***DUNDEE won** after penalty shootout.*
Cory Morgan scored game-winning shot.
Game 2 *27 Mar* **Dundee-Bracknell**   **5-5ot**
***DUNDEE won** after penalty shootout.*
John Dolan scored game-winning shot.
***DUNDEE qualify** for final, two games to nil.*

Second semi-final

Game 1 *26 Mar* Guildford-Fife   **1-3**
Game 2 *27 Mar* Fife-Guildford   **1-3**
Game 3 *31 Mar* Guildford-Fife   **6-3**
***GUILDFORD qualified** for final,*
two games to one.

FINAL
best of five games

Game 1 *2 Apr* Guildford-Dundee   **0-4**
Game 2 *3 Apr* Dundee-Guildford   **5-2**
Game 3 *6 Apr* Guildford-Dundee   **2-3**

DUNDEE STARS are Playoff champions
three games to nil.

LEADING PLAYOFF SCORERS

	GP	G	A	Pts	Pim
Lukas Smital BRK	12	10	9	19	38
Cory Morgan DUN	15	10	9	19	18
Scott Barnes DUN	15	10	8	18	62
Patric Lochi DUN	14	7	11	18	6
Ratislov Palov GUI	15	6	12	18	4
Judd Medak FIF	13	5	12	17	36
Milos Melicherik GUI	16	4	13	17	18
Jozef Kohut GUI	15	9	7	16	38
Peter Campbell BRK	12	8	7	15	6
Peter Konder GUI	16	4	10	14	12
Adrian Saul FIF	13	7	8	15	6
David Longstaff NEW	10	8	7	15	6

LEADING PLAYOFF NETMINDERS

	GPI	Mins	SoG	GA	Sv%
Jamie McLennan GUI	7	385	192	13	93.2
Stevie Lyle BRK	12	750	413	31	92.5
Miroslav Bielik GUI	9	540	324	25	92.3

Qualification: 360 minutes

CHAMPIONSHIP FINALS - SUMMARIES

Game One, Saturday 2 April

GUILDFORD FLAMES	0	(0-0-0)
DUNDEE STARS	4	(0-3-1)

Scoring:

0-1 DUN Dolan (Lochi, Corbett)		22.28
0-2 DUN Wishart (Morgan, Barnes)		22.54
0-3 DUN Dolan (Lochi)		30.54
0-4 DUN Corbett (Borgatello)		44.58

Netminding:

Bielik GUI	10-8-10 28	*save%*	85.7
Lindsay DUN	6-6- 7 19	*save%*	100.0

Penalty minutes: Flames 8, Stars 16.
Referee: Andy Carson.   *Attendance*: 1,264
Linesmen: Dalton, Cavanagh.

Game Two, Sunday 3 April

DUNDEE STARS	5	(1-2-2)
GUILDFORD FLAMES	2	(1-0-1)

Scoring:

0-1 GUI Kohut (Melicherik, Konder)		1.21
1-1 DUN Marshall (Morgan)		11.57
1-2 DUN Lochi (Dolan, Corbett)		24.21
1-3 DUN Dolan (Corbett, Lochi)		25.11
1-4 DUN Dolan (Lochi, Corbett)		40.52
1-5 DUN Barnes (Morgan, Wishart)		48.57
2-5 GUI Durco (Melicherik, Reilly) pp		58.04

Netminding:

Lindsay DUN	14-13-11 38	*save%*	94.7
Bielik GUI	12-17-15 44	*save%*	88.6

Referee: Moray Hanson.   *Attendance*: 2,108
Linesmen: Drennan, Mizen.

Game Three, Wednesday 6 April

GUILDFORD FLAMES	2	(2-0-0)
DUNDEE STARS	3	(2-0-1)

Scoring:

1-0 GUI Melicherik (Oliver)	pp	4.52
1-1 DUN Barnes (Shmyr, Borgatello)	pp	7.08
1-2 DUN Lochi (Borgatello)		12.00
2-2 GUI Reilly (Cross)		13.40
2-3 DUN Morgan (Wishart)	pp	53.58

Netminding:

McLennan GUI	11- 5-12 28	*save%*	89.3
Lindsay DUN	5-10- 4 19	*save%*	89.5

Referee: Simon Kirkham.   *Attendance*: 1,504
Linesmen: Darnell, Young.

THE FINALISTS

DUNDEE STARS

Evan Lindsay, Stephen Murphy; Cristiano Borgatello, Jeff Marshall, Paddy Ward, Chad Reekie, Scott Corbett, Andy Samuel, John Dolan, Gary Wishart, Cory Morgan, Patric Lochi, Jason Shmyr (capt), David Smith, Scott Barnes, Ali Haddanou.
Manager/Coach: Roger Hunt.

GUILDFORD FLAMES

Tom Annetts, Miroslav Bielik, Jamie McLennan; Paul Dixon (capt), Neil Liddiard, Adam Walker, Stan Marple, Juraj Durco, Milos Melicherik, Jozef Kohut, Peter Konder, Ratislav Palov, David Oliver, Nick Cross, Marian Smerciak, Jason Reilly, Nicky Chinn, Andrew Hemmings.
Manager/Coach: Stan Marple.

PAST PLAYOFF WINNERS

2002-03	Coventry Blaze
2001-02	Dundee Stars
2000-01	Guildford Flames
1999-2000	Fife Flyers
1998-99	Fife Flyers
1997-98	Guildford Flames
1996-97	Swindon IceLords (Premier Lge)
	Fife Flyers (Northern Premier Lge)

STARS' STARS

Left: **CORY MORGAN** scored the winning goal for Dundee Stars in the third and final playoff game against Guildford Flames; *right*: **JOHN DOLAN** who scored four times for Dundee against Flames.

Photos: Tony Boot

Four-goal Dolan leads Stars

Dundee Stars produced one of the most dramatic fightbacks in recent playoff history to win the John Brady Bowl for the British National League championship.

Coming from fifth in the league and fourth in the playoff quarter-finals, **Roger Hunt**'s men knocked off the hot favourites, Bracknell Bees, in the semis, then wiped out Guildford Flames in three straight in the final.

It was the second playoff success in Stars' short history; they captured the prize in their inaugural year of 2001-02.

"This win is probably sweeter than 2001-02 because that team [under player-coach **Tony Hand**] was expected to win things," said a team spokesman. "And a lot of credit must go to Roger. He stuck to what he believed because he knew he was on the right track."

Stars' best individual performances came from late signing **Cory Morgan** who beat Flames' locked-out NHL neminder **Jamie McLennan** for the winning goal in Game Three of the final; and Dundee's own keeper **Evan Lindsay** whose superb play was one of the reasons his team went so deep into the playoffs.

And there was the remarkable **John Dolan**, the promising young Dundonian who scored the winning penalty shot against Bracknell and beat Flames four times in Games One and Two.

Defending champs Guildford Flames started as favourites, helped by the fact that they had home ice advantage throughout the semis and final after finishing second in the quarter-finals. (Stars played only two home games.)

But Flames won only one of their four contests in the Spectrum, a comfortable 6-3 semi-final victory which knocked out Fife Flyers. The Kirkcaldy side had been shaken by the loss of their player-coach **Mark Morrison** who broke a leg in Game Two when someone fell on top of him after he went down to stop a shot.

Guildford then had the worst possible start to the finals, being shutout in their own barn, with Lindsay facing only 19 shots on his net. Surprisingly, only 1,300 fans turned up to watch while the next night in Dundee, Stars attracted over 2,000, their biggest crowd of the season.

The league winning Bees suffered 'winners syndrome' and were unable to lift themselves for the playoffs. After losing only once to Stars in four league and two playoff games, they drew both semi-final games and still couldn't clinch victory in overtime.

⌧ Ignoring last season's mass stay-away by their fans, the league went with an even longer playoff schedule this time, substituting a best-of-five series in the semis and finals for the usual home-and-away legs.

With all the games being played between Scotland and southern England based sides, it was a relief for everyone's wallets - apart from the coach companies - that neither series went the full five games.

WINTER CUP

Two teams from the English Premier League accepted invitations to join the qualifying round of this British National League competition (previously known as the Findus Cup) which was played in the first three months of the season.

After each team had played the other home and away, the top four were drawn into the semi-finals with the first placed team meeting the fourth placed and the second playing the third.

The semi-finals and final were played over two legs, home and away.

QUALIFYING ROUND STANDINGS

	GP	W	L	OL	D	GF	GA	Pts
Bracknell Bees	16	13	2	1	0	94	48	27
Newcastle Vipers	16	12	3	0	1	63	43	25
Fife Flyers	16	10	2	3	1	71	47	24
Hull Stingrays	16	9	7	0	0	52	45	18
Dundee Stars	16	8	7	1	0	63	47	17
Edinburgh Cap's	16	8	7	0	1	64	71	17
Guildford Flames	16	7	6	2	1	56	50	17
MK Lightning	16	2	14	0	0	41	83	4
P'boro' Phantoms	16	1	15	0	0	30	100	2

QUALIFYING ROUND RESULTS
See next page

SEMI-FINALS
First semi-final, first leg, 12 January 2005
HULL-BRACKNELL   **3-3** (3-1,0-1,0-1)
First semi-final, second leg, 19 January
BRACKNELL-HULL   **6-1** (1-0,4-1,1-0)
BRACKNELL BEES win 9-4 on aggregate

Second semi-final, first leg, 15 January
FIFE-NEWCASTLE   **1-2** (0-1,0-0,1-1)
Second semi-final, second leg, 19 January
NEWCASTLE-FIFE   **3-4ot**
                        (0-0,0-1,3-3,0-0)
5-5 on aggregate. **NEWCASTLE VIPERS win** after penalty shootout. Game winning shot by **Matt Beveridge**.

FINAL
First leg, 20 February 2005
NEWCASTLE-BRACKNELL   **1-5** (0-1,0-1,1-3)
Second leg, 23 February
BRACKNELL-NEWCASTLE   **3-0** (2-0,0-0,1-0)

BRACKNELL BEES win Winter Cup
8-1 on aggregate

THE WINNING TEAM
BRACKNELL BEES
Dan Green, Stevie Lyle; Jan Krulis, Richard Hardy, Luke Reynolds, Mark Galazzi, Greg Owen, Peter Campbell, Ross McDougall, Lee Richardson, Mark Richardson, Danny Meyers, Dwight Parrish, Matus Petricko, Danny Hughes, Martin Masa, Lukas Smital, Mike Ellis, Ryan Aldridge, Mike Rees.
Manager/Coach: Mike Ellis.

CUP FINAL SUMMARIES
First leg, 20 February 2005

NEWCASTLE VIPERS	1	(0-0-1)
BRACKNELL BEES	5	(1-1-3)

Scoring:
0-1 BRK Campbell (Krulis)   6.39
0-2 BRK Rees (Petricko, Campbell) pp   26.02
0-3 BRK Smital (Krulis)   pp   46.58
1-3 NEW Wilson (Beveridge)   47.11
1-4 BRK M Rich'dson (Parrish, Aldridge) pp 50.54
1-5 BRK Smital (Parrish)   52.01
Netminding:
Teskey NEW   10-6-10 26   save% 80.76
Lyle BRK   7-5- 7 19   save% 94.74
Penalty minutes: Vipers 30 (McAllister - 10m abuse), Bees 8.
Referee: Andy Carson.   Attendance: 1,992
Linesmen: Steve Brown, Dave Emmerson.

Second leg, 23 February

BRACKNELL BEES	3	(2-0-1)
NEWCASTLE VIPERS	0	(0-0-0)

Scoring:
1-0 BRK Owen (Galazzi)   00.27
2-0 BRK Campbell (Petricko, Parrish) 03.45
3-0 BRK Campbell (unass.)   pp   56.37
Netminding
Lyle BRK   12-10- 7 29   save% 100.00
Teskey NEW   13-20-10 43   save% 93.02
Penalty minutes: Bees 6, Vipers 16.
Referee: Nigel Boniface.   Attendance: 2,730
Linesmen: Tom Darnell, Lee Young.

PAST CUP FINALISTS
2004 **Newcastle Vipers** beat Guildford Flames 6-1 at the Telewest Arena, Newcaslte
2003 **Newcastle Vipers** beat Coventry Blaze 3-0 at the Telewest Arena, Newcastle.
2002 **Fife Flyers** beat Coventry Blaze 6-3 at the National Ice Centre, Nottingham.
All sponsored by Findus.

Left: **MARK RICHARDSON**, Bracknell Bees, captained the GB under-20s and was voted the Best Young British Player by the ice hockey writers; *right*: Bracknell's All-Star forward, **LUKAS SMITAL**, was the Winter Cup's top scorer. *Photos*: Bob Swann.

Bees ice trophy number two

Bracknell Bees, icing their best team since their Superleague winning side in 1999-2000, won the Winter Cup in front of one of their biggest crowds of the season, two weeks after they clinched the league title.

GB international **Greg Owen**, scored the winning goal in the Hive after only 27 seconds and Canadian **Peter Campbell** added two more as **Stevie Lyle** shutout Newcastle Vipers - the *Findus* Cup holders - 3-0.

The result was almost academic as Bees had thumped Vipers 5-1 in their own barn three days earlier, with Campbell again on target while **Lukas Smital** had two.

Owen, whose wife Hannah gave birth to a baby girl shortly after Bees' first leg win in Newcastle, said: "I thought of Amelie the moment I scored. I'm saving the puck for her."

Vipers' general manager, **Clyde Tuyl**, said: "It just wasn't going to be our final. We came up against a quality hockey club in Bracknell and we had no reply to what they threw at us. They have been the best team in the league by some distance this season."

Bees only rarely stumbled during the tournament with three losses in the preliminary round and a surprising 3-3 tie in Hull in the quarter-finals.

Vipers enjoyed the same success in the cup as they had in the league, finishing runners-up after the first round. But they needed overtime and ten penalty shots before settling their semi-final battle with third place Fife Flyers.

After their one-goal defeat in Kirkcaldy, Flyers fought back with **Adrian Saul** scoring the second leg winner with less than two minutes left to force the semi into overtime.

After this proved scoreless, **Matt Beveridge** and **Paul Ferone** converted penalty shots for Vipers and **Judd Medak** and **John Haig** for Flyers.

Into sudden death shots and Beveridge beat **Scott Hay** for the winner with Vipers' sixth attempt overall. The downside was that the Wednesday night game was watched by little over a thousand fans in the vast northern arena.

Rick Strachan's Hull Stingrays, who snatched the last semi-final place from Dundee and Edinburgh, were a trifle unlucky to come up against the barnstorming Bees.

But Bracknell knew they'd been in a contest after the first period in Hull when Stingrays led 3-1 on goals from **Evgeny Alipov, Andrei Nikolaev** and **Slava Koulikov**. After that Hull goalie **Ladislav Kudrna** had a torrid time with Smital and **Danny Meyers** tieing the score. Back at the Hive it was one-way traffic again.

QUALIYING ROUND RESULTS

Winter Cup

	BRK	DUN	EDI	FIF	GUI	HUL	MIL	NEW	PET
Bees	**	5-3 11/9	9-2 13/11	4-3ot (7) 5/12	3-1 31/10	6-5 20/10	10-1 26/9	6-0 6/11	10-1 4/9
Stars	6-3 19/12	**	3-1 4/12	2-4 24/10	5-1 12/12	2-4 2/10	6-2 27/11	3-4ot (2) 19/9	10-2 10/10
Capitals	4-12 12/9	2-3 17/10	**	3-3ot 3/10	5-4ot (5) 14/11	2-4 31/10	8-3 11/12	1-4 9/10	5-2 19/9
Flyers	5-2 18/12	4-2 2/11	3-4ot (1) 11/9	**	3-4 30/11	3-2 30/10	6-4 19/9	1-5 23/10	6-1 9/10
Flames	4-5 5/9	6-2 3/10	4-5ot (4) 16/10	3-5 19/9	**	0-1 21/11	7-1 5/12	3-3ot 11/9	6-2 30/10
Stingrays	0-2 28/11	4-2 23/10	2-3 27/11	2-5 19/12	3-4 12/9	**	5-3 5/5	5-2 14/11	5-4 3/10
Lightning	4-6 20/11	2-3* 6/11	5-8 2/10	3-8 12/12	1-3 23/10	2-3 24/11	**	0-3 4/12	3-1 16/10
Vipers	5-4ot (3) 2/10	5-1 12/9	8-3 8/9	4-3ot (6) 28/11	5-3 17/10	3-2 18/9	4-2 10/10	**	4-1 15/9
Phantoms	4-7 27/10	0-8 14/11	2-8 18/9	2-9 26/9	1-3 20/11	2-5 11/12	0-7 7/11	5-4 18/12	**

score at 25.39 when game abandoned due to bad ice. Game awarded 5-0 to visiting Dundee Stars.

LEADING CUP SCORERS

	GP	G	A	Pts	Pim
Dino Bauba EDI	16	18	22	40	73
Peter Campbell BRK	17	19	18	37	8
Todd Dutiaume FIF	17	15	17	32	16
Lukas Smital BRK	18	9	23	32	18
Matus Petricko BRK	19	7	24	31	22
Adrian Saul FIF	18	10	20	30	24
Martin Masa BRK	19	13	15	28	20
Marty Johnson EDI	11	9	19	28	12
Karry Biette FIF	16	15	13	28	14

LEADING CUP NETMINDERS

Stevie Lyle BRK	17	942	425	33	92.2
Doug Teskey NEW	20	1220	697	55	92.1
Scott Hay FIF	18	1098	613	49	92.0

Qualification: 400 minutes

OVERTIME GAME WINNING GOALS

See Results Chart above

1	EDI	Dino Bauba (unassisted)		69.15
2	NEW	D Longstaff (Beveridge, Wilson)	pp	64.15
3	NEW	Simon Leach (Ruggles, Beveridge)		61.16
4	EDI	Dino Bauba (Cingel)		63.37
5	EDI	Dino Bauba (Kieras)	pp	64.01
6	NEW	S Johnson (Trumbley, Weaver)	pp	65.38
7	BRK	M Rees (L Richardson, Meyers)	pp	63.07

SIN BIN

Player Penalties	GP	Pim	Ave
Dino Bauba EDI	16	73	4.56
Jozef Kohut GUI	16	65	4.06

CROSSOVER GAMES

A series of inter-league games between the UK's top two leagues was arranged with the encouragement of the International Ice Hockey Federation with the aim of bringing about one national league.

The seven Elite League sides met each of the seven British National League teams home and away with the results and the points being credited to the respective leagues. Sides from the same league did not play each other.

The table below is for information only.

It was the first time sides from the rival circuits had played against each other in competitive games since the Superleague was created in 1996.

A politically sensitive competition, it was given no official title. The Elite League described it as the Cross League and it was sometimes referred to as the National Cup .

FINAL STANDINGS

	GP	W	L	D	OL	GF	GA	Pts
Belfast Giants BEL	14	12	1	1	1	67	27	26
Cardiff Devils CAR	14	12	2	0	0	62	31	24
Nottingham Panthers NOT	14	11	3	0	1	55	27	23
Coventry Blaze COV	14	10	3	0	1	57	31	21
London Racers LON	14	9	4	1	0	46	33	19
Basingstoke Bison BAS	14	9	4	0	1	59	48	19
Sheffield Steelers SHE	14	8	5	1	0	39	29	17
Bracknell Bees BRK	14	7	5	1	1	48	33	16
Guildford Flames GUI	14	4	8	1	1	33	44	10
Dundee Stars DUN	14	4	10	0	0	29	56	8
Hull Stingrays HUL	14	4	10	0	0	22	52	8
Fife Flyers FIF	14	3	10	0	1	40	69	7
Newcastle Vipers NEW	14	2	10	1	1	24	56	6
Edinburgh Capitals EDI	14	0	13	0	1	30	75	1

Elite League teams in bold.   Points system as for leagues.
Teams tied on points separated by goal difference.

Confusing and surprising

Belfast Giants won this most confusing of tournaments - even by the quirky standards of British ice hockey - at home on 24 February when **Roman Gavalier** scored the winning goal at 5.29 of overtime to give Giants a 4-3 victory over the BNL's Guildford Flames.

Giants' game was confusing, too, as the fans had been led to believe that the rules of the home team's league applied to this one-season competition and the Elite League normally played only five minutes OT. No official rules were published by either league.

Moreover, Giants were not presented with any trophy to mark their success as the inter-league games were only a 'ghost' competition, with points from the games being counted towards each side's league. Worse, the whole purpose of the Crossover Games - to bring the leagues together - ultimately failed.

This failure was not due to the competition itself. On the contrary, this was greeted by most fans as a welcome opportunity to see more visiting teams.

The BNL fans probably got the better of the deal because although their teams were usually beaten by the Elite sides, they were able to see a different style of hockey; the suggestion that the Elite teams should use fewer imports in the Crossover Games was never taken up.

Besides, there were plenty of upsets, especially in the early part of the season when the surprise element gave the BNL sides an advantage, and before the Elite teams had benefited from their more intense schedule.

REMEMBER THIS?

"I think our supporters would sooner be watching the likes of Milan rather than Hull or Basingstoke on a Saturday night." **Neil Black**, owner of Nottingham Panthers, in November 2002. [Sorry, Neil. Couldn't resist this. - ed.]

On the first full weekend of competition, 18-19 September, the BNL teams won four of the five games, with Dundee Stars and the low budget Hull Stingrays both upsetting the Elite League champs, Sheffield Steelers.

Steelers' new coach, **Rob Stewart**, admitted: "We weren't prepared to work hard at both ends of the ice. Going down 3-0 from five shots left us a big hill to climb."

The Sheffield *Star* criticised the team for their lack of passion, and club owner **Norton Lea** for failing to publicise the inter-league games.

The next night, Hull goalie **Ladislav Kudrna** was in top form as the surprising Stingrays entertained Steelers in front of 1,100 fans, the largest crowd seen in Hull Arena for some time. The Slovak keeper stopped 27 of 28 Steelers' shots as Stingrays pipped Steelers 2-1.

Mr Lea's indifference to these games become even more obvious a couple of days later when Steelers hosted their opposite numbers, Fife Flyers, the reigning BNL champs, at the new iceSheffield rink next door to the Arena.

While the move was probably due to the Arena not being available, the scheduling did nothing to encourage Sheffield fans to watch games against the other league's teams, especially as the contest was held in mid-week.

The game attracted only about 1,000 fans with many regulars staying away partly for fear of not getting into the 1,500-seat rink, and partly because their season tickets weren't valid and the tickets cost £13, the same as in the Arena.

Still, as Steelers only managed a 2-1 win despite outshooting Flyers 35-20, maybe it was as well that not too many fans were around to witness their team's latest debacle.

The next day, 23 September, the BNL's biggest victory in the entire tournament was racked up by Bracknell Bees, who beat more Elite sides than any other BNL team. At home to their local rivals, Basingstoke Bison, Bees scored six times in the last period, including a hat-trick from Brit **Danny Hughes**.

That brought the score in games to 6-2 in favour of the BNL, but on the third weekend, the Elite won four of the five games. Bees had the only victory, winning the return game at Basingstoke 5-1.

It was not only Norton Lea who was unhappy with the Crossover Games. When Guildford Flames jammed the blueline in Coventry to hold the Blaze 2-1, Blaze coach **Paul Thompson** said: "You can't do anything about opposition teams coming in here and the way they play, but that's the most negative we've ever seen Guildford. We spent about 70 per cent of the game in their zone but we weren't penetrating."

As the season went on, however, these defensive tactics were gradually broken down by the Elite sides. It fell to Cardiff Devils to tally the most goals against a BNL team on 6 February when they hammered eleven past the hapless Fife Flyers in Wales.

OVERTIME GAME WINNING GOALS
See Results Chart

1	HUL	Scott Wray (Burgess, Glowa)	63.10
2	CAR	Kirk DeWaele (Sacratini)	63.49
3	FIF	Euan Forsyth (Haig)	61.19
4	DUN	Mark Scott (unass.)	62.54
5	LON	Mark Thomas *no other details available*	
6	BRK	Peter Campbell (L Richardson)	65.54
7	NOT	Paul Moran *no other details available*	
8	BEL	Gavalier (Nasvall, Johnson)	65.29
9	COV	Wade Belak (McNamara, Tait)	64.56

But as this came on the same weekend as Dundee shutout Elite triple winners, Coventry, 1-0 at home, and Newcastle Vipers pushed Nottingham Panthers into overtime before conceding 2-1, it was obvious that the games had also raised the play of the BNL sides.

On 13 February, even one of the coaches became confused after Bees shutout Steelers in Bracknell 6-0, with **Stevie Lyle** having a 26-shot shutout. Sheffield's **Paul Heavey** declared: "It looks like they are in the wrong league, or we are - depending on how you look at it."

It is unlikely that the Crossover Games would have continued even if the British National League had survived. The format attracted too many critics among the Elite League owners who hated the defensive hockey the BNL clubs employed, the smaller crowds in their rinks and, of course, losing.

But they exposed the BNL's goalies to a wider audience. Both Bracknell's Lyle (with Steelers) and Hull's Kudrna (Panthers) ended up in the Elite League playoffs.

RESULTS CHART

	BAS	BEL	BRK	CAR	COV	DUN	EDI	FIF	GUI	HUL	LON	NEW	NOT	SHE
BAS	*	#	1-5 25/9	#	#	2-3ot (4) 15/1	7-2 22/1	7-2 10/10	2-5 18/9	7-2 27/2	#	3-2 12/2	#	#
BEL	#	*	4-3 12/2	#	#	6-0 30/10	8-1 23/10	5-2 27/12	4-3ot (8) 24/2	2-0 17/12	#	6-3 1/1	#	#
BRK	10-3 23/9	3-3ot 4/12	*	3-4ot (2) 14/11	3-1 18/9	#	#	#	#	#	5-2 9/10	#	4-2 3/10	6-0 13/2
CAR	#	#	3-2 19/9	*	#	5-1 10/2	6-3 10/10	11-2 6/2	4-1 19/12	1-2 19/2	#	4-1 27/12	#	#
COV	#	#	3-0 12/12	#	*	4-2 2/1	7-2 20/11	4-3ot (9) 27/2	2-1 26/9	9-2 30/1	#	9-1 3/10	#	#
DUN	3-7 30/1	2-4 26/9	#	1-6 16/10	1-0 6/2	*	#	#	#	#	3-4 17/2	#	1-3 27/1	1-3 21/11
EDI	4-6 24/10	1-6 12/12	#	2-3 13/2	3-4 28/11	#	*	#	#	#	2-3ot (5) 25/1	#	4-7 5/12	2-7 9/11
FIF	4-6 26/2	6-5ot (3) 11/12	#	4-6 12/2	2-4 27/11	#	#	*	#	#	3-4 15/2	#	4-2 4/12	3-6 20/11
GUI	2-0 1/1	1-5 6/10	#	3-4 18/12	3-4 4/12	#	#	#	*	#	4-1 17/11	#	1-5 20/2	6-4 16/1
HUL	2-3 5/12	1-3 22/1	#	1-3 17/10	4-3ot (1) 16/10	#	#	#	#	*	3-1 27/10	#	2-6 26/9	2-1 19/9
LON	#	#	3-1 22/10	#	#	4-6 23/1	4-2 7/1	3-1 20/2	2-1 26/11	8-0 13/2	*	5-0+	#	#
NEW	2-5 31/10	1-6 23/1	#	5-2 24/11	4-3 13/11	#	#	#	#	#	2-2ot 26/1	*	1-2ot (7) 6/2	1-4 26/9
NOT	#	#	1-2ot (6) 30/1	#	#	6-2 23/2	5-1 25/11	5-2 14/11	7-2 2/10	2-0 11/9	#	2-1 12/1	*	#
SHE	#	#	3-1 10/10	#	#	2-3 18/9	2-1 6/11	1-2* 22/9	0-0ot 16/2	3-1 23/1	#	3-0 30/10	#	*
	BAS	BEL	BRK	CAR	COV	DUN	EDI	FIF	GUI	HUL	LON	NEW	NOT	SHE

Results counted towards teams' respective league standings.
Teams did not meet in Crossover Games.
* played at iceSheffield.
+ Forfeit to London Racers. Newcastle unable to fulfil fixture due to BNL playoffs.
Elite League teams in bold.

ENGLISH LEAGUES

The English leagues - the Premier and the National - comprised the sport's third tier and are designed for clubs with low budgets whose declared aim is developing local players.

The Premier League was first established in 1997-98 to accommodate the non-Superleague clubs who were unable to afford the increasing cost of competing in the British National League (BNL). The low budget teams now compete in the National League's north and south conferences.

In the Premier League, teams met four times, twice at home and twice away. The National League sides played each other twice, once home and once away.

LEADING SCORERS

Premier League	GP	G	A	Pts	Pim
Andrew Power ROM	27	32	46	78	145
Claude Dumas TEL	32	36	30	66	32
Nick Poole MIL	23	19	42	61	26
Kyle Amyotte ROM	22	31	29	60	48
Duane Ward CHE	28	25	35	60	87
Brock Harrison SWI	31	17	40	57	70
Danny Marshall ROM	29	19	36	55	34
Jason Coles WIG	29	36	16	52	85
Justyn Schollar SWI	31	20	32	52	63
Scott McKenzie CHE	29	22	24	46	12
National League North					
John Ross SHE	16	18	33	51	12
Bobby Haig BLA	15	22	26	48	68
Les Millie SHE	14	22	22	44	34
Richard Oliver SHE	13	19	21	40	2
Stefan Dodwell NOT	16	23	16	39	30
National League South					
Mike Allaby INV	17	36	34	70	2
Andy Smith INV	17	29	28	57	2
Derek Flint OXF	18	29	26	55	4
Adam Smith INV	17	15	26	41	39
Alan Green OXF	17	18	18	36	34

FINAL STANDINGS

Premier League	GP	W	L	D	GF	GA	Pts
MK Lightning MIL	32	23	6	3	149	75	49
P'boro' Phantoms PET	32	18	10	4	136	95	40
Wightlink Raiders WIG	32	17	9	6	117	102	40
Romford Raiders ROM	32	17	13	2	144	113	36
Swindon Wildcats SWI	32	15	14	3	106	102	33
Slough Jets SLO	32	14	15	3	122	108	31
Ch'ford Chieftains CHE	32	10	14	8	128	130	28
Telford Wild Foxes TEL	32	11	16	5	139	136	27
Solihull Kings SOL	32	2	30	0	63	243	4
National Lge North							
Sh'ffield Scimitars SHE	16	16	0	0	146	24	32
Nottingham Lions NOT	16	13	3	0	113	51	26
Blackburn Hawks BLA	16	9	5	2	110	62	20
Whitley Warriors WHI	16	8	6	2	87	75	18
Bill'ham Bombers BIL	16	8	6	2	77	43	18
Flintshire Freeze FLI	16	8	7	1	88	89	17
Kingston Jets KIN	16	2	12	2	60	95	6
Sun'land Chiefs SUN	16	3	13	0	49	119	6
Bradford Bulldogs BRD	16	0	15	1	25	197	1
National Lge South							
Invicta Dynamos INV	18	17	0	1	170	33	35
Oxford City Stars OXF	18	13	3	2	123	77	28
Str'tham Redskins STR	18	9	4	5	91	51	23
Cardiff Devils CAR	18	8	6	4	88	66	20
M K Thunder MIL	18	7	7	4	51	66	18
Bracknell Hornets BRK	18	8	8	2	78	84	18
Bas'stoke Buffalo BAS	18	8	10	0	77	96	16
Har'gey G'hounds HAR	18	5	11	2	72	111	12
P'boro' Islanders PET	18	4	12	2	52	112	10
Slough H Hawks SLO	18	0	18	0	25	131	0

Tied teams separated by the results between them.

OFFICIAL WEBSITE
www.eiha.co.uk

LEADING NETMINDERS

Premier League	GPl	Mins	SoG	GA	Sv%
Chris Douglas SWI	29	1709	1052	86	91.8
Allen Sutton MIL	21	1219	486	45	90.7
Toby Cooley WIG	22	1380	738	71	90.4
Stephen Wall PET	31	1842	884	90	89.8
Tom Wills SLO	27	1575	842	92	89.1
National Lge North					
Paul Jones SHE	12	608	201	16	92.O
Ricky Ashton BIL	15	830	421	37	91.2
National Lge South					
James Tanner STR	17	720	493	34	93.1
Ian Rowlands INV	17	715	336	24	92.9

FAIR PLAY

Premier League	GP	Pims	Ave
Chelmsford Chieftains	32	487	15.2
Milton Keynes Lightning	32	540	16.9
Wightlink Raiders	32	597	18.6
Solihull Kings	32	619	19.3
Telford Wild Foxes	32	661	20.6
Slough Jets	32	857	26.8
Swindon Wildcats	32	878	27.4
Peterborough Phantoms	32	947	29.6
Romford Raiders	32	997	31.1

PAST (PREMIER) LEAGUE WINNERS

2003-04	Milton Keynes Lightning
2002-03	Peterborough Phantoms
2001-02	Invicta Dynamos
2000-01	Swindon Phoenix
1999-00	Chelmsford Chieftains
1998-99	Solihull Blaze
1997-98	Solihull Blaze
1996-97	Wightlink Raiders
1995-96	Wightlink Raiders
1994-95	Wightlink Raiders
1993-94	Wightlink Raiders
1992-93	Solihull Barons
1991-92	Medway Bears
1990-91	Oxford City Stars
1989-90	Bracknell Bees
1988-89	Humberside Seahawks
1987-88	Romford Raiders

Lightning weather storms

Milton Keynes Lightning banished increasing worries over the future of their rink and retained their English Premier League title by a comfortable nine-point margin over their closest rivals, **Peterborough Phantoms**.

Led by player-coach, **Nick Poole**, one of the league's finest playmakers with 42 assists in 23 games, MK also overcame an injury crisis which briefly knocked out some of their leading players, including last term's top scorer, **Gary Clarke**.

Veteran **Doug McEwen** reckoned Phantoms allowed their rhythm to be upset by playing the British National League teams in the Winter Cup during the early part of the campaign. By mid-season, their disillusioned coach, **Kevin King**, had quit.

Only a disastrous 8-1 January defeat by Phantoms pushed **Wightlink Raiders** into third. As Lightning and Phantoms can be considered big budget teams at this level, Raiders, who play out of the smallest rink in the top three leagues, were rightly pleased with their high finish.

It was also a fitting time for their veteran defender, **Matt Coté**, to bid farewell to the sport.

Romford Raiders could be happy with their placing, too, after their roster underwent big changes when they were taken over by Chelmsford's **Ollie Oliver**. Among their signings were Chieftains' captain, **Andrew Power**, who ended as the league's top scorer.

In the middle of the most competitive league for years were **Swindon Wildcats**, again led by coach **Daryl Lipsey**. He brought in a couple of his talented and personable pals, forwards **Brock Harrison** and **Justyn Schollar**, as well as Romford's Brit, **Chris Douglas**. Douglas was the league's best netminder, Swindon's crowds went up and so did their league position.

Only four points separated the next three sides. Yugoslav forward **Zoran Kozic** and Canadian goalie **Tom Wills** formed the backbone of **Slough Jets** who finished one spot higher than last year.

Chelmsford Chieftains, who had lost many of their best players as well as their coach to their Essex rivals, iced a fairly inexperienced line-up under the coaching of player **Andy Hannah**.

Though **Telford Wild Foxes** managed only eighth place in the nine-team league, it was their most successful season since their formation in 2001. Player-coach **Claude Dumas** not only got the best out of his young team but also finished as runner-up in the league scoring.

Only **Solihull Kings** struggled, with two wins in 32 games, both coming during a purple patch in November when **Steve Chartrand** briefly came out of retirement to help his old club.

RESULTS CHART

ENGLISH PREMIER LEAGUE

	CHE	MIL	PET	ROM	SLO	SOL	SWI	TEL	WIG
Chieftains		1-6 17/10	1-4 12/9	2-2 26/12	3-4 16/1	14-0 2/1	6-3 9/1	7-5 6/11	2-2 26/9
	**	0-2 28/11	1-6 30/1	5-1 27/2	1-1 6/2	10-3 20/2	3-4 23/1	6-4 8/1	0-3 24/10
Lightning	3-1 25/9		4-2 28/12	5-4 9/10	2-2* 23/1	12-0 8/1	4-1 19/9	5-6 14/11	1-3 19/12
	7-2 19/2	**	2-0 5/3	3-5 29/1	4-2 12/2	3-1 2/3	2-0 26/2	5-0 15/1	8-1 6/2
Phantoms	2-4 29/1	3-3 27/12		4-5 27/11	2-2 31/10	9-0 2/10	3-4 2/1	4-2 4/12	2-3 17/10
	8-5 12/2	5-4 6/3	**	5-4 15/1	4-0 19/12	10-3 27/2	8-4 16/1	9-4 6/2	8-1 23/1
Raiders	13-5 27/12	3-4 3/10	3-4 9/1		3-3 25/9	7-1 17/10	2-5 5/12	10-4 4/9	5-0 16/1
	8-1 19/12	6-5 30/1	6-2 13/2	**	4-6 24/10	6-3 6/2	7-5 20/2	2-3 19/9	5-3 6/3
Jets	7-4 13/11	5-7 22/1	5-2 5/2	4-2 11/9		6-3 18/9	4-1 26/9	8-2 27/11	3-7 9/1
	4-7 15/1	1-5 13/2	2-3 26/2	2-6 7/11	**	14-0 20/11	3-1 10/10	6-3 5/3	3-5 19/2
Kings	0-6 3/1	1-11 11/9	1-6 23/10	4-7 12/2	2-1 14/11		1-5 3/10	1-7 23/1	3-6 7/11
	4-9 5/2	7-11 16/1	1-2 21/11	1-5 19/2	2-9 30/1	**	0-3 6/3	0-7 10/2	3-1 28/11
Wildcats	4-2 18/9	2-6 5/2	4-2 6/11	4-1 2/10	2-1 9/10	11-0 11/12		2-2 30/10	1-3 30/1
	3-3 4/12	0-4 27/2	2-4 28/11	4-6 22/1	5-2 8/1	7-4 5/3	**	3-2 19/2	4-1 12/2
Wild Foxes	5-5 11/12	2-5 24/10	5-5 5/12	1-2 18/9	2-4 17/10	13-4 20/1	6-1** 5/9		4-3 3/10
	3-3 26/2	2-4 9/1	4-4 20/2	9-1 5/2	5-2 6/3	7-2 22/1	5-7 29/1	**	6-4 13/3
Raiders	4-4 22/1	3-3 2/1	4-1 25/9	6-3 13/11	6-1 29/1	7-3 18/12	2-1 16/10	6-5 2/10	
	5-5 5/3	1-1 20/2	2-3 8/1	@	5-2 27/2	11-5 15/1	3-3 13/2	6-4 12/3	**
	CHE	MIL	PET	ROM	SLO	SOL	SWI	TEL	WIG

Second figure is date of game
@ game on 13 Nov. played for 4 points.
* actual score. Game awarded to 5-0 to Jets as Lightning iced an ineligible player.
** score at 54.45 when game was abandoned. Result allowed to stand.

PREMIER LEAGUE PLAYOFFS

At the end of the league games, the top eight teams in the Premier League qualified for the Playoffs.

The league winner was placed in group A along with the fourth, fifth and eighth placed teams, with the remaining sides going into group B. Each team played the other in their group home and away and the top two in each group met in the semi-finals.

In the semi-finals, the winner of one group played the runner-up in the other group. For the first time, the semis and the final were played over one weekend in the same venue, at Coventry's Skydome.

QUARTER-FINAL STANDINGS

Group A	GP	W	L	D	GF	GA	Pts
MK Lightning	6	5	1	0	36	20	10
Romford Raiders	6	4	2	0	35	22	8
Telford Wild Foxes	6	2	4	0	20	35	4
Swindon Wildcats	6	1	5	0	15	29	2
Group B							
Peterboro' Phantoms	6	5	1	0	25	16	10
Slough Jets	6	4	2	0	26	13	8
Ch'ford Chieftains	6	3	3	0	23	26	6
Wightlink Raiders	6	0	6	0	16	35	0

QUARTER-FINAL RESULTS

Group A	MIL	ROM	SWI	TEL
MK Lightning	-	4-5	8-3	8-2
Romford Raiders	6-8	-	3-4	9-2
Swindon Wildcats	2-3	1-4	-	2-6
Telford Wild Foxes	2-5	3-8	5-3	-
Group B	CHE	PET	SLO	WIG
Ch'ford Chieftains	-	1-4	0-3	7-5
P'boro' Phantoms	8-4	-	3-2	3-2
Slough Jets	3-4	5-2	-	9-2
Wightlink Raiders	3-7	2-5	2-4	-

SEMI-FINALS

Saturday 16 April 2005 at Milton Keynes

MK LIGHTNING	2	(0-1-1)
SLOUGH JETS	1	(0-1-0)

Scoring
0-1	SLO	Towalski (Kozic)		21.27
1-1	MIL	Clarke (Poole)		31.07
2-1	MIL	Clarke (Poole)	pp	58.02

Netminding
Sutton MIL	6-6-12 24	save%	95.83
Wills SLO	5-7-13 25	save%	92.00

Penalty minutes: Lightning 12, Jets 24 (Chinn 2+10 spearing).
Referee: Toni Scialdone   *Attendance*: 1,300
Linesmen: Martin Vana, Roman Szucs.

P'BORO' PHANTOMS	4	(2-1-1)
ROMFORD RAIDERS	3	(1-1-1)

Scoring
1-0	PET	Yardley (McEwen, L Buckman)	09.54
1-1	ROM	Power (Marshall)	pp	12.33
2-1	PET	Morgan (unass.)		15.45
3-1	PET	L Buckman (Hammill, McEwen)	pp	27.38
3-2	ROM	Cowmeadow (Marshall, Kaminskas)		31.36
3-3	ROM	Power (Whiting)		50.40
4-3	PET	J Buckman (Morgan)		55.47

Netminding
Wall PET	11-16- 8 35	save%	91.43
Moffat ROM	15-16-16 47	save%	91.49

Penalty minutes: Phantoms 14, Raiders 46 (Power 2+10 spearing, Williams 2+game - rough)
Referee: Dave Cloutman   *Attendance*: 1,300
Linesmen: Antony Decaux, Dan Doubleday.

THIRD PLACE PLAYOFF

Sunday 17 April at Coventry Skydome
Romford Raiders-Slough Jets   6-4

FINAL

Sunday 17 April at Coventry Skydome

MK LIGHTNING	7	(3-2-2)
P'BORO' PHANTOMS	2	(0-0-2)

Scoring:
1-0	MIL	Irvine (unass.)		06.00
2-0	MIL	Poole (McEwan)		09.09
3-0	MIL	Skinnari (Wales)		19.20
4-0	MIL	Carr (McEwan, Carpenter)		23.46
5-0	MIL	Clarke (Poole, Newman)	pp	37.22
5-1	PET	Hammill (McEwen, Armstrong)		43.45
5-2	PET	D Cotton (Hopper)		51.56
6-2	MIL	Newman (Clarke)		53.20
7-2	MIL	Wales (unass.)		56.55

Netminding:
Sutton MIL	9- 9 -9 27	save%	92.59
Wall PET	21-14-17 52	save%	86.54

Penalty minutes: Lightning 24 (Irvine 2+10 ch/behind), Phantoms 24 (Morgan 2+10 ch/behind).
Referee: Dave Cloutman.   *Attendance*: 1,550
Linesmen: Antony Decaux, Martin Vana.

MILTON KEYNES LIGHTNING are Playoff champions

THE FINALISTS

MILTON KEYNES LIGHTNING

Allen Sutton, Mark Woolf; Steve Carpenter, Michael Wales, Bari McKenzie, Gary Clarke, Kurt Irvine, Dean Campbell, Adam Carr, Jamie Randall, Chris McEwan, Dwayne Newman (capt), Mikko Skinnari, Greg Randall, Simon Howard, Ross Bowers, Nick Poole.
Coach: Nick Poole. Manager: Vito Rausa.

PETERBOROUGH PHANTOMS

James Moore, Stephen Wall; James Morgan, Jake Armstrong, Julian Smith, Doug McEwen, Andrew Munroe, Darren Cotton, Grant Hendry, Jason Buckman, Antti Kohvakka, Steven Maule, James Ferrara, Karl Hopper, James Ellwood, Jon Cotton, Jesse Hammill (capt), Lewis Buckman, Marc Long.
Coach: Jon Kynaston. Manager: Phil Wing.

LEADING PLAYOFF SCORERS

	GP	G	A	Pts	Pim
Nick Poole MIL	8	7	16	23	4
Andrew Power ROM	8	10	12	22	88
Kyle Amyotte ROM	8	8	14	22	0
Gary Clarke MIL	8	13	7	20	4
Danny Marshall ROM	8	9	11	20	2
Duncan Cook CHE	6	6	7	13	8
Zoran Kosic SLO	8	6	5	11	4
Norman Pinnington SLO	8	4	7	11	36
Andrius Kaminskas ROM	8	5	5	10	63
Jason Coles WIG	6	4	6	10	16
Marc Long PET	8	3	7	10	14

LEADING PLAYOFF NETMINDERS

	GPI	Mins	SoG	GA	Sv%
Tom Wills SLO	7	418	222	15	93.2
Andy Moffat ROM	8	480	326	30	90.8
Gregg Rockman CHE	6	359	270	25	90.7

Qualification: 120 minutes

Lightning strike down Phantoms

Milton Keynes Lightning's 7-2 final victory over *Peterborough Phantoms* left Lightning as the most dominant team in the league during the three seasons since their formation.

Their April win in the Coventry Skydome completed a league and playoff double, their playoff championship was a three-peat for Planet Ice's flagship team, and it was their second successive double.

Their one-sided margin of victory was similar to last year when they shot down Slough Jets by a ten-goal difference over two legs.

In Coventry, Lightning went 5-0 ahead before Phantoms' long-serving Canadian, **Jesse Hammill**, finally beat **Allen Sutton** early in the last period. **Darren Cotton** got their second but that was all they could manage.

At the final whistle, Lightning defenceman **Simon Howard**, their assistant coach, was jubilant: "The first period was what we call total hockey. Every player executed our game plan perfectly."

Phantoms' coach, **Jon Kynaston**, admitted: "We were second best physically and in terms of our work rate. We can play so much better."

If the result was disappointing, so was the final crowd of only 1,550 in the 2,600-capacity Skydome. But this was the first time the league had staged a one weekend, one venue format.

A day earlier the semis had provided exciting entertainment with both losing sides putting up brave fights before succumbing to one-goal defeats.

Phantoms needed an unassisted backhander in the last five minutes from **Jason Buckman** to get past a determined *Romford Raiders* side who had tied the game at 3-3 through an **Andy Power** goal in the 51st minute.

In the first game of the playoff weekend, *Slough Jets* went down to two goals from Lightning's super sniper, **Gary Clarke** - including the winner with two minutes left - after an early one from their young Brit, **Matt Towalski**.

Jets were certain they'd scored the game-tying goal 21 seconds from time, but referee, **Toni Scialdone**, disallowed it.

The quarter-finals were as competitive as the league with only *Wightlink* Raiders out of the running after their squad was hit with a nasty bug.

■ Like the Elite League, the EPL decided to hold a third place playoff before the final. Jets and Raiders were more sporting than their counterparts and treated the contest seriously. But the teams shared seven roughing penalties in the game which Raiders won in the last period.

PREMIER CUP

In this invitational tournament played during the league season, three sides from the English National League joined the Premier League sides, excluding Milton Keynes and Peterborough who decided to compete in the BNL Winter Cup.

In the preliminary round, the ten teams competed in two geographically divided groups, each team playing the other in its own group four times, twice at home and twice away.

The top team in each group went straight into a home-and-away final to decide the cup's destination.

PRELIMINARY ROUND STANDINGS

North	GP	W	L	D	GF	GA	Pts
Swindon Wildcats	16	13	2	1	89	34	27
Telford Wild Foxes	16	13	2	1	105	48	27
Sheffield Scimitars	16	6	10	0	71	67	12
Blackburn Hawks	16	3	10	3	39	105	9
Solihull Kings	16	1	12	3	31	81	5
South							
Romford Raiders	16	10	3	3	80	48	23
Chelmsford Chieftains	16	9	5	2	68	62	20
Slough Jets	16	6	5	5	52	51	17
Wightlink Raiders	16	6	8	2	51	47	14
Invicta Dynamos	16	2	12	2	41	84	6

Tied teams separated by results between them.

FINAL

First leg, *12 March 2005*
SWINDON-ROMFORD 0-2 (0-0,0-0,0-2)
Scorers: ROM Kaminskas, Marostega 1g; Power 2a; Marshall, Amyotte 1a.
Netminding: Douglas SWI 46, Moffat ROM 31.
Penalty minutes: Wildcats 20, Raiders 32 (Power 2+10 elbows).
Men of Match: Moffat ROM, Douglas SWI.
Referee: Dave Cloutman. *Attendance*: 948

Second leg, *13 March 2005*
ROMFORD-SWINDON 3-3 (0-1,2-2,1-0)
Scorers: ROM Amyotte 2g; Power 1+2; Marshall 2a. SWI Harrison 1+1; Forshee, Becker 1g; Schollar 2a.
Netminding: Moffat ROM 28, Douglas SWI 46.
Penalty minutes: Raiders 10, Wildcats 12.
Men of Match: Amyotte ROM, Forshee SWI.
Referee: Dave Cloutman. *Attendance*: 1,021

Romford Raiders win Premier Cup
5-3 on aggregate

NATIONAL LEAGUE PLAYOFFS

The top four teams in each group of the National League qualified for the Playoffs, in which they met the other teams in their group once at home and once away. The winning team in each group played again, home and away, to decide the Championship.

FIRST ROUND STANDINGS

North	GP	W	L	D	GF	GA	Pts
Sheffield Scimitars	6	6	0	0	41	9	12
Nottingham Lions	6	4	2	0	29	28	8
Blackburn Hawks	6	1	4	1	18	30	3
Whitley Warriors	6	0	5	1	13	34	1
South							
Invicta Dynamos	6	6	0	0	46	13	12
Streatham Redskins	6	3	3	0	20	23	6
Cardiff Devils	6	3	3	0	29	23	6
Oxford City Stars	6	0	6	0	15	51	0

FINAL

First leg, *22 May 2005*
SHEFFIELD-INVICTA 6-0 (1-0,3-0,2-0)
Scorers: Millie 3g; D Wood 1+1; Hardy, Oliver 1g; Goodman, Ross 2a; Ashton, Duncombe 1a.
Penalty minutes: Scimitars 28, Dynamos 102 (Martin 34, Low 30, bench 22).
Netminding: Jones SHE *shots* 26, *save%* 100.0; Silvester/Rowlands INV *shots* 39, *save%* 84.6.
Referee: M Litchfield. *Attendance*: 573.
Second leg, *29 May 2005*
INVICTA-SHEFFIELD 3-4 (1-1,0-2,2-1)
Scorers: INV Andrew Smith, Shaw 1+1; Carey 1g; Low, Lake, Beerling 1a. SHE Millie 2g; Woolhouse, Oliver 1g; Butterworth, Johnson, Goodman, Morgan, Bingham.
Penalty minutes: Dynamos 37 (Baxter 27), Scimitars 41 (Abel 27).
Netminding: Rowlands INV *shots*: 36, *save%* 88.9; Jones SHE *shots*: 35, *save%* 77.1.
Referee: Matt Thompson. *Attendance*: Unknown.

SHEFFIELD SCIMITARS
are English National League Playoff Champions *10-3 on aggregate*

SHEFFIELD SCIMITARS *left to right, back row*: Paul Jones, Jon Woolhouse, Stuart Brittle, Simon Butterworth, John Ross, James Goodman, Matt Street, Steve Duncombe, Ryan Johnson, Neil Abel, Carl Ashton, Darren Maynard; *front row*: Shaun Ashton, Les Millie, Will Barron, Andrew Chapman, Neil Hardy, Steve Bingham, Richard Oliver (mascot).

Scimitars' near perfect record

Sheffield Scimitars completed the first Treble in their history when they successfully retained their Playoff crown to add to their league (north) and English Cup titles.

It was the first Treble in the English National League since Whitley Warriors turned the trick in 2001-02. Under player-coach **Neil Abel** the team from the iceSheffield complex were unbeaten all season, dropping only one point in these competitions, a draw with Billingham Bombers in the Cup.

They won the Playoffs with a performance almost identical to their 2003-04 victory. **Les Millie** was their big scorer again, this time with five goals against Invicta Dynamos whom Sheffield beat last time out.

But this time their margin of victory was far more decisive with a crushing 6-0 win in the first leg at home, Millie scoring three unanswered goals in the second period.

Their brave if mostly doomed run-outs against the Premier League sides in the Premier Cup may well have helped the Scimitars to raise their game in their own league.

In the final of the English Cup, Sheffield met Invicta again and beat them 8-3 on aggregate, 4-0 in Kent and 4-3 at home.

SHEFFIELD SCIMITARS

Paul Jones, Darren Maynard; Greg Wood, Simon Butterworth, Neil Abel, Shaun Ashton, Neil Hardy, Jon Woolhouse, Ryan Johnson, James Goodman, Ben Morgan, Will Barron, Richard Oliver, John Ross (captain), Andrew Chapman, Steven Duncombe, Stephen Bingham, Danny Wood, Carl Ashton, Les Millie.
Coach: Neil Abel. *Manager*: Shirley Lockwood.

LEADING PLAYOFF SCORERS

	GP	G	A	Pts	Pim
Andy Smith INV	8	15	15	30	0
Les Millie SHE	8	11	9	20	52
John Ross SHE	8	8	10	18	8
Peter Carey INV	8	8	9	17	16
Stuart Low INV	8	5	12	17	44

LEADING PLAYOFF NETMINDERS

	GPI	Mins	SoG	GA	Sv%
Paul Jones SHE	8	395	149	12	91.9
Jon Silvester INV	8	123	66	6	90.9

SCOTTISH COMPETITIONS

SCOTTISH NATIONAL LEAGUE

	GP	W	L	D	GF	GA	Pts
Dundee Stars	14	11	1	2	74	44	24
Solway Sharks SOL	14	10	3	1	99	47	21
Edinburgh Capitals EDI	14	9	4	1	70	39	19
Paisley Pirates PAI	14	7	4	3	77	41	17
North Ayr Bruins AYR	14	6	8	0	53	56	12
Kirkcaldy Kestrels KIR	14	4	8	2	52	73	10
Dundee Tigers	14	3	8	3	42	83	9
Elgin Tornadoes ELG	14	0	14	0	39	123	0

LEADING SCORERS

	GP	G	A	Pts	Pim
Tommy Boll SOL	14	16	19	35	8
Terry Robertson SOL	14	23	9	32	6
Robert Chalmers SOL	12	23	7	30	16
Mark Gallagher SOL	14	9	20	29	27
Andrew Samuel, Stars	11	17	7	24	2
Paul McGurnaghan, Stars	14	4	18	22	2
Stuart McCaig PAI	12	12	7	19	36
John Churchill PAI	11	6	13	19	8
Paul Guilcher, Tigers	14	10	5	15	10
Gordon Latto KIR	14	4	11	15	0

SCOTTISH CUP

QUARTER-FINALS
Dundee Tigers-Elgin Tornadoes   6-4
North Ayr Bruins-**Edinburgh Capitals**   3-6
Solway Sharks-Dundee Stars   7-4
Kirkcaldy Kestrels-**Paisley Pirates**   3-4

SEMI-FINALS
Edinburgh Capitals-Dundee Tigers   6-0h, 7-2a
Capitals won 13-2 on aggregate
Paisley PIrates-Solway Sharks   9-1h, 6-6a
Pirates won 15-7 on aggregate

FINAL *23 April 2005, Linx Ice Arena, Aberdeen*
Edinburgh Capitals-Paisley Pirates   0-5

PAISLEY PIRATES are Scottish Cup champions

OTHER CUPS

AUTUMN CUP
Solway Sharks beat Kirkcaldy Kestrels   15-8
on aggregate (5-7a, 10-1h)

SPRING CUP
Edinburgh Capitals beat Solway Sharks   4-2
at Murrayfield

CAPITAL CUP
Fife Ice Arena, 4 January 2005 - No details available.

CALEDONIAN CUP
Not played in season 2004-05.

YOUTH INTERNATIONALS

UNDER-19 HOME INTERNATIONAL

Players born 1 January 1986 or later
Nottingham Arena, 10 April 2005

ENGLAND UNDER-19	4	(3-0-1)
SCOTLAND UNDER-19	3	(1-1-1)

Scorers: ENG Richardson 3g; Phillips 1+1; Briggs, Butterworth 1a.   SCO Rich 1+1; McPherson, Johnstone 1g; Mitchell 1a.
Penalty minutes: England 10, Scotland 14.
Shots on Goal: Craze/Fone ENG 29, Findlay SCO 38.   *Referee*: James Ashton.

The Frank Dempster Trophy

The eighth annual Home International at this level was the first to be played for the **Frank Dempster** Memorial Trophy, named in honour of the former chairman of the Scottish Ice Hockey Association who died during the season.

Bracknell Bee **Mark Richardson** helped England to race to a 3-1 first period lead with a straight hat-trick in seven minutes and his team went on to record their seventh victory over the Auld Enemy.

THE TEAMS
ENGLAND UNDER-19
Nathan Craze CAR, Stephen Fone SHE; Ryan Watt BAS, James Patterson BIL, Chad Briggs BLA, Mark Richardson BRK, Steve Fisher, Ricky Lewis CAR, Kevin Phillips HUL, James Cook NOT, Dean Tonks NOT, Craig Peacock PET, Simon Butterworth, Chace Ferrand, Scott Huntington, Nick Manning SHE, Greg Martyn, Graham Newell SWI, Aaron Nell (Okanagan Academy, Canada), Chris Wilcox (Banff Academy, Canada).
Coaches: Mark Beggs SWI, Mick Mishner.
Manager: Steve Taylor.

SCOTLAND UNDER-19
Blair Daly FIF, Daryl Findlay PAI; Chris Turley AYR, Scott McKenzie CHE, Craig Johnstone, Chad Reekie DUN (capt), Ross Dalgleish, Ross Donaldson, Grant McPherson, Jamie Mitchell, Lee Mitchell, Chris Wands FIF, Ryan McNeil, Chris Wilson, Graeme McCamley, Ryan McGinley PAI; Matthew Rich (Notre Dame, USA).
Coach: Martin Grubb FIF
Managers: Millar & Heather Wands.

ENGLAND UNDER-16

Players born 1 January 1989 or later
CHRIS VERWIJST TOURNAMENT
Tilburg, Netherlands, 1-3 April 2005
Qualifying Round
1 Apr	England-Switzerland	1-2 (0-0,1-1,0-1)
	England-Netherlands	6-0 (0-0,5-0,1-0)
2 Apr	England-Slovenia	3-2 (0-1,2-0,1-1)

Final Round
2 Apr	England-Japan	10-1 (5-1,3-0,2-0)
3 Apr	England-Hungary	2-0 (0-0,0-0,2-0)

ENGLAND GOAL SCORERS

	GP	G	A	Pts
Dean Tonks	5	6	2	8
Jason Falsetta	5	1	5	6
Jamie Lane	5	2	3	5
Daniel Murdy	5	1	4	5
Adam Holton	5	1	3	4
Daniel Wood	5	3	0	3
Jonathan Boxill	5	2	1	3
Daniel Hammond	5	1	2	3
Evander Grinnell	5	2	0	2
Carl Thompson	5	2	0	2
Ben Davies	5	1	0	1

Tonks and Jaszczyk star

England's top scorer, **Dean Tonks** of Nottingham Lions, was voted to the All-Star team and goalies **Andrew Jaszczyk**, also Lions, and Phantoms' **Euan King** each had a shutout as England, with only one defeat, finished fifth on their 18th entry into this highly rated Dutch tournament.

ENGLAND UNDER-16
Andrew Jaszczyk NOT, Euan King PET; Ben Davies CAR, Stevie Lee HUL, Lloyd Gibson, Mike Holland, Daniel McAleese SHE, Adam Holton SLO; Daniel Hammond CHE, Jason Falsetta GUI, Dean Tonks NOT, Evander Grinnell ROM, Daniel Wood SHE, Carl Thompson SLO, Jonathan Boxill, Jamie Line, Tom Mills SWI, Daniel Murdy WHI.
Coaches: Paul Simpson, Robert Wilkinson.
Manager: Karen Pyatt.

ENGLAND under-19 *left to right*, *back row*: Dean Tonks, Nick Manning, Chad Briggs, Chris Wilcox, James Patterson, Steve Fisher, Simon Butterworth, Chace Ferrand, Scott Huntington, James Cooke, Craig Peacock, Kevin Phillips, Aaron Nell, Nicky Lewis; *front row*: Steven Fone, Ryan Watt, Mark Richardson, Graham Newell, Nathan Craze, Greg Martyn.   *Photo:* Diane Davey.

SCOTLAND under-19 *left to right*, *back row (standing):* Daryl Findlay, Ryan McNeil, Chris Wilson, Lee Mitchell, Chris Wands, Grant McPherson, Graeme McCamley, Blair Daly, Craig Johnstone, Chris Turley, Ryan McGinley; *front row*: Matthew Rich, Chad Reekie, Jamie Mitchell, Ross Dalgleish, Ross Donaldson, Scott McKenzie.   *Photo:* Diane Davey.

HALL OF FAME

Kevin Conway

Category - Player

Kevin Conway is one of the most talented players to come to this country from Canada in the sport's modern era.

In 20 campaigns, ending in season 2003-04, he scored a prodigious total of 2,617 points (1,355 goals) in 738 competitive games at all levels. He also played a key role in the successful British national team of the 1990s.

His first British club was Ayr Bruins whom he joined in 1985-86 with his good friend, **Tim Salmon**. The pair had finished among the leading scorers in their final year in Canadian major junior A.

In his first campaign here, in the three-import, *Heineken*-sponsored British League, he led the scoring in the Premier Division with 227 points (129 goals), and in 1987 he helped Durham Wasps to win the *Heineken* Championships at Wembley Arena.

The following season, reunited with Salmon, he tallied his highest ever single-season points total with 252 in 29 games as Telford Tigers won the *Heineken* Division One title. He was voted BIHWA's Player of the Year.

After enjoying a promotion run with Cleveland Bombers, in 1991-92 he moved south to Basingstoke, again with buddy Salmon. In his debut season, he hit the magic century-mark in goals for the fourth time in his British career.

After seven seasons with the club, during which they gained promotion to the Premier Division and spent two seasons in Superleague, he was their all-time leading scorer with a total of 950 points (481 goals).

In honour of his outstanding achievements with the club, Bison retired his number ten shirt and raised it to the rafters.

But he wasn't finished. In 1999-2000 he won a English League Grand Slam with Chelmsford Chieftains and ended his career with three seasons in Milton Keynes and Solihull.

He was capped 58 times for Britain, beginning in 1992, and was a member of the 1993 squad that memorably won promotion to the world A pool. He also played in two Olympic qualifiers. His all-time scoring total of 66 points (33 goals) is second only to **Tony Hand**'s.

Born on 13 July 1963 at Sault St. Marie, Ontario, Kevin has remained in England and is now coach of the Kingston (Hull) River Rats, the reigning under-10 champions, whose side includes his eight-year-old son, Scott.

Annette and Allan Petrie

Category - Builder

Since **Annette** and **Allan Petrie** formed the Great Britain Supporters Club in 1993, it has raised tens of thousands for the national teams at all levels. This season alone the members, who currently number over 400, donated over £10,000, including £5,000 for a training camp for the national senior men's team.

The husband-and-wife pair are helped by a five-strong committee and GBSC has representatives at most British clubs. Funds are raised by the sale of merchandise, raffles and special events organised during the championships.

But the support is not only financial. The GBSC is the world's only fan club for a national team and its members are renowned for their fanatical support of their country wherever they go. There must be many games over the past decade that Britain have won thanks to the constant chanting of "GB, GB" as the British fans out-number the rest of the spectators.

With the team fighting to win promotion to the elite level, many of the countries visited have been in the less well-known parts of eastern Europe. But wherever Britain goes, the fans follow, enjoying facilities as good or better than their heroes, thanks to Allan and Annette's superb organising abilities.

The idea for a GB Supporters Club came during Britain's triumphant promotion run in 1993. Annette and Allan took 25 fans to Eindhoven, Netherlands only to discover that others had paid over the odds for their trip while some had come independently. This produced the impetus for a recognised fan club.

The British Ice Hockey Association, the then governing body, were contacted, and they gave their permission for the creation of an official club. The GBSC was launched later that year at the Olympic Qualifying competition in Sheffield.

Keith Kewley

Category - Veteran

Keith Kewley captained and coached three different Scottish teams to championship titles in the Forties and Fifties. He was also instrumental in developing some of the finest native players of the time.

Born at Stratford, Ontario on 10 July 1925, Kewley played in Canada before coming to Scotland in 1946, aged 21, and joined Dunfermline Vikings in the revived Scottish National League. He went on to become captain and then coach of the Vikings, and coach of Ayr Raiders and Paisley Pirates.

A keen student of the game, he became a full-time coach only a year after his arrival. His meticulous preparation and innovative development of strategy and set plays set him apart from most of his older coaching rivals.

Keith inherited his love of the game from his father, Claude, a Toronto sports journalist who was the Canadian scout of the Scottish Ice Hockey Association, responsible for selecting the line-ups of the seven teams of the SNL until 1949. Four of his six sons were to play successfully in Scottish ice hockey - Keith, Herb, Hal and Danny.

Keith was particularly supportive of young Scottish players and brought some outstanding home-grown talent into the Canadian-dominated line-ups. His reasons were not wholly altruistic.

Some 50 years before the similarly import-dominated Superleague, he realised that a small roster of 10 or 12 Canadian players, playing in a punishing schedule of 60-plus games, was going to need replacements during the season. The cost-effective option was to develop the local youngsters to provide cover.

Brennan, his fellow Hall of Famer, recalled his first coaching session with Kewley when he was just 17: "I learned more in that hour than I had picked up in the previous four years," he said.

Keith Kewley, now 80, became a highly respected coach in St Thomas, Ontario for many years after he returned to Canada in the mid-1950s with British hockey in decline.

Thomas 'Tuck' Syme

Category - Veteran

'Tuck' Syme was one of Britain's outstanding home-grown defenceman. In the eight post-war seasons of the Canadian-dominated professional Scottish National League, he was the only Scot to receive All-Star recognition.

He played for Britain in the Winter Olympics and World Championships and caught the eye of the NHL's legendary Montreal Canadiens.

Thomas Woods Syme was born in the Fife mining village of Blairhall on 15 May 1928 and followed his father and brother into the Blairhall Colliery. At the same time, he started skating at the nearby Dunfermline rink.

He broke into the senior Vikings side during season 1946-47 and his talent was developed by his coach Keith Kewley. Only two years later,

aged just 19, he was selected to play for Britain in the Winter Olympics at St Moritz, Switzerland.

In 1950, joined by his elder brother James, known as 'Tiny', he was capped again for his country, this time for the World Championships in London where GB finished fourth (in the world). The hard-hitting defencemen (belying the nickname 'Tiny') each stood 6ft, 2in and weighed around 190 pounds.

In between times, 'Tuck' had enjoyed a season in Canada with the Guelph Biltmores, a farm team of the New York Rangers. So, many years before **Tony Hand** was drafted by Edmonton Oilers, 'Tuck' was effectively a property of the Rangers. Indeed, he even played in an exhibition match against them.

However, again like Hand, 'Tuck' became homesick and returned to his native Scotland to establish himself as one of the league's top players. He assisted Vikings to the Canada Cup in 1950-51 and the Autumn Cup in 1952-53.

When Vikings folded in 1953, 'Tuck' and 'Tiny' teamed up again with coach Kewley at Paisley Pirates. 'Tuck' was made captain of the Pirates (a rare honour for a non-Canadian at that time) and led them to the Treble of league, Autumn Cup and Canada Cup.

He was probably the highest paid sportsman in the country at that time. Paisley paid him £19 per week, while football legend **George Young** - the captain of Glasgow Rangers and Scotland - was receiving only £14.

'Tuck' tried his luck again in Canadian hockey, joining the Val d'Or Miners of the minor pro Quebec League in 1954. His wages had increased to $50 per week – but he had to combine hockey with work 7,200 feet underground in the local goldmine!

He recalled playing in an exhibition match against the legendary Montreal Canadiens, facing Maurice **'Rocket' Richard** and **Jean Beliveau**. 'Tuck' so impressed the Montreal management that they wanted to see him at their training camp. The invite was withdrawn when they discovered his age, 27, and felt he was too old, and his hockey career came to an end.

'Tuck' Syme played 380 games in his eight seasons in Scotland, scoring 133 points (46 goals) and accumulating 594 penalty minutes.

*Written by **David Gordon**, **Martin C Harris** and **Stewart Roberts**. Research by **David Gordon**, **Martin C Harris** and **Graham Merry**.*

*The current Hall of Fame was established in 1986 by the British Ice Hockey Writers' Association, under their secretary **Tony Allen**. The original Hall was created in 1950 by Canadian journalist and player **Bob Giddens**. Biographies of all Hall members are on the BIHWA website at www.bihwa.co.uk.*

Clockwise from top left: former GB defenceman **THOMAS 'TUCK' SYME**, *right*, receives his Hall of Fame certificate from BIHWA's **David Gordon**; GB Supporters Club founders **ALLAN** and **ANNETTE PETRIE** display their certificate; ex-GB forward **KEVIN CONWAY**; veteran player and coach **KEITH KEWLEY**.

TRIBUTES

Frank Dempster

BILL BRITTON

Bill Britton, the respected general secretary of the English Ice Hockey Association, was involved with ice hockey at all levels.

In his home town of Nottingham where he rarely missed a Panthers' game, he is credited with helping the Elite League to gain recognition by the governing body, Ice Hockey UK.

"Bill was one of the sport's diplomats and no matter what was thrown at him, he was never flustered," said Panthers' manager, **Gary Moran**, on the club's website.

His boss at the EIHA, **Ken Taggart**, also paid him a warm tribute. "Bill ran the English Leagues for us and, most important, he was the one who set up the English Premier League for our stronger clubs. We're going to miss him real bad." Other tributes to Bill came from the Women's League, which he chaired, and the British Universities IHA to which he also devoted much of his time.

In the 1990s he represented the EIHA on the old British Ice Hockey Association, and served on the disciplinary committees of both bodies.

Bill, who was 74 when he died on 18 June 2005, served on the EIHA for 21 years, starting soon after its formation in 1982. But he had been around the sport since 1949 when he saw his first Panthers' game.

A sports enthusiast, he was a director of Grantham FC and played cricket for an RAF XI during his national service. When he received an offer to play for Nottingham CCC, he turned it down on the grounds that the pay wasn't enough.

Married to Sheila, he spent his working life mostly in financial services, retiring as an independent financial advisor.

FRANK DEMPSTER

Frank Dempster, who died on Christmas Eve 2004, aged 67, was a leading figure in the sport, wearing a multitude of hats as player, coach and administrator for many years. He was highly respected both within these shores and at international level.

Born in Ayr on 13 March 1937, he was educated at the town's former Newton Academy, where football was his first sport. The old Ayr Ice Rink on Beresford Terrace, in the post-war glory years of the Ayr Raiders, became an important part of Frank's early life, as it was for thousands of local youngsters. He spent much of his time working on the maintenance of the rink, and it was there where he first played ice hockey towards the end of the Fifties.

He eventually became a member of the Ayr Rangers which won the Scottish League in 1962-63, and he added another string to his bow by contributing reports to the *Ice Hockey Herald*, the sport's regular magazine of the time.

In those days, Frank also guested for many teams. Such was his enthusiasm: "anywhere you could get a game," was how he described hectic late-night 400-mile-plus journeys to play in Southampton or Brighton.

He retired from playing when the old rink closed in April 1972 and took over as club secretary, helping to re-establish the team - now the Bruins - at Limekiln Road in 1974.

He was bench coach of the Bruins when they won the Icy Smith Cup, the British club championship, in 1976. This was the year in which he became a personal member of the British Ice Hockey Association while continuing to serve as Ayr's representative on the old Northern Ice Hockey Association.

Meanwhile, he found time to serve as manager of the Bruins and various Scottish and British national sides, as well as coaching young players. When the Scottish Ice Hockey Association was reformed in 1979, Dempster was elected president. He was chairman of the Association at the time of his passing.

It would be difficult to find anybody who worked harder or for longer hours for ice hockey than Frank, particularly as his efforts were mostly expended during some difficult years for the sport. His contributions were duly recognised with his induction to the British Ice Hockey Hall of Fame in 1992.

He is survived by his wife June, daughter Sharon, son-in-law John, and grandsons Sean and Ryan.

BILL GLENNIE

Hall of Famer **Bill Glennie** was one of the truly great players of the post-World War Two era.

Born in Portage La Prairie, Manitoba, he first came to England with the Canadian Army during the war with his buddy, **Wyn Cook**. Stationed in Hampshire, both men married English girls.

After spending the first peace-time season back in North America with Washington Lions of the Eastern Hockey League, Bill and Wyn returned to the UK and signed for Harringay Greyhounds.

They started as they meant to go on. Greyhounds won the playoff title, Cook was fourth in the scoring and Glennie sixth. Bill was voted right-wing on the All Star team, an honour he went on to achieve year after year.

He became player-coach of Greyhounds' sister team, the Racers, during the Fifties and took them to the league title.

Other highlights of his career include playing on the English National League (ENL) Select team which beat Canada and the USA to win the Churchill Cup; and leading Racers to victory in 1955 over the previously unbeaten Penticton Vees, who won the World Championships that year, competing as Canada.

Bill himself always regarded his taking the first Western team to Moscow in 1955 as the outstanding memory of his hockey playing years.

Tall and rangy (175 pounds and six feet tall in his prime), he was a tough, two-way skater who developed a devastating defensive move in which he circled behind his own defence to check an unsuspecting attacker.

Always a big scorer, he tallied over 1,000 points in this country, scoring 516 goals and 527 assists In 613 games in ENL competitions. He took 538 penalty minutes.

At one time early in his career he wore spectacles, but Brighton Tigers' 'artful dodger', **Bobby Lee**, knocked them off one night and 'accidentally' skated over them. After that, Bill wore contact lenses.

Off the ice, he was a quiet and thoughtful man who played the piano and loved golf which he was good enough to have played professionally. His most regular golf partner was **Marsh Key**, the Scots-born centreman with Dundee and Harringay.

Bill so impressed his employers, the Greyhound Racing Association, the owners of Harringay Stadium, that when he retired from playing they appointed him to an executive post. Eventually he became general manager of the Powderhall Stadium in Edinburgh and he and his wife, Doris, made their permanent home along the coast in Longniddry.

He died there on 11 March 2005, three days before his 80th birthday.

GEORGE KOVAC

George Kovac kept goal at Wembley and Dundee during the immediate post-war years.

From December 1946 the Canadian from Winnipeg was the starting netminder for Wembley Monarchs. He placed fourth overall in the English National League averages and was the only keeper to register two shutouts that winter. In May he provided a superb performance in the six-match series between Wembley All Stars and the visiting Ottawa All Stars.

For the next three winters he plied his trade in the Scottish National League for Dundee Tigers. Season 1947-48 was the most successful as Tigers won the playoffs and the Scottish Canada Cup and he was named to the All-Star 'B' team. Two years later he backstopped Dundee to the Scottish Autumn Cup.

George was a likeable, cheerful man and a consistent performer in goal who was renowned for his fearless dives at the skates of opponents. In his 203 matches in Britain he achieved a goals-against average of 4.84 with five shutouts.

In 1940 he had volunteered for the Army and landed on the beaches of France on D-Day with the Regina (Saskatchewan) Rifles. There he was concussed and temporarily deafened and blinded by an exploding shell. After recovering in hospital, he was discharged from the army in Canada six months later.

He died in his native country aged 83 in November 2004. He is survived by Joan, his wife of 60 years, son Keith and two grandchildren.

TOMMY MCINROY

Britain's top goal scorer in the 1939 World Championships, Scotsman **Tommy McInroy**, passed away on 24 July 2005, aged 88. He was GB's oldest surviving international.

McInroy, from Perth, was 21 when he scored his first international goal in a 3-1 victory over Belgium in Britain's opening game. GB finished eighth in the world that year.

Remarkably, Mac - as he was known to his teammates - had only learned to skate two years earlier at the newly opened Perth rink, under the tutelage of Perth Panthers' Canadian coach, **Les Tapp**. Such was his rapid development that he was a regular with the Canadian-dominated Panthers by the end of their first season.

His meteoric rise was described in the *Daily Record* of the time: 'McInroy has come to the fore with a sensational rush. His selection [for GB] is something of a romance, when we think that two years ago he couldn't even skate, far less play the world's fastest game.

'He has all the necessary attributes. He skates fast, can stickhandle reasonably well, marks his wing, and, unlike the great majority of home-bred players, has a powerful and accurate shot. In fact, we might call him a natural in this respect.'

Thomas Scott McInroy was born in June 1917 at Rosemount Farm, Blairgowrie, where his father worked as a ploughman. Educated at Rattray School, he served an apprenticeship as a slater/roughcaster. During a particularly bad winter which meant a quiet spell for the building trades, Tommy applied himself assiduously to his new sport at the Perth rink.

He spent the 1937-38 season with the newly-formed Perth Blackhawks, and at the time of his national team call-up, he had moved to another new rink, in Kirkcaldy where he joined the first year Fife Flyers.

After the war he returned to Scotland and played mostly with Fife's second string, the Kirkcaldy Flyers, where he was a great influence on the younger team members.

Tommy was the forerunner of a number of Perth players who went on to appear for Britain in world tournaments: **Ian Forbes**, brothers **Jimmy** and **Laurie Spence**, **George Watt**, **Sam MacDonald** and **Graeme Farrell**.

He was also a fine all-round cricketer, having played for Blairgowrie and Perthshire, and in the immediate post-war years he turned out for the North Inch side.

During World War Two, Tommy was a corporal in the 6th Battalion of the Black Watch serving in Algeria, Tunisia, Sicily, Italy and Greece.

His ice hockey career ended in 1949 when he moved north to work in Lossiemouth, which was to become his home for the next 56 years. Predeceased by his wife Nancy, daughter Heather, and son Kenneth, he is survived by grandchildren and great-grandchildren in Elgin and Blackpool.

JIMMY MITCHELL

Jimmy Mitchell was an outstanding Scottish born and bred defenceman, playing for Britain and, most famously, for Fife Flyers in the Forties and Fifties. He was born on 13 January 1925 at Kirkcaldy where he learned to skate at the age of 14. Only the Second World War, when he served in the Black Watch, prevented him from joining Flyers until he was 21.

Between 1946 and 1954 he played over 400 games in the virtually all-Canadian Scottish National League, which Flyers won in consecutive seasons, 1948-50. During that time he recorded 34 goals and 99 assists, with a paltry 123 penalty minutes.

After one season in the new British National League when travelling increased enormously, Jimmy spent two years out of hockey. Then he agreed to take on the role of player-coach of Edinburgh Royals who went on to win the North British League. Though he started the 1958-59 season with Royals in the British Autumn Cup, he finished it on the Continent.

A spell with Whitley Bay Bees followed, then for two seasons in 1961-63, he turned out for **Ken Bailey**'s Altrincham Aces which had a strong Scottish contingent. He was capped six times for Britain in the 1951 World Championships in Paris after having a trial for GB's 1948 Olympic team.

A coach builder by trade, he moved to Coventry in 1959 and enjoyed a few games at Solihull in the early Seventies.

Jimmy Mitchell died at Windygates, Fife on 28 May 2001, aged 76.

GRAHAM NURSE

Graham Nurse was one of this sport's greatest enthusiasts. But his love of the game was too much for him to settle for simply being a fan.

From the early Sixties until shortly before his untimely death at the age of 58 in 2004, he threw himself into organising, whether it was a club, a league or a national body. Being a sociable character, his passion rubbed off on others.

His closest friend, **Keith Purvis**, who worked with Graham at Altrincham, has penned this tribute for the Annual:

'Graham started skating at the Altrincham ice rink when it opened in 1960 and he followed the Aces from their formation in 1961. Over the next 30 years he did almost everything for the team, except actually play.

'When he introduced me to the club in 1970, I soon realised his commitment to and love of the sport. In 1981, he instigated a number of meetings which culminated in the formation of the English National League in season 1981-82.

Graham Nurse

'I recall us travelling to meet **Bill, Tom** and **Francis Smith**, the brothers who ran the three north-east rinks at the time, and persuading them that the future of the teams they controlled - Cleveland Bombers, Durham Wasps and Whitley Warriors - lay in England and not Scotland.

'Graham chaired the league which was an immediate hit with the fans and soon expanded into the British (*Heineken*) League.

'In season 1989-90, his network of friends enabled him to create the first Ice Hockey Players Association. Ironically, only a lack of interest from the players themselves caused this early attempt to fail. It did, however, illustrate the concern he felt for the players, something that lasted throughout his involvement with ice hockey.

'In the early Nineties, Graham moved away from the Aces (or Trafford Metros as they were then) to the newly formed Blackburn Blackhawks, another club he helped to create, this time in a 3,000-seat arena.

'The climax of his career came in 1995 when he found himself in the vast 17,500-seat arena which had recently opened in Manchester. Another friend, Cardiff Devils' legendary **John Lawless**, was setting up the Manchester Storm.

'John asked Graham to put together the off-ice team for home games at the arena, a job which he did with pride. As the ultimate organiser, the chance to work with such a professional team was beyond anything either of us could have dreamed of in those early years. He revelled in his role, only 'retiring' at the end of the Storm's penultimate season.

'Graham was a perfect gentleman and he will be sadly missed.'

Graham Nurse passed away on 29 August 2004, after a short but brave battle with a peculiarly virulent cancer. Though he was divorced from Michelle, whom he married in 1967, they remained friends. He also left a son, Mike, and a daughter, Vicky.

GORDON (MOOSE) SHERRITT

Gordon Sherritt was a defenceman with Harringay Greyhounds in 1939-40, the only war-time British campaign.

Greyhounds won the English National League and National Tournament against competition from four other teams, all London-based. Gordon, who contributed 10 goals and four assists, was rewarded with a place on the All-Star 'B' team.

A 6ft 1in blueliner from Canada, he was a neat body checker with hip and shoulder. He went on to play eight NHL games in 1943-44 with Detroit Red Wings where he received his nickname.

Gordon finished his hockey career in 1949 with Minneapolis Millers of the United States Hockey League. He died on 12 March 2005, aged 85, and the new rink in his adopted town of Monticello, Minnesota is to be named the 'Moose' Sherritt Ice Arena in his memory.

JIMMY SPENCE

Jimmy Spence was one of ice hockey's finest Scottish born players, skating for various clubs during his 23-year career and appearing in three World Championships for Britain. Only the severe downturn in the sport's fortunes during the Sixties and Seventies prevented him from going on to claim further honours.

A centreman, he proved to be a natural talent from the start as he scored on his senior debut with the Canadian-dominated Perth Panthers at the tender age of 15. In his five seasons in the semi-pro Scottish National League between 1950 and 1955 he scored 310 points (161 goals) in 245 games and had a measly 66 penalty minutes.

In his final Perth campaign he was the club's top scorer (10th in the league) with 43 goals and 81 points. After the demise of the SNL, Jimmy moved south to another Panthers' side in Nottingham where his 71 points helped them to the double of Autumn Cup and British National League titles in 1955-56.

When his two-year spell of national service ended in 1958 he returned to the now amateur sport in Perth and enjoyed spells with Glasgow Flyers and Paisley Mohawks. In the winter of 1961-62 he came south again, this time joining the newly formed Altrincham Aces where he spent two seasons.

With few rinks left in ice hockey, he played just a handful of games for Fife Flyers in 1963-66. Eventually, in 1971 he signed for Dundee Rockets where he was united on a Golden Oldie line with two other Perth-based players, **Sammy McDonald** and **Mike Mazur**.

Spence was runner-up in Northern League scoring for the next two seasons and won the Earl Carlson Trophy in 1972-73 with most points from all league competitions.

He was first selected to play for his country in 1961 when GB won promotion to Pool A. While he missed out the next year against the top nations in Colorado, USA, he did turn out for the national team again in 1965 and 1973. His GB record stands at 13 goals and 16 points.

His defenceman brother **Laurie Spence** played for Britain in 1953.

Jimmy Spence was born in Edinburgh on 21 March 1935 and moved to Perth with his family a year later when his father was appointed ice master at the newly opened rink.

This gave the youngster plenty of opportunity to hone his skating skills. At the age of 11 he joined the pee-wee Panther Cubs before moving to the intermediate Blackhawks. He played twice at under-18 level for Scotland against England.

Respected as a gentleman both on and off the ice, in his working life he was a senior electrician at Dewar's of Perth. He died suddenly at his home in Perth on 9 September 2004, aged 69, leaving a wife, Margaret, and four children.

KEN SWINBURNE

British ice hockey lost one of its great unsung heroes with the death on 6 May 2005 of **Ken Swinburne** following a short illness.

Although he never stepped onto the ice in skates, Kenny still managed to gather an impressive medals tally in his role of equipment manager with the all-conquering Durham Wasps.

Initially a fan, Kenny became a fixture on the Wasps' bench - and later with the many Newcastle teams - and could be seen standing on the bench, showing no emotion, just chewing his gum waiting to be needed.

Whether it was a piece of stick tape, some elastoplast, a lace or whatever, it's a fair bet that Kenny would have it to hand within seconds from his famous 'utility belt'. Former Durham great **Peter Johnson** said he could never remember a time when Ken was unable to produce something for the required 'fix'.

■ **ALAN DRACKETT**, the younger brother of *The Ice Hockey Annual's* **Phil Drackett**, died in May 2005 after a short illness. Long time fans will know Alan better as **Alan Dane** who was the Streatham reporter for the weekly newspaper, *Ice Hockey World*, in the Fifties. Alan adopted the pen-name to avoid confusion with his brother who also wrote for the paper.

■ **STEVE RANSON**, the equipment manager of Slough Jets for several years, died suddenly on 25 June 2005 after suffering a heart attack. He was 50. The owner of a chauffeuring business in Cippenham, he left a wife, Karen, and two teenage daughters. [*Steve is second from the left in the back row of the Jets' team photo on page 101 of the Annual.*]

He was a familiar face to almost everyone in British ice hockey and was well liked by all who knew him. He was as popular in Whitley Bay as he was in Durham, and there could perhaps be no greater tribute to the man than that!

HARRY TODD

Former Nottingham Panthers' director, **Harry Todd**, who died in March 2005 aged 79, was connected with ice hockey in Nottingham for most of his life.

He played for Nottingham Wolves in the Midlands Intermediate League (1951-55), initially as a forward and later dropping back to the blueline. A great hockey enthusiast, Harry was on the ice whenever possible with the Wolves, who became homeless in the late Fifties.

He had a few games for Altrincham Aces in season 1963-64 and took Nottingham legends **Chick Zamick** and **Les Strongman** to play for the Cheshire club when Panthers folded.

He was delighted when hockey returned to Nottingham Stadium in 1980 and as he had always taken a keen interest in the players, he became involved with the burgeoning youth programme. He was made a director of the Panthers in the mid-1980s.

He owned the successful Surfside and Alpine sports equipment shop on Mansfield Road in Woodthorpe before retiring.

*Written and researched by **Phil Drackett**, **David Gordon**, **David Hall**, **Martin C Harris** and **Stewart Roberts**.*

INTERNATIONAL ROUND-UP

HONOURS ROLL-CALL 2004-05

World Cup
CANADA

World Champions
CZECH REPUBLIC

World Junior U20 Champions
CANADA

World Junior U18 Champions
USA

European Champions Cup
AVANGARD OMSK, Russia

Continental Cup
HKm Zvolen, Slovakia

Stanley Cup
Not competed for due to player lockout.

Omsk are Europe's Champs

Jaromir Jagr scored the overtime winner as Russia's Avangard Omsk came from behind to beat Finnish champion Karpat Oulu 2-1 in the final of the inaugural European Champions Cup on 16 January 2005 in St Petersburg, Russia.

In front of over 10,000 fans in the St Petersburg Ice Palace, Jagr, the only NHL player with Omsk, scored the winner off a pass from **Maxim Sushinsky** at 14:38 of the extra period.

Jagr, a Czech international, had a contract with the NHL's New York Rangers which would have paid him US$11 million in season 2004-05, but he was unable to play for them when the league closed down for the season due to a labour dispute.

■ Omsk is owned by Russian oil billionaire, **Roman Abramovich**, who - need we remind you - also owns Chelsea Football Club.

■ The Champions Cup is the long awaited replacement for the European Hockey League which folded in 2000 after only four seasons.

The compact Cup format, with the champion clubs of Europe's top six nations meeting in a major city over a long weekend, is considered a great improvement over a league format. With Europe's top domestic leagues playing 50-60 games a season, there are few dates left for an on-going league-style championship.

The IIHF's aim now is to create a global competition matching the European club champions with the Stanley Cup winners and crowning a true world club champion.

GB to meet Israel in 2006

Israel, the middle-eastern country which has only one rink, won promotion to Division I of the World Championships after capturing the gold medal in Division II.

The victory, in Belgrade, Serbia & Montenegro, was one of the biggest feats that international ice hockey has ever seen.

Coached by Canadian **Jean Perron** who led the Montreal Canadiens to a Stanley Cup in 1986, Israel defeated Iceland 4-2 on 10 April 2005 to clinch the division title.

Israeli standouts were goalie **Evgeny Gussin**, who allowed 11 goals in five games, and forward **Oren Eizenman**, who had ten goals and 14 points in five games. Three of his goals were game winners.

A month earlier Perron had led Israel's World under-18 team to a third-place finish in Division III in Sofia, Bulgaria.

Israel's recreational, college and minor league players, mostly immigrants from North America or Russia, can now look forward to facing Division I teams, including Britain, who are made up largely of full-time professional players.

WORLD CHAMPIONSHIPS

Great Britain - the story so far

The 1930s produced what is unquestionably the British game's finest hour. In February 1936, Great Britain upset the ice hockey world in Garmisch-Partenkirchen, Bavaria by winning the Triple Crown of Olympic, World and European titles. Their five victories included a 2-1 defeat of Canada, the reigning world champions.

The players were hand-picked by the Canadian coach, **Percy Nicklin**, and **John F (Bunny) Ahearne**, the secretary of the British Ice Hockey Association. The import rules were a lot different then: though all the players had been born in Britain, all but two of them lived in Canada where they had learned the game.

The World and European Championships were held in London the following year when GB retained their European title and were runners-up in the world, a feat they repeated in 1938. They remained among the leading ten nations in the world until 1951, winning four European crowns.

After the sport went into a decline in this country, the national team's performances suffered similarly until GB was relaunched in 1989 with a purely home-grown side.

The revival swiftly brought success. In 1993 in Eindhoven, boosted by ten dual nationals and guided by coach **Alex Dampier**, GB were promoted to the elite 12-nation A Pool.

They survived at this level for only one year, however, returning to Pool B (now Division I) in 1995, though not before they had memorably competed in Milan against the major hockey powers of Canada and Russia.

GB have remained in this division ever since, twice seeing promotion snatched from them - in 1999 under coach **Peter Woods** and in 2001 under Geneva's **Chris McSorley**, one of Europe's leading coaches.

The absence of opportunities for native British talent in the professional Superleague and the addition of half-a-dozen former Soviet countries to the World Championship roster led to GB slipping to 25th in the world in 2004.

When McSorley resigned shortly before the 2005 Championships, his place was taken by his assistant, **Rick Strachan**, whose selection of an almost entirely home-grown side was partly dictated by the absence of eligible dual nationals from the import-heavy domestic leagues.

■ GB's World Championship record since 1989 is shown at the end of this section.

Great Britain 2005

DIVISION I, Group A
Debrecen, Hungary, 17-23 April, 2005

FINAL STANDINGS

	GP	W	L	D	GF	GA	Pts
Norway NOR	5	4	0	1	43	8	9
Poland POL	5	3	1	1	16	8	7
Hungary HUN	5	2	1	2	15	6	6
Britain GBR	5	2	3	0	19	15	4
Japan JPN	5	2	3	0	14	14	4
China CHN	5	0	5	0	5	61	0

Norway are promoted to the World Championships proper in 2005; **China** are relegated to Division II.

GB'S 2005 WORLD RANKING: 25TH*

*The IIHF world rankings are based on the past four years' results - 100 per cent of 2005, 75 per cent of 2004, and 50 per cent and 25 per cent of the first two years respectively.

GB's ranking is unchanged from 2004.

RESULTS

	NOR	POL	HUN	JAP	CHI
GB	3-8	0-2	3-0	3-5	10-0
NOR		3-2	2-2	5-0	25-1
POL			1-1	2-1	9-3
HUN				3-0	9-0
JAP					8-1

GREAT BRITAIN

Goal: Stephen Murphy (Bjorkloven, Sweden), Joe Watkins (London).

Defence: Leigh Jamieson (Belfast), #James Pease (Coventry), Kyle Horne (Fife), Neil Liddiard (Guildford), #Kevin Phillips, #Adam Radmall (Hull), #Mark Thomas (London), Jonathan Weaver (Newcastle).

Forwards: #Marc Levers (Belfast), *Mike Ellis, #Mark Richardson (Bracknell), Jonathan Phillips, #Warren Tait (Cardiff), Russell Cowley, Ashley Tait (Coventry) capt, David Clarke, Paul Moran, Matt Myers (Nottingham), #Paul Sample (Sheffield), Colin Shields (Greenville Grrrowl, ECHL).

Coach: Rick Strachan (Hull), *assistant*: Roger Hunt (Dundee). *Manager*: Stuart Robertson.

* dual national (1)   # new cap (8)

FAIR PLAY CUP

Penalty minutes per team
Poland 74, Hungary 76, Norway 80, Japan 99, **GB 110**, China 112.

BRITAIN'S POINTS SCORERS

	GP	G	A	Pts	Pim
David Clarke	5	2	6	8	4
Mike Ellis	5	3	4	7	6
Jonathan Weaver	5	2	4	6	6
Ashley Tait	5	2	3	5	8
Colin Shields	4	2	2	4	6
Leigh Jamieson	5	2	2	4	6
Matt Myers	5	3	0	3	10
Marc Levers	5	1	2	3	0
Warren Tait	5	1	2	3	0
Mark Richardson	5	1	0	1	0
Russ Cowley	5	0	1	1	2
Adam Radmall	5	0	1	1	2
Paul Moran	5	0	1	1	4
Neil Liddiard	5	0	1	1	14

BRITAIN'S NETMINDING

	GPI	Mins	SoG	GA	Sv%
Stephen Murphy	5	248	158	7	95.57
Joe Watkins	1	50	36	6	83.33
Empty net goals			2	2	2
TEAM TOTALS	5	300	196	15	92.35

BRITAIN'S GAME SUMMARIES

17 April 2005, Fonix Hall, Debrecen, Hungary

BRITAIN-POLAND   **0-2 (0-0,0-1,0-1)**

Scoring:
0-1 POL Plachta (Laszkiewicz) 2pp   30.43
0-2 POL Garbocz   en   59.44
Shots on goal:
Murphy GB   11-20-10 41 *save%* 95.1
Radziszewski POL   1- 8-17 26 *save%* 100.0
Penalty minutes: GB 20, Poland 12.
Goals/powerplays: GB 0/5, Poland 1/9.
GB man of match: Murphy.
Referee: Bachelet FRA.   *Attendance*: 300.
Britain defended bravely but were unable to prevent the first Polish victory since 1997. GB have beaten the Poles three times since then.

GB's BEST PLAYER
STEPHEN MURPHY
selected by the GB Supporters Club

Coach Strachan was not downhearted: "A lot of the guys haven't played at this level before," he said, "but their confidence rose as the game went on. It was a great start for us."

Goalie Murphy was Britain's man of the match despite being injured in the 15th minute when Ellis clattered into him during a pile-up in front of the net.

Clarke with six shots and Shields (5) were GB's outstanding forwards.

Weaver had a golden opportunity to put Britain ahead after 42 seconds only for the Polish keeper to pull off a brilliant save, which was matched by his stops on Clarke in the first minute of the middle session and on Richardson with three minutes left.

GB were short-handed nine times and Strachan agreed that the officiating in internationals is stricter than in domestic games.

But he insisted his men were learning to cope with it. "The guys worked hard and that can mean you get penalised. But we weren't so bad later in the game."

18 April 2005, Fonix Hall, Debrecen, Hungary

NORWAY-BRITAIN   **8-3 (4-1,2-1,2-1)**

Scoring:
1-0 NOR Ask (Spets)   9.25
2-0 NOR Hansen (Trygg, Spets)   9.59
2-1 GB Myers (A Tait, Clarke)   pp   16.36
3-1 NOR Martinsen (Ask, Bastiansen)   17.10
4-1 NOR Vikingstad (Trygg, Olsen)   18.04
5-1 NOR Skasdammen (Bastiansen, Knold)
                                          22.38
6-1 NOR Knold (Trygg)   pp   24.54

6-2 GB Weaver (A Tait, Clarke) pp   35.17
7-2 NOR Vikingstad (Olsen, Thoresen) pp 46.53
7-3 GB Ellis (Clarke)   pp   51.19
8-3 NOR Hallem (Trygg, Hansen)   57.33
Shots on goal:
Murphy/Watkins GB 17-14-13 44 *save %* 81.82
Grotnes NOR   5- 4- 7 16 *save %* 81.25
Penalty minutes: Norway 24, Britain 28
Powerplays/goals: Norway 7/2, GB 6/3.
GB Man of Match: Weaver.
Referee: Pellerin CAN   *Attendance*: 300

Britain's powerplay was the only part of their game that held together as they slumped to their worst championship defeat in ten years.

In 1995, Britain lost 9-2 to Denmark in Bratislava, Slovakia during the one-year tenure of coach **George Peternousek**.

GB have yet to beat Norway in six meetings between the two nations since 1989.

The regular powerplay unit of Weaver, Shields, Clarke and Ashley Tait was on the ice for all three of GB's goals with Weaver scoring once, Clarke connecting for three assists and Tait for two.

The contest was effectively decided in the first period with the aggressive, fast skating Norwegians forcing GB into errors.

Goalie Murphy was in the wars again when he was struck in the helmet on Norway's first goal and was replaced by Watkins after Hansen made it 2-0 on Norway's eighth shot in ten minutes. Strachan explained that he wanted to rest Murphy - "my number one goalie" - and saw no point in him risking further injury in "a game we couldn't win".

The defence offered little protection to Watkins and the final two periods were a formality. "I knew the Norwegians were a quality team and that our young defencemen would struggle," said the coach. "When Norway scored early their confidence dipped, but they'll learn by their mistakes."

GB's woes increased when forward Sample was taken to hospital after suffering a suspected broken wrist and was later ruled out for the rest of the tournament.

20 April 2005, Fonix Hall, Debrecen, Hungary

JAPAN-BRITAIN   5-3 (0-0,2-1,3-2)

Scoring:
1-0 JAP Keller (Suzuki, Kabori) pp   22.59
1-1 GBR Shields (Clarke, Ellis) pp   28.22
2-1 JAP Osawa (Kon)   30.02
2-2 GBR A Tait   43.24
2-3 GBR Shields (Ellis)   pp   51.50
3-3 JAP S Sato (Miyauchi)   57.34
4-3 JAP Kon (Nishiwaki, Suzuki)   59.00
5-3 JAP Takeshi Saito (Iwata)   en   59.50

Shots on goal:
Kikuchi JAP   7- 7- 7 21   *save%*   85.71
Murphy GB   9-17-14 40   *save%*   87.50
Penalty minutes:
Japan 47 (Tetsuya Saito 5m roughing + game misc.), GB 28.
Powerplays/goals: Japan 8/1, GB 7/2
GB man of match: Shields.
Referee: Bachelet FRA.   *Attendance*: 500.

Playing their best game of the tournament so far, Britain were leading 3-2 with eight minutes left when the Japanese launched a surprise attack.

BRITAIN *left to right,* *back row:* Jan Musil (doctor), Warren Tait, Marc Levers, Kevin Phillips, Mark Richardson, Paul Sample, Adam Radmall, Claire Goodwin (physio); *middle row:* Jason Ellery (equipment), NeilLiddiard, Matt Myers, Mark Thomas, Leigh Jamieson, James Pease, Kyle Horne, Russ Cowley, Paul Moran, Mark Elliot (physio); *front row:* Joe Watkins, Jonathan Philips, Jonathan Weaver, Ashley Tait, Rick Strachan (head coach), Roger Hunt (asst. coach), David Clarke, Mike Ellis, Colin Shields, Stephen Murphy.

Photo: Diane Davey

Scoring three times in under three minutes, their 5-3 win gave them their second victory over GB in three games. GB last beat Japan in 1993.

Coach Strachan, admitting that the manner of the defeat was "totally disheartening", pointed out that 16 of his 22-man team were under-25.

He said his decision to ice fewer players might also have contributed to the outcome. "We had to win this game to have a chance at a medal so I went with our nine best guys. We got outstanding performances from some of them, but the other side of it is they were tired by the end and this cost us the game."

Bracknell Bees' player-coach, Ellis, was one of the players Strachan relied on and he enjoyed his best game. The team's only dual national, and at 31 the oldest player on the squad, he laid on all three goals and couldn't be faulted during the Japanese fightback as he was taking a breather on the bench when they scored their equalising and winning goals.

The game was littered with petty fouls, forcing the referee to speak firmly to the team captains after seven minutes, but it made little difference as he handed out 25 minors, one major and a game misconduct. But for once, the opposition (also a young team) spent almost twice as much time in the box as GB.

22 April 2005, Fonix Hall, Debrecen, Hungary

HUNGARY-BRITAIN   0-3 (0-0,0-1,0-2)

Scoring:
0-1 GB Weaver (A Tait, Shields)   pp   35.50
0-2 GB Jamieson (Shields, Weaver)   54.32
0-3 GB A Tait (Ellis, Liddiard)   57.24
Shots on goal
Szuper HUN   4-10- 8 22   save% 86.36
Murphy GB   11-15-24 50   save% 100.0
Penalty minutes: Hungary 8, GB 10.
Powerplays/goals: Hungary 4/0, GB 3/1.
GB man of match: Clarke.
Referee: Pellerin CAN.   *Attendance*: 4,800.

Britain's dramatic 3-0 victory was not only a surprise, it was also their first win over the vastly more experienced Hungarian side since 1999.

Strachan successfully employed the same defensive system which had turned his low budget club side, Hull Stingrays, into giant killers, and Murphy performed heroics as Hungary rained 50 shots on his net to no avail.

The noisily partisan crowd were silenced by Weaver's 36th minute powerplay goal. The Newcastle defender redirected Ashley Tait's cross-ice pass with a slapshot to the top corner past Hungary's Levente Szuper, who has NHL experience.

Both goals in the final period came on breakaways. Defender Jamieson coolly rounded Szuper for his first world championship goal,

then Tait, with a defender wrapped over him, also made the keeper look distinctly unlike the 'Superman' he is dubbed by the Hungarian fans.

Hungary were unlucky to have a goal disallowed moments into the third period. Murphy allowed a hard shot from the blueline to slip from his grasp and over his line. GB were saved only by the ref who had blown the play dead a split-second earlier.

Pat Cortina, Hungary's coach (who coached Italy in last year's championships), pointed to a 35th minute roughing penalty taken by Ladanyi, one of his most experienced forwards, as the game's turning point. "This was one of the things that shows this team is not yet ready, mentally or physically, for the A pool," he said.

The reason for the unexpected result was partly psychological. For GB it was a "meaningless game", said Strachan. Regardless of the outcome against Hungary, they still had to beat China in their final game. "I told them to go out and just enjoy the atmosphere," he said.

The pressure was all on the Hungarians who, in front of their packed home crowd, needed not only points but also a bucketful of goals. The Norwegians had upped the ante in the promotion stakes by putting 25 past China earlier that day.

23 April 2005, Fonix Hall, Debrecen, Hungary

BRITAIN-CHINA   10-0 (0-0,6-0,4-0)

Scoring:
1-0 GB Ellis (Clarke, Weaver)   pp   21.58
2-0 GB Myers (Cowley, Moran)   22.33
3-0 GB Myers (Jamieson)   sh   25.03
4-0 GB Clarke (Weaver)   32.04
5-0 GB W Tait (Levers)   pp   38.58
6-0 GB Ellis (W Tait, Levers)   39.37
7-0 GB Clarke (Weaver, Radmall)   43.29
8-0 GB Levers (Jamieson)   49.18
9-0 GB Richardson (Clarke)   55.15
10-0 GB Jamieson (Ellis, W Tait)   57.31
Shots on goal
Murphy GB   7-11- 3 21   save% 100.0
Yu CHI   13-13-11 37   save% 72.97
Penalty minutes: Britain 24, China 22.
Powerplays/goals: GB 6/2, China 7/0.
GB Man of Match: Horne.
Referee: Bachelet FRA.   *Attendance*: 700.

It was a very long 22 minutes before Mike Ellis finally broke GB's duck, then within another three minutes Myers had put them 3-0 up. Warren Tait, Levers and Richardson tallied their first goals at this level, and the game ended with Murphy celebrating his second shutout.

A smiling Strachan had a McSorleyism to sum up the game - "We came out flat, we thought it would be easy. So in the interval I told 'em 'there's no Gretzky's or Lemieux's here, so get your work boots on'."

"The future's bright for GB"

STEWART ROBERTS

All the wacky goings-on in Britain's domestic leagues were forgotten in Hungary as we watched GB's first home-grown team (bar one player) since 1989, with eight new caps and an average age of 23, play some entertaining and competitive hockey.

Two shutouts, including a famous victory over their hosts, left Britain only just out of the medals.

Coach **Rick Strachan**, a former GB defenceman, and his assistant, Dundee's **Roger Hunt**, must take a lot of credit for the team's performances. Strachan, the coach of the BNL's Hull Stingrays and an assistant GB coach in Oslo, was thrust into the national role (officially on a temporary basis) when **Chris McSorley** quit on the eve of the tournament.

'Strachs' enjoyed the games. "It was an excellent week," he said. "Coming here with a young team and not really knowing what to expect, I think we surprised a lot of people. If we hadn't given up those late goals against Japan, we could have had a bronze medal.

"The kids are getting more ice-time at domestic level and it showed this week. The future's bright for GB."

That said, there's no question that there were some weak links; the team will win promotion

only when our best home-grown guys are joined by at least a handful of dual nationals.

The current dearth of dual nats is due to the policies of our leading clubs who have virtually stopped recruiting imports with British ancestry. Bracknell Bees' player-coach **Mike Ellis** was one of the few available.

Strachan, one of GB's most loyal players, retired from playing in 2002 with 66 caps. That he quickly earned his players' respect was reflected by the consistency of GB's play and their professionalism on and off the ice. They only struggled against Norway, who went on to win promotion.

It was only politics - some members of the governing body were believed to have pressed for Coventry Blaze coach, **Paul Thompson**, to take over the post - that caused a four-month delay in Rick's confirmation as coach. The August decision by Ice Hockey UK will be popular with players and fans.

■ Over a hundred fans made the journey to this quiet and charming town in eastern Hungary and helped to create plenty of noise in the 5,000-seat, state-of-the-art arena.

■ Chris McSorley gave the demands of his club side, Geneva Eagles, as his main reason for resigning after four Worlds. In his letter to Ice Hockey UK, he urged them to create a strong and properly funded national programme which 'will pay enormous dividends'. We will all miss his professionalism, his enthusiasm, his friendliness and his colourful quotes.

BRITAIN'S RECORD 1989-2004

2004 Division I/A, Oslo, Norway
Coach: **Chris McSorley** (Geneva)
Hungary 3-5, Norway 4-4, Belarus 4-5,
Netherlands 1-4, Belgium 6-0.
World Ranking: 25th. Group standing: 5th.

2003 Division I/B, Zagreb, Croatia
Coach: **Chris McSorley** (Geneva)
France 2-2, Italy 2-4, Estonia 3-4, Croatia 7-1,
Norway 2-3.
World Ranking: 21st. Group standing: 5th

2002 Division I/B,
Szeskesfehervar and Dunaujvaros, Hungary.
Coach: **Chris McSorley** (Geneva)
Denmark 3-5, Hungary 1-4, Romania 5-2,
China 8-3, Norway 1-2.
World Ranking: 20th. Group standing: 4th

2001 Pool B, Ljubljana, Slovenia
Coach: **Chris McSorley** (London)
Estonia 6-2, Croatia 10-1, Slovenia 3-3,
China 12-1, Kazakhstan 11-2.
World Ranking: **18th**. Group Standing: 2nd.

2000 Pool B, Katowice, Poland
Coach: **Peter Woods** (Superleague)
Estonia 5-6, Slovenia 3-3, Netherlands 9-0,
Poland 6-4, Denmark 5-4, Kazakhstan 3-1,
Germany 0-5.
World Ranking: 19th. Group standing: 3rd

1999 Pool B, Copenhagen, Denmark
Coach: **Peter Woods** (Superleague)
Slovenia 2-1, Kazakhstan 1-0, Germany 2-3,
Estonia 6-2, Poland 4-3, Hungary 4-2,
Denmark 5-5.
World Ranking: 18th Group standing: 2nd

1998 Pool B, Ljubljana/Jesenice, Slovenia.
Coach: **Peter Woods** (Superleague).
Ukraine 1-6, Denmark 7-1, Estonia 4-5,
Slovenia 3-5, Poland 4-3, Norway 3-4,
Netherlands 10-3.
World Ranking: 22nd Group standing: 6th

1997 Pool B, Katowice/Sosnowiec, Poland
Coach: **Peter Woods** (Basingstoke)
Poland 3-4, Kazakhstan 2-4, Netherlands 8-2,
Denmark 9-1, Austria 2-2, Switzerland 2-3,
Belarus 2-6.
World Ranking: 18th Group standing: 6th

1996 Pool B, Eindhoven, Netherlands
Coach: **Peter Woods** (Basingstoke).
Latvia 5-6, Switzerland 2-7, Poland 4-2,
Netherlands 6-2, Japan 3-3, Denmark 5-1,
Belarus 4-2.
World Ranking: 16th. Group standing: 4th

1995 Pool B, Bratislava, Slovakia.
Coach: **George Peternousek** (unatt.)
Slovakia 3-7, Romania 0-2, Netherlands 3-2,
Denmark 2-9, Japan 3-4, Poland 4-3, Latvia 4-8.
World Ranking: 19th. Group standing: 7th

1994 Pool A, Bolzano, Italy.
Coach: **Alex Dampier** (Sheffield)
Russia 3-12, Germany 0-4, Italy 2-10,
Canada 2-8, Austria 0-10, Norway 2-5.
World Ranking: 12th. Group standing: 12th

1993 Pool B, Eindhoven, Netherlands.
Coach: **Alex Dampier** (Sheffield).
Poland 4-3, Denmark 4-0, Japan 5-4,
Bulgaria 10-0, Netherlands 3-2,
Romania 10-4, China 14-0.
World Ranking: 13th. Group standing: 1st

1992 Pool C, Hull, England.
Coach: **Alex Dampier** (Nottingham).
Australia 10-2, S Korea 15-0, Belgium 7-3,
N Korea 16-2, Hungary 14-3.
World Ranking: 21st. Group standing: 1st

1991 Pool C , Copenhagen, Denmark.
Coach: **Alex Dampier** (Nottingham).
China 5-6, N Korea 7-2, Denmark 2-3,
Belgium 11-0, Hungary 3-3, Bulgaria 4-5,
S Korea 7-1, Romania 6-5.
World Ranking: 21st. Group standing: 5th

1990 Pool D, Cardiff, Wales.
Coach: **Alex Dampier** (Nottingham)
Australia 14-0, 13-3; Spain 13-1, 17-3.
World Ranking: 26th. Group standing: 1st

1989 Pool D, Belgium.
Coach: **Terry Matthews** (Whitley Bay).
New Zealand 26-0, Romania 6-6, Belgium 5-6,
Spain 8-4.
World Ranking: 27th. Group standing: 3rd

WORLD CHAMPIONSHIPS 2005

Vienna & Innsbruck, Austria, 30 April-15 May
1 Czech Rep., 2 Canada, 3 Russia, 4 Sweden,
5 Slovakia, 6 USA, 7 Finland, 8 Switzerland,
9 Latvia, 10 Belarus, 11 Ukraine,
12 Kazakhstan, 13 Slovenia, 14 Denmark,
15 Germany, 16 Austria.
Germany and *Austria* are relegated to Div I in
2006.

DIVISION I, Group B
Eindhoven, Netherlands, 17-23 April
1 Italy, 2 France, 3 Netherlands, 4 Estonia,
5 Lithuania, 6 Romania.
Italy is promoted to the World Championships in
2006; *Romania* is relegated to Division II.

DIVISION II
Group A
Zagreb, Croatia, 10-16 April
1 Croatia, 2 Australia, 3 (South) Korea,
4 Bulgaria, 5 New Zealand, 6 Turkey.
Croatia is promoted to Division I in 2006;
Turkey is relegated to Division III.
Group B
Belgrade, Serbia & Montenegro, 4-10 April
1 Israel, 2 Serbia, 3 (North) Korea, 4 Belgium,
5 Spain, 6 Iceland.
Israel is promoted to Division I; *Iceland* is
relegated to Division III.

DIVISION III
See next page.

IRELAND *left to right*, *back row (standing)*: Mick Higgins (manager), Dave Kelly, Mark Bowes, Garrett MacNeill, Ross Killen, Johnny Keaney, Patrick McCabe, Robert Leckey; *middle row*: John Crawley (trainer), Mexican interpeter, Gareth Roberts, O'Connor Lyne, Gareth Martin, Stevie Hamill, Stephen Cooper, Larry Jurovich, Tony Griffen (asst. trainer), Cliff Saunders (IIHA president); *front row*: Emmett Dowling, Keith Daly, David Gibson, Jim Tibbetts (asst. coach), David Morrison, Jim Graves (head coach), Philip Darcy, Willie Morrison, Kevin Kelly.

Ireland 2005

DIVISION III
Mexico City, Mexico, 7-13 March 2005

FINAL STANDINGS

	GP	W	L	D	GF	GA	Pts
Mexico MEX	4	4	0	0	60	3	8
South Africa RSA	4	3	1	0	47	12	6
Luxembourg LUX	4	2	2	0	49	16	4
Ireland IRL	4	1	3	0	32	20	2
Armenia ARM	4	0	4	0	5	142	0

Mexico are promoted to Division II in 2005.

RESULTS

	MEX	RSA	LUX	ARM
Ireland	1-6	4-5	4-8	23-1
Mexico		4-2	2-0	48-0
South Africa			7-3	33-1
Luxembourg				38-3

IRELAND
Emmet Dowling, Kevin Kelly; Larry Jurovich, David Kelly, Robert Leckey BEL, O'Connor Lyne, Patrick McCabe, Garrett MacNeill USA, David Morrison BEL; Mark Bowes, Stephen Cooper, Keith Daly, David Gibson BEL, Stephen Hamill BEL, Jonathan Keaney BEL, Ross Killen, Gareth Martin BEL, Willie Morrison BEL, Darcy Phillip, Gareth Roberts BEL. *Coaches:* Jim Graves, Jim Tibbetts. *Manager:* Michael Higgins.

IRELAND'S LEADING SCORERS

	GP	G	A	Pts	Pim
Gareth Martin	3	7	5	12	2
Gareth Roberts	4	7	5	12	4
David Gibson	4	3	4	7	0
Stephen Hamill	3	4	2	6	2
Willie Morrison	4	2	4	6	8

IRELAND'S NETMINDING

	GPI	Mins	SoG	GA	Sv%
Kevin Kelly	4	210	94	19	79.79
Emmet Dowling	1	30	3	1	66.67
TEAM TOTALS	4	240	97	20	79.38

The Irish keep battling

Dundonald's own **Gareth Martin** was the star of Team Ireland's second entry into the World Championships, *writes* **Wayne Hardman**.

The 22-year-old forward, who played for Belfast Giants in 2003-04, was joint top scorer and was voted the team's most valuable player.

He might have added to his tally but he and **Stevie Hamill** were injured in a feisty game against South Africa. Hamill was cross-checked head-first into the boards and was unconscious before he hit the ice. Both missed the last game against their hosts. Ireland were already without **Mark Morrison** and **Graeme Walton** who were needed by the Giants.

Martin was the only Team Ireland player to have played professionally with the Giants. He made hockey history as the first Belfast born player to score at the Odyssey, but he was not re-signed last season when **Tony Hand** took over the coaching.

"Half of our team is from the north, the other half is from the south. We have Protestant players and Catholics, and everybody gets along because they all love hockey." *Kevin Kelly.*

Goalie **Kevin Kelly** had perhaps the best story to tell as he spent most of the season in Canada as a rent-a-goalie, renting his skills out to any team who needed a keeper and were prepared to help pay his bills.

Kelly did this as practice time was hard to come by in a country with only two ice rinks, though Giants gave the squad time at a nominal rate on the weekends when they were at home.

Coach **Jim Graves**, a Canadian ex-goalie now resident in Belfast where he used to work with the Giants, arranged the following friendlies -

November **Luxembourg- Ireland 5-3**
     ***Ireland-New York Tourists 13-11**
25 January ***Belfast Giants-Ireland 7-4**
19 February **Peterboro' Phantoms-Ireland 20-1**
20 February **Streatham Redskins-Ireland 5-2**
* played at the Odyssey Arena
☒ The team were fined 8,000 Swiss francs (almost £4,000) after goalie Kevin Kelly failed to remove his face mask during the playing of the National Anthem.
■ Ireland's coaching staff were aided by another Jim, Bostonian **Jim Tibbetts**, coach of the French under-20s.
Ed's note - Ireland's players were listed by the IIHF as registered with 'Dublin', except the eight shown on the left as 'BEL' who were listed as registered with Belfast Giants. Oddly, none of the eight appeared on Giants' roster.

CLARKE David   b. 5-Aug-81

Club	Year	Comp	GP	G	A	Pts	PIM
Pet	2000	WC	7	0	0	0	2
New	2001	WC	5	2	0	2	6
Lon	2002	WC	5	0	1	1	10
Gui	2003	WC	5	0	0	0	8
Not	2004	WC	5	4	3	7	2
Not	2005	WC	5	2	6	8	4
		Totals	32	8	10	18	32

COWLEY Russell   b. 12-Aug-83

Club	Year	Comp	GP	G	A	Pts	PIM
Cov	2003	WC	5	0	0	0	0
Cov	2004	WC	5	0	0	0	4
Cov	2005	WC	5	0	1	1	2
		Totals	15	0	1	1	6

ELLIS Mike   b. 21-May-73

Club	Year	Comp	GP	G	A	Pts	PIM
Bas	2000	WC	7	1	1	2	0
Bas	2001	WC	5	0	2	2	10
Bas	2002	WC	5	0	1	1	0
Bas	2003	WC	5	0	0	0	8
Brk	2004	WC	5	0	0	0	0
Brk	2005	WC	5	3	4	7	6
		Totals	32	4	8	12	24

HORNE Kyle   b. 30-Sep-80

Club	Year	Comp	GP	G	A	Pts	PIM
Fif	2001	WC	5	0	2	2	4
Fif	2003	WC	5	0	0	0	0
Fif	2005	WC	5	0	0	0	0
		Totals	15	0	2	2	4

JAMIESON Leigh   b. 30-Jul-85

Club	Year	Comp	GP	G	A	Pts	PIM
Bel	2004	WC	5	0	1	1	4
Bel	2005	WC	5	2	2	4	6
		Totals	10	2	3	5	10

LEVERS Marc   b. 30-Jun-81

Club	Year	Comp	GP	G	A	Pts	PIM
Bel	2005	WC	5	1	2	3	0

NETMINDER
MURPHY Stephen   b. 11-Dec-81

Club	Year	Comp	GP	GPI	Mins	GA	GAA
Fif	2001	WC	5	1	30	1	2.00
Dun	2002	WC	3	1	60	2	2.00
Dun	2003	WC	2	0	0	0	0.00
Swe	2005	WC	5	5	248	7	1.69
		Totals	15	7	338	10	1.78

LIDDIARD Neil   b. 7-Mar-78

Club	Year	Comp	GP	G	A	Pts	PIM
Pet	2000	OQ	3	0	0	0	0
Pet	2000	WC	7	0	0	0	0
Bas	2001	WC	5	2	2	0	4
Bas	2002	WC	5	0	0	0	8
Gui	2005	WC	5	0	1	1	14
		Totals	25	2	3	5	26

MORAN Paul   b. 3-Aug-74

Club	Year	Comp	GP	G	A	Pts	PIM
Not	2004	WC	5	1	0	1	2
Not	2005	WC	5	0	1	1	4
		Totals	10	1	1	2	6

MYERS Matt   b. 6-Nov-84

Club	Year	Comp	GP	G	A	Pts	PIM
Car	2004	WC	5	1	2	3	2
Not	2005	WC	5	3	0	3	10
		Totals	10	4	2	6	12

PEASE James   b. 28-Aug-81

Club	Year	Comp	GP	G	A	Pts	PIM
Cov	2005	WC	5	0	0	0	2

PHILLIPS Jonathan   b. 14-July-82

Club	Year	Comp	GP	G	A	Pts	PIM
Car	2003	WC	5	0	1	1	6
Car	2004	WC	5	2	0	2	10
Car	2005	WC	5	0	0	0	14
		Totals	15	2	1	3	30

PHILLIPS Kevin   b. 5-Jan-86

Club	Year	Comp	GP	G	A	Pts	PIM
Hul	2005	WC	5	0	0	0	2

RADMALL Adam   b. 17-Feb-84

Club	Year	Comp	GP	G	A	Pts	PIM
Hul	2005	WC	5	0	1	1	2

RICHARDSON Mark   b. 1-Oct-86

Club	Year	Comp	GP	G	A	Pts	PIM
Brk	2005	WC	5	1	0	1	0

SAMPLE Paul   b. 26-May-82

Club	Year	Comp	GP	G	A	Pts	PIM
Del	2004	WC	5	1	0	1	4
She	2005	WC	2	0	0	0	0
		Totals	7	1	0	1	4

SHIELDS Colin   b. 27-Jan-80

Club	Year	Comp	GP	G	A	Pts	PIM
NAHL	2001	WC	5	6	2	8	4
UoM	2002	WC	5	2	3	5	4
UoM	2003	WC	5	4	1	5	2
UoM	2004	WC	5	0	2	2	6
ECHL	2005	WC	4	2	2	4	6
		Totals	24	14	10	24	22

TAIT Ashley   b. 9-Aug-75

Club	Year	Comp	GP	G	A	Pts	PIM
Not	1995	WC	2	0	0	0	4
Not	1995	OQ	3	1	1	2	0
Not	1996	WC	7	1	1	2	10
Kin	1998	WC	7	2	0	2	4
Not	1999	WCQ	4	0	0	0	4
Not	2000	OQ	3	0	0	0	6
Not	2000	WC	7	3	4	7	10
Not	2001	WC	5	2	4	6	4
Not	2002	WC	5	1	1	2	0
Cov	2003	WC	5	0	3	3	0
Cov	2004	WC	5	2	1	3	2
Cov	2005	WC	5	2	3	5	8
		Totals	58	14	18	32	52

TAIT Warren   b. 17-Apr-81

			GP	G	A	Pts	PIM
Car	2005	WC	5	1	2	3	0

THOMAS Mark   b. 23-Jul-83

			GP	G	A	Pts	PIM
Lon	2005	WC	5	0	0	0	16

WEAVER Jonathan   b. 20-Jan-77

Club	Year	Comp	GP	G	A	Pts	PIM
New	1998	WC	7	1	5	6	0
Man	1999	WC	7	0	2	2	2
USA	1999	WCQ	4	0	0	0	2
Ayr	2001	WC	5	7	2	9	0
Ayr	2002	WC	3	0	0	0	0
Fif	2003	WC	5	2	1	3	4
New	2005	WC	5	2	4	6	6
		Totals	36	12	14	26	14

NETMINDER
WATKINS Joe   b. 27-Oct-79

Club	Year	Comp	GP	GPI	Mins	GA	GAA
Bas	1999	WCQ	1	0	0	0	0.00
Bas	2000	WC	6	4	240	10	2.50
Brk	2002	WC	4	2	120	6	3.00
Brk	2003	WC	4	2	119	5	2.52
ECHL	2004	WC	5	3	180	9	3.00
Lon	2005	WC	5	1	50	6	7.20
		Totals	25	12	709	36	3.04

WORLD CHAMPIONSHIP AND OLYMPIC QUALIFYING APPEARANCES 1989-2005

	Years	GP	G	A	Pts	PIM
ADEY Paul	1995-2001	55	28	24	52	65
BAILEY Chris	2003	4	0	0	0	25
BENNETT Ivor	1989	4	0	1	1	2
BERRINGTON Paul	2002-03	10	2	3	5	8
BIDNER Todd	1993	4	1	1	2	4
BISHOP Mike	1995-2000	36	5	8	13	109
BOBYCK Brent	1999-2000	7	0	1	1	0
BOE Vince	1999-2000	11	0	3	3	22
BREBANT Rick	1994-2002	32	10	13	23	78
CAMPBELL Scott	1999-2003	13	0	1	1	60
CHARD Chris	1995	1	0	0	0	0
CHINN Nicky	1993-2000	40	6	8	14	109
CLARKE David	2000-05	32	8	10	18	32
CONWAY Kevin	1992-99	58	33	33	66	54
COOPER Ian	1989-2000	80	30	31	61	128
COOPER Stephen	1989-2000	61	11	27	38	54
COTE Matt	1994-2000	29	0	2	2	16
COWLEY Russell	2003-05	15	0	1	1	6
CRAIPER Jamie	1990-92	17	12	8	20	34
CRANSTON Tim	1993-97	39	11	13	24	91
DIXON Paul	1995-2005	59	4	16	20	26
DURDLE Darren	1996-2000	22	3	6	9	36
EDMISTON Dean	1991-92	12	3	4	7	15
ELLIS Mike	2000-05	32	4	8	12	24
FERA Rick	1993-94	17	7	17	24	34
GALAZZI Mark	2003	4	0	0	0	25
GARDEN Graham	1995-2000	27	5	5	10	28
HAND Paul	1989-92	18	7	5	12	41
HAND Tony	1989-2002	59	40	79	119	34
HARDING Mike	1999-2000	7	1	3	4	4
HOAD Jeff	2002-04	14	6	5	11	14
HOPE Shannon	1992-98	53	1	8	9	88
HORNE Kyle	2001-05	15	0	2	2	4
HUNT Simon	1995-96	11	3	1	4	26
HURLEY Darren	1999-2003	36	9	8	17	138
IREDALE John	1989-93	24	6	8	14	12
JAMIESON Leigh	2004-05	10	2	3	5	10
JOHNSON Anthony	1990-93	28	15	13	28	20
JOHNSON Shaun	1992-2001	16	2	7	9	6
JOHNSON Stephen	1990-93	23	10	12	22	6
JOHNSTONE Jeff	1999-2000	14	4	3	7	6
KENDALL Jason	2000	3	0	0	0	0
KELLAND Chris	1990-94	31	10	8	18	44
KIDD John	1989	4	2	1	3	0
KINDRED Mike	1995	5	0	1	1	2
KURTENBACH Terry	1993-96	29	1	7	8	6
LAKE Ryan	2004	5	0	1	1	0
LAMBERT Dale	1993	4	0	0	0	4
LARKIN Bryan	1997	7	0	1	1	6

	Years	GP	G	A	Pts	PIM
LATTO Gordon	1976-89	21	2	2	4	10
LAWLESS John	1990-91	12	5	10	15	22
LEE Phil	1989-90	8	2	0	2	0
LEVERS Marc	2005	5	1	2	3	0
LIDDIARD Neil	2000-05	25	2	3	5	26
LINDSAY Jeff	1995-96	22	0	1	1	22
LITTLE Richard	1996-97	10	5	2	7	18
LONGSTAFF David	1994-2004	75	24	35	59	74
MacNAUGHT Kevin	1990-92	17	14	16	30	16
MALO Andre	1993-2000	37	2	7	9	40
MARSDEN Doug	1997	7	0	1	1	8
MASON Brian	1990-94	34	10	10	20	37
McEWEN Doug	1993-2001	49	13	13	26	32
MOODY Scott	2003-04	9	1	0	1	6
MORAN Paul	2004-05	10	1	1	2	6
MORGAN Neil	1995-98	35	11	11	22	16
MORIA Steve	1995-2000	49	22	13	35	30
MORRIS Frank	1994-95	13	1	1	2	10
MORRISON Scott	1993-95	25	15	8	23	16
MULVENNA Glenn	2000	7	0	0	0	18
MEYERS Danny	2004	5	1	1	2	2
MYERS Matt	2004-05	10	4	2	6	12
NEIL Scott	1981-93	37	23	12	35	18
NELSON Craig	2002	5	0	0	0	10
ORD Terry	1989	4	0	1	1	0
O'CONNOR Mike	1992-94	22	4	5	9	52
OWEN Greg	2003	5	0	0	0	20
PAYNE Anthony	1995	6	1	0	1	0
PEASE James	2005	5	0	0	0	2
PENNYCOOK Jim	1977-89	23	10	9	19	4
PENTLAND Paul	1989	4	0	0	0	0
PHILLIPS Jonathan	2003-05	15	2	1	3	30
PHILLIPS Kevin	2005	5	0	0	0	2
PICKLES Andy	2001	5	0	1	1	2
PLOMMER Tommy	1995-96	7	3	0	3	4
POPE Brent	2003-04	8	0	0	0	37
POUND Ian	1995	7	0	0	0	10
PRIEST Merv	1996-2000	30	6	7	13	30
RADMALL Adam	2005	5	0	1	1	2
REID Alistair	1989	4	1	2	3	0
RHODES Nigel	1989	4	2	0	2	2
RICHARDSON Mark	2005	5	1	0	1	0
ROBERTSON Iain	1991-95	27	4	3	7	2
SAMPLE Paul	2004-05	7	1	0	1	4
SAUNDERS Lee	1995-96	8	0	1	1	0
SCOTT Patrick	1993-97	31	10	9	19	24
SHIELDS Colin	2001-2005	24	14	10	24	22
SMITH Damian	1992-95	14	3	4	7	10
SMITH David	1995	5	1	0	1	0
SMITH Paul	1981-89	11	0	1	1	13

	Years	GP	G	A	Pts	PIM
SMITH Peter	1989-91	14	7	2	9	10
SMITH Stephen	1989	4	2	1	3	2
STEFAN Gary	1990-92	17	12	10	22	28
STONE Jason	1998	6	0	0	0	0
STRACHAN Rick	1995-2002	66	7	10	17	20
TAIT Ashley	1995-2005	58	14	18	32	52
TAIT Warren	2005	5	1	2	3	0
TASKER Michael	2001-02	10	2	3	5	8
THOMAS Mark	2005	5	0	0	0	16
THOMPSON Paul	1998	6	1	1	2	8
THORNTON Steve	1999-2004	26	6	23	29	14
WAGHORN Graham	1991-96	19	1	3	4	16
WARD Colin	2004	5	3	0	3	2
WEAVER Jonathan	1998-2005	36	12	14	26	14
WEBER Randall	1998	7	0	2	2	6
WILSON Rob	1998-2004	34	11	22	33	32
WISHART Gary	2002	5	0	2	2	4
YOUNG Scott	1999-2002	16	5	4	9	56

NETMINDERS	Years	GP	GPI	Mins	GA	GAA
CAVALLIN Mark	2003-04	9	5	300	16	3.20
COWLEY Wayne	1999-2000	10	3	160	10	3.75
FOSTER Stephen	1995-2000	31	16	855	61	4.28
GRAHAM David	1989-91	10	6	330	18	3.27
GRUBB Ricky	1995	1	1	40	5	7.50
HANSON Moray	1989-94	9	6	317	32	6.06
HIBBERT Jim	2000	1	1	20	3	9.00
LYLE Stevie	1995-2002	39	26	1495	63	2.53
McCRONE John	1989-94	23	19	957	57	3.57
McKAY Martin	1990-94	15	8	418	28	4.02
MORRISON Bill	1995-99	33	17	1000	38	2.28
MURPHY Stephen	2001-05	15	7	338	10	1.78
O'CONNOR Scott	1992-2003	9	5	198	4	1.21
SMITH Jeff	1990	3	1	60	2	2.00
WATKINS Joe	1999-2005	25	12	709	36	3.04

2005 players shown in bold
Detailed records are in The Ice Hockey Annual 2003-04 & 2004-05

MIKE ELLIS scores GB's third goal against their strongest opponents, Norway, who won promotion out of Division I. *Inset*: Coach **RICK STRACHAN** holds his first championship press conference.

Photos: Diane Davey

WORLD JUNIOR CHAMPIONSHIPS

U20 CHAMPIONSHIPS

Division I, iceSheffield, England, 13-19 December 2004.

Age limit is under 20 years on 1 January 2005

FINAL STANDINGS

Group A	GP	W	L	D	GF	GA	Pts
Norway	5	5	0	0	29	12	10
Kazakhstan	5	4	1	0	29	15	8
Austria	5	3	2	0	12	16	6
France	5	2	3	0	18	19	4
Italy	5	1	4	0	11	16	2
Britain	**5**	**0**	**5**	**0**	**8**	**29**	**0**

Norway promoted to the World Championships in 2006, **Britain relegated** to Division II.

GB UNDER-20'S GAME SUMMARIES

13 Dec **BRITAIN-AUSTRIA** 0-1 (0-0,0-0,0-1) *GB man of match:* Lawrence. *Penalty minutes:* GB 18, Austria 14. *GB netminder:* Lawrence (42 shots). *Attendance:* 286.

14 Dec **FRANCE-BRITAIN** 5-3 (3-1,0-1,2-1) *GB man of match:* Jamieson. *GB scorers:* Jamieson, K Phillips, Brittle 1g; Thompson 2a; Richardson 1a. *Penalty minutes:* France 16, GB 20. *GB netminder:* Lawrence (45 shots). *Attendance:* 297.

16 Dec **BRITAIN-ITALY** 0-3 (0-2,0-0,0-1) *GB man of match:* K Phillips. *Penalty minutes:* GB 30 (Jamieson 10m misc.), Italy 16. *GB netminder:* Lawrence (38). *Attendance:* 363.

18 Dec **NORWAY-BRITAIN** 10-3 (4-1,2-1,4-1) *GB man of match:* McKenzie. *GB scorers:* Thompson, Jamieson, Duncombe 1g; McKenzie, Richardson 1a. *Penalty minutes:* Norway 42 (Trygg 10m misc.), GB 42 (Duncombe, Reekie 10m misc.). *GB netminder:* Woolhouse (53 shots). *Attendance:* 500.

19 Dec **KAZAKHSTAN-BRITAIN** 10-2 (1-0,6-0,3-2) *GB man of match:* Moore. *GB scorers:* Thompson, Richardson 1g; D Phillips, McKenzie, Duncombe 1a. *Penalty minutes:* Kazakhstan 26, GB 74. *GB netminder:* Lawrence (47), Woolhouse (27). *Attendance:* 326.

BRITAIN UNDER-20

Geoff Woolhouse NOT, Davey Lawrence SHE; Leigh Jamieson BEL, Chad Reekie DUN, Euan Forsyth FIF, Luke Boothroyd, Dave Phillips, Kevin Phillips HUL, Steve Duncombe SHE, Shane Moore SWI, Kurt Reynolds (USA); Shaun Thompson BAS, Mark Richardson BRK, capt, Lee Mitchell FIF, Adam Walker GUI, Bari McKenzie MIL, Andrew Thornton NEW, Simon Butterworth, Chace Farrand SHE, Adam Brittle, Tom Carlon TEL, Lewis Day (Canada). *Head coach:* Roger Hunt DUN. *Asst coach:* Mick Mishner WHI. *Manager:* Jim Laing (unatt).

RESULTS

	NOR	KAZ	AUT	FRA	ITA
GBR	**3-10**	**2-10**	**0-1**	**3-5**	**0-3**
NOR		3-5	5-0	5-4	4-2
KAZ			8-3	5-3	3-2
AUT				3-2	5-1
FRA					4-3

GB UNDER-20'S POINTS SCORERS

	GP	G	A	Pts	Pim
Shaun Thompson	5	2	2	4	6
Mark Richardson	5	1	2	3	0
Leigh Jamieson	5	2	0	2	32
Steve Duncombe	5	1	1	2	22
Bari McKenzie	5	0	2	2	16
Adam Brittle	5	1	0	1	0
Kevin Phillips	5	1	0	1	6
David Phillips	5	0	1	1	16

GB UNDER-20'S NETMINDING

	GPI	Mins	SoG	GA	Sv%
Davey Lawrence	4	223	172	16	90.7
Geoff Woolhouse	2	77	80	13	83.7
GB TOTALS	**5**	**300**	**252**	**29**	**88.5**

BRITAIN UNDER-20 *left to right, back row:* Adam Brittle, Adam Walker, Shane Moore, Lee Mitchell, Jim Laing (manager), Kurt Reynolds, Luke Boothroyd, Bari McKenzie, Chad Reekie; *middle row:* Jason Ellery, Shaun Thompson, Simon Butterworth, Steve Duncombe, Tom Carlon, Chace Farrand, Dave Phillips, Euan Forsyth, Lewis Day, Andrew Thornton, physio; *front row:* Davey Lawrence, Kevin Phillips, Mick Mishner (asst. coach), Mark Richardson, Roger Hunt (coach), Leigh Jamieson, Geoff Woolhouse.

Photo: Gary Apsley

'A learning experience'

Coach **Roger Hunt** put a brave face on this disappointing tournament as GB's under-20s, competing for the first time at this level, lost all their five games. "It was a learning experience," he said. "In the end the guys had nothing left in the tank. The pace was different and the physical side was not the same."

The one aspect of the European game which invariably leaves even our best players struggling is the speed. The continentals don't waste energy on hard checking, they rely on their speed to get them out of trouble. Even GB's most skilful players couldn't keep up.

That said, the first three games were competitive. Against France, Britain staged a gutsy comeback from 3-0 down to draw 3-3 before succumbing to two late markers.

The Italian game was a thriller, too. Poor **Mark Richardson**, one of the brightest talents on display, missed his penalty shot at the end of

---

GB under-20s BEST PLAYERS
ADAM BRITTLE
selected by the GB Supporters' Club
KEVIN PHILLIPS
Selected by the IIHF

---

the second period which would have brought GB to within one goal. The Italians needed an empty netter at the end before they could relax.

The remaining two games showed just how far GB have to go to be competitive at world level. As always, the lack of pre-championship warm-up games is one drawback but giving our younger players more ice-time at the top level in this country would also help.

Belfast's **Leigh Jamieson** and top scorer, **Shaun Thompson** 17, of Basingstoke were the only GB players who enjoyed anything like regular shifts with their Elite League club.

Some of the opposition's players in iceSheffield were being watched by NHL scouts!

Although Britain won the right to stage this championship against stiff competition from the Italians, they must have made a sizeable loss. According to **Bob Wilkinson** of Ice Hockey UK, the governing body received £53,000 from the International Ice Hockey Federation.

However, he calculated that they needed 600 fans at each GB game to break even and they only came close to that once - for the Saturday night game against Norway. The other contests drew barely half that number.

Hunt preferred to look to next year when GB return to Division II. "We'll have 17 of this year's players back and we also have some good guys coming through [in the under-18s]. We've had a taste of this level, and it was an eye-opener."

U18 CHAMPIONSHIPS

Division I, Maribor, Slovenia, 3-9 April 2005

Age limit is under 18 years on 1 January 2005

FINAL STANDINGS

Group A	GP	W	L	D	GF	GA	Pts
Belarus	5	4	1	0	23	10	8
Slovenia	5	3	2	0	22	14	6
Kazakhstan	5	3	2	0	19	14	6
France	5	3	2	0	11	14	4
Austria	5	2	3	0	15	25	4
Britain	5	1	4	0	10	23	2

Belarus promoted to the World Championships in 2006, Britain relegated to Division II.

RESULTS

	BEL	SLO	KAZ	FRA	AUT
GB	0-5f	1-7	2-4	3-2	4-5
BEL		5-3	3-2	2-3	8-2
SLO			5-3	4-1	3-4
KAZ				4-1	6-3
FRA					4-1

GB UNDER 18'S POINTS SCORERS

	GP	G	A	Pts	Pim
Joe Greener	4	1	3	4	4
John Dewar	4	1	3	4	35
Tom Carlon	4	2	1	3	4
Oliver Bronnimann	4	2	0	2	2
Shaun Thompson	4	2	0	2	2
Lewis Day	4	1	1	2	0
Ben O'Connor	4	0	2	2	10
David Phillips	4	1	0	1	18
Shane Moore	4	0	1	1	8

GB UNDER-18'S NETMINDING

	GPI	Mins	SoG	GA	Sv%
Martin Clarkson	2	75	41	3	92.7
Joe Dollin	3	165	98	15	84.7
GB TOTALS	4	240	139	18	87.1

GB UNDER-18'S GAME SUMMARIES

3 Apr **BRITAIN-BELARUS   0-5**
Britain disqualified for not being ready to play.

4 Apr **AUSTRIA-BRITAIN   5-4 (1-2,0-0,4-2)**
GB man of match: Carlon. *GB scorers*: Thompson 2g; Carlon 1+1; D Phillips 1g; Moore, Greener, O'Connor 1a. *Penalty minutes*: Austria 8, GB 10. *GB netminder*: Dollin (37 shots).

6 Apr **BRITAIN-KAZAKHSTAN   2-4 (1-0,1-2,0-2)**
GB man of match: Thompson. *GB scorers*: Dewar, Lewis 1+1; Greener 1a. *Penalty minutes*: GB 18, KAZ 14. *GB netminder*: Dollin (32).

7 Apr **SLOVENIA-BRITAIN   7-1 (2-1,2-0,3-0)**
GB man of match: Bronnimann.   *GB scorer*: Bronnimann 1g; Dewar 1a.   *Penalty minutes*: Slovenia 10, GB 79 (Towe 2+10 ch/behind, D Phillips 10m misc., Dewar game).   *GB netminders*: Dollin (29), Clarkson (8).

9 Apr **FRANCE-BRITAIN   2-3 (0-1,1-1,1-1)**
GB man of match: Clarkson.   *GB scorers*: Greener 1+1; Carlon, Bronnimann 1g; O'Connor, Dewar 1a. *Penalty minutes*: France 10, GB 12. *GB netminder*: Clarkson (33).

Clarkson, 16, backs bag-less GB kids to French victory

Someone up there doesn't want GB to do well internationally.

As if our national squads don't have enough to put up with, the airline managed to leave the under-18s' bags on the tarmac at Gatwick Airport!

When they still hadn't arrived by face-off time of the opening game in Slovenia, the IIHF had no option but to award the points to GB's opponents, Belarus.

It was a game that they would probably have lost, anyway, as Belarus won promotion, but the chance to play as a team for the first time would have given **Mike Urquhart** and his lads a far better chance against the Austrians.

As it was, **David Phillips** and **Shaun Thompson** gave Britain the lead after nine minutes, only for the Austrians to force their way back into the game, going 3-2 up early in the third. In a wild last ten minutes, Thompson tied it up again, but Rotter and Schlacher, with their second goals for Austria, put the game virtually out of reach.

Tom Carlon breathed life into his team-mates in the final two minutes but they couldn't find the equaliser.

As well as icing six players from the under-20s, this squad boasted some of the most exciting young talent at this age level for years, especially among the forwards.

Carlon had ten goals this time last year when GB won promotion from Division II.

BRITAIN UNDER-18

Martin Clarkson CAR, Joe Dollin GUI; David Savage GUI, Luke Boothroyd, David Phillips HUL, Julian Smith PET, Ben Morgan SHE, Shane Moore SWI; Shaun Thompson BAS, Robert Dowd BIL, Iain Beattie EDI, Daniel Scott NOT, James Ferrara PET, Andrew Turner, Greg Wood SHE, Tom Carlon, Matt Towe TEL, Lewis Day, John Dewar, Ben O'Connor (Canada), Oliver Bronnimann (Geneva), Joe Greener (USA).
Head coach: Mike Urquhart NOT. *Asst coach*: Peter Russell CAR. *Manager*: Ian Turner (unatt.).

Former Swindon junior, **John Dewar; Ben O'Connor**, 16, son of former Durham Wasp dual national, **Mike O'Connor**; Yorkshire lad **Lewis Day** and Basingstoke teenager **Joe Greener** are all young men in a hurry to prove themselves by competing during the season in North America.

Three of them: Dewar, Greener and Lewis, combined to rock the Kazakhs in the next game with two goals by the 22nd minute. But then their opponents woke up, outshooting GB 23-8 in the final two periods.

Oliver Bronnimann, who has a Swiss parent and played for Geneva's junior side, scored his first ever goal for GB (assisted by Dewar) of an otherwise forgettable game against the host nation. Any chance Britain had of getting close to the Slovenians was damaged when they took 79 penalty minutes. Dewar was responsible for 20 of them when he was thrown out at the end of the game.

Then at last, after five defeats in Sheffield and an abandoned game and a couple of close calls in Slovenia, a GB junior team managed to gain a victory - and it was over the French! (It's not been their year, has it?)

GB opened with Greener notching his first international goal. Then his pass to Carlon made it 2-1, and it was Bronnimann from Dewar for 3-1. After Treille brought the French to within one goal at 57.23, France got a bit panicky; their goalie, Buysse, was in and out of his net like a yo-yo. But GB held on.

The game - and maybe the tournament - was a coming-out party for Cardiff goalie, **Martin Clarkson**, at 16 the youngest player on the team. In his first full 60-minute spell in a GB international, he was voted man of the match with a sparkling 94 per cent as he batted away 31 shots in his net. The next **Stevie Lyle**?

■ As if the lack of kit bags wasn't handicap enough, few GB fans were able to cheer on the team as the tournament ended only a week before the senior side played their opening game in Hungary.

CONTINENTAL CUP

The Continental Cup was established in 1997 as a replacement for the European Cup (inaugurated 1965). The name was changed to avoid confusion with the European League (1996-2000).

Similar to football's Champions League, entry in the Cup is open to clubs who have won their country's national league.

There were 14 Eastern European nations among the 20 who agreed to compete in the 2004 competition.

Costs are kept down by gathering clubs together geographically as far as possible and allowing games to be played by groups of teams in one venue, rather than home and away.

The 2004 cup was played over three qualifying rounds in September, October and November, with Hungary hosting the four-team final in January.

British teams have entered the competitions each year since 1983, apart from 1997 and 2003.

Britain's 2004 representatives were Nottingham Panthers who accepted an invitation after Sheffield Steelers, the Elite League winners, declined theirs on cost grounds. Panthers were seeded into the Second Round.

We give below details of Nottingham's games.

SECOND ROUND

Group D in Amiens, France

	GP	W	L	D	GF	GA	Pts
Milan Vipers ITA	3	2	0	1	15	4	5
Nottingham Panthers GBR	3	2	0	1	6	3	5
Amiens Gothiques FRA	3	1	2	0	4	7	2
Olympia Ljubljana SLO	3	0	3	0	2	13	0

Teams tied on points separated by overall goal difference.

RESULTS

15 Oct	**Panthers**-Milan	2-2 (1-0,0-0,1-2)
	Ljubljana-Amiens	0-3 (0-1,0-2,0-0)
16 Oct	Ljubljana-**Panthers**	0-1 (0-0,0-1,0-0)
	Amiens-Milan	0-4 (0-1,0-1,0-2)
17 Oct	Milan-Ljubljana	9-2 (3-0,5-2,1-0)
	Amiens-**Panthers**	1-3 (0-2,1-0,0-1)

PANTHERS' GAME SUMMARIES

15 October 2004, Amiens Coliseum, France

PANTHERS-MILAN VIPERS   2-2 (1-0,0-0,1-2)

Scoring:
1 NOT Ahlroos (Kalmikov)   8.59
2 MIL Kallarson (Laszkiewicz, Rickmo)   49.21
3 NOT Kalmikov (Ivan, Ahlroos)   50.21
4 MIL Helfer (Kallarson, Felicetti)   52.23
Shots on Goal:
Cruickshank NOT 17-19-17   53   save % 96.2
Eriksson MIL   10- 7-10   27   save % 92.6
Men of Match: Cruickshank NOT, Kallarson MIL.
Penalty minutes:
Panthers 34 (Craighead 5+game - rough), Milan 34 (Smith 5+game - rough).
Referee: Bachelet FRA.   *Attendance:* 1,300

16 October 2004, Amiens Coliseum, France

LJUBLJANA-PANTHERS   0-1 (0-0,0-1,0-0)

Scoring:
1 NOT Ivan (Krulis) pp   37.28
Shots on Goal:
Satosaari LJU   16-14-11 41   save %   97.6
Cruickshank NOT   5- 4- 7 16   save % 100.0
Men of Match: Satosaari LJU, Myers NOT.
Penalty minutes: Ljubljana 76 (Ladiha 5+game - spear; Groznik 5+game - rough; Cvetec 2+10 xch-behind), Panthers 22.
Referee: Bachelet FRA.   *Attendance:* 1,250

17 October 2004, Amiens Coliseum, France

AMIENS-PANTHERS   1-3 (0-2,1-0,0-1)

Scoring:
1 NOT Kalmikov (Cadotte, Ricci) sh   7.32
2 NOT Craighead (Krulis, Ahlroos) pp   9.31
3 AMI Rozenthal (Marcos, Zwikel)   35.07
4 NOT Craighead   56.40
Shots on Goal:
Mindjimba AMI   29   save %   89.7
Cruickshank NOT   42   save %   97.6
Men of Match: Nortas AMI, Ivan NOT.
Penalty minutes: Amiens 16, Panthers 32 (Craighead 10misc - unsport.)
Referee: Oswald.   *Attendance:* 3,000.

Back-up cock-up

The in-fighting behind the scenes at the Amiens Coliseum proved to have as big an influence on the outcome of this tournament as injuries and the quirky refereeing calls did in the games.

Before the contest began, the Slovenian team, Olympia Ljubljana, asked to use their three newly signed locked-out NHL players.

Gary Moran, Panthers' general manager, told *Powerplay*: "The Slovenian's plans were thwarted by Panthers' management and the decisive chairmanship of the IIHF's tournament director [Frenchman **Patrick Francheterre**]." But the British insistence on fair play was lost on the Slovenians who plotted their revenge.

After two games each, Milan and Nottingham had similar records. To help ensure the Italians won their last game and the group, Ljubljana iced their reserve goalie against Vipers who won by seven goals. As Panthers later managed only a two-goal defeat of their hosts, this was enough for Milan to win the competition.

NOTTINGHAM PANTHERS

Curtis Cruickshank, #Geoff Woolhouse; *Jan Magdosko, Calle Carlsson (capt), Jan Krulis, Scott Ricci, +Paul Moran; David Clarke, Kim Ahlroos, Matt Myers, Richard Wojciak, Konstatin Kalmikov, Mark Cadotte, +Roman Tvrdon, Daniel Scott, John Craighead, Marek Ivan, #Sean Yardley, #Adam Carr, #Rhys McWilliams.

Coach: Paul Adey.   *Manager:* Gary Moran.
+ *injured in first game,* * *did not play - groin injury,* # *did not ice.*

Straight-faced, Olympia had claimed that their number one keeper, Newcastle's **Tomi Satosaari**, was injured, but then foolishly gave themselves away when back-up **Andrej Hocevar** really was injured in the last period and Satosaari skated sheepishly into the Slovenian net.

Adey was incensed and said that Panthers would protest to the IIHF. "Teams have to compete," he fumed. "Anything less than that makes a mockery of the outcome." Whether they protested or not, nothing was changed and Panthers lost out on goal difference.

⊠ After the problems encountered by the GB team in the 2000 World Championships in the Slovenian capital, Ljubljana, fans can expect some especially heated rivalries whenever these two nations' players meet in future.

☑ Three previous British teams have topped their first round groups: **Dave Whistle**'s Belfast Giants who reached the 2002 finals, **Chris McSorley**'s London Knights who won a silver medal in 2000, and **John Lawless**'s Cardiff Devils who reached the 1994 semi-finals.

PAST BRITISH PERFORMANCES

2003 No entry.

2002 **BELFAST GIANTS**, *coach:* **Dave Whistle**
Superfinal in Milan, Italy and Lugano, Switzerland: lost 0-2 to Lugano, beat Davos SWI 4-2, lost 3-4 to Slovan Bratislava SVK.
Third Round in Belfast, N Ireland: beat Valerengen NOR 3-0, beat Rouen FRA 8-0, beat Linz AUS 5-3.

   (AYR) SCOTTISH EAGLES, *coach:* **Paul Heavey**. *Second Round in Rouen, France:* beat Storhamar Dragons NOR 2-1, beat Riga LAT 2-1. (Third game cancelled due to bad ice.)
Eagles qualified for Third Round but club folded.

2001 **LONDON KNIGHTS**, *coach:* **Bob Leslie**.
Third Round in Oslo, Norway: lost 2-5 to Jukurit FIN, beat Anglet FRA 5-3, drew 4-4 with Valerengen.

   SHEFFIELD STEELERS, *coach:* **Mike Blaisdell**. *Second Round in Anglet, France:* beat Herning, DEN 5-3, beat Grenoble FRA 4-1, lost 3-4 to Anglet.

2000 **LONON KNIGHTS** *coach* **Chris McSorley**
Third Round in Storhamar, Norway: drew 1-1 with Valerengen, beat Minsk BEL 5-0, beat Storhamar Dragons 9-1.
Final Round in Zurich, Switzerland: lost 0-1 to Zurich Lions, beat Slovan Bratislava 5-2, beat Munich Barons GER 4-1.

1999 **CARDIFF DEVILS**, *coach:* **Paul Heavey**.
Second Round in Cardiff, Wales: beat Lyons Lions FRA 9-2, beat Nottingham Panthers 5-3, lost 2-8 to Lada Togliatti RUS.

   NOTTINGHAM PANTHERS, *coach:* **Mike Blaisdell**. *Second Round in Cardiff, Wales:* beat Lada Togliatti 8-6, lost 3-5 to Cardiff Devils, beat Lyon Lions 5-3.

   SHEFFIELD STEELERS, *coach:* **Don McKee**. *Third Round in Sheffield, England:* drew 4-4 with Angers Ducs FRA, drew 3-3 with Storhamar Dragons, beat Avangard Omsk RUS 4-2.

1998 **SHEFFIELD STEELERS**, *coach:* **Don McKee**. *Second Round in Omsk, Russia:* drew 4-4 with Ust Kamenogorsk KAZ, lost 1-5 to Avangard Omsk, lost 1-3 to Lada Togliatti.

   CARDIFF DEVILS, *coach:* **Paul Heavey**. *Second Round in Cardiff, Wales:* lost 2-3 to Olympia Ljubljana, lost 2-4 to Dunaujvaros HUN, beat Podhale Nowy Targ POL 5-3.

1997 No entry.
1983-96 See *The Ice Hockey Annual 1997-98.*

Roll of Honour (Modern Era)

)*Winners and runners-up in all major domestic club competitions since the start of the Modern Era.*
Compiled exclusively for the Annual *by **Gordon Wade** with contributions from **Martin Harris**.*
The Roll of Honour for the years before season 1982-83 is in The Ice Hockey Annual 1998-99.

SEASON	COMPETITION	WINNER	RUNNER-UP	NOTES
2004-05	Elite League Playoff Ch'ship	Coventry Blaze	Nottingham Panthers	Won 2-1ot at Nottingham
	Elite League	Coventry Blaze	Belfast Giants	7-team league
	Challenge Cup	Coventry Blaze	Cardiff Devils	Won 11-5 on agg. (6-1h,5-4a)
	Crossover Games	Belfast Giants	Cardiff Devils	Inter-league games with BNL
	British Nat'l Lge Ch'ship	Dundee Stars	Guildford Flames	Won best-of-five series, 3-0
	British National League	Bracknell Bees	Newcastle Vipers	7-team league
	Winter Cup	Bracknell Bees	Newcastle Vipers	Win 8-1 on agg. (5-1a,3-0h)
	Eng Premier Lge Ch'ship	Milton Keynes Lightning	Peterboro' Phantoms	Won 7-2 at Coventry
	Eng Premier Lge	Milton Keynes Lightning	Peterboro' Phantoms	9-team league
	Eng Premier Cup	Romford Raiders	Swindon Wildcats	Won 5-3 on agg. (2-0a,3-3h
	Eng Nat'n'l Lge Ch'ship	Sheffield Scimitars	Invicta Dynamos	Won 10-3 on agg. (6-0h, 4-3a)
	Eng Nat'n'l Lge, North	Sheffield Scimitars	Nottingham Lions	9-team league
	Eng Nat'n'l Lge, South	Invicta Dynamos	Oxford City Stars	10-team league
	English Cup	Sheffield Scimitars	Invicta Dynamos	Won 8-3 on agg (4-0a,4-3h)
2003-04	Elite League Playoff Ch'ship	Sheffield Steelers	Nottingham Panthers	Won 2-1 at Nottingham
	Elite League	Sheffield Steelers	Nottingham Panthers	New 8-team league
	Challenge Cup	Nottingham Panthers	Sheffield Steelers	Won 4-3 on agg. (1-1h,3-2ot a)
	British Nat'l Lge Ch'ship	Guidford Flames	Bracknell Bees	Won 9-7 on agg. (5-4a,4-3h)
	British National League	Fife Flyers	Guildford Flames	7-team league
	Findus Cup	Newcastle Vipers	Guildford Flames	Won 6-1 at Newcastle
	Eng Premier Lge Ch'ship	Milton Keynes Lightning	Slough Jets	Won 12-2 on agg. (7-0a, 5-2h)
	Eng Premier League	Milton Keynes Lightning	Peterborough Phantoms	9-team league
	Eng Premier Cup	Peterborough Phantoms	*Wightlink* Raiders	Won 7-2 on agg. (3-1a,4-1h)
	Eng Nat'n'l Lge Ch'ship	Sheffield Scimitars	Invicta Dynamo	Won 8-5 on agg. (4-3a,4-2h)
	Eng Nat'n'l Lge, North	Flintshire Freeze	Sheffield Scimitars	10-team league
	Eng Nat'n'l Lge, South	Invicta Dynamo	Oxford City Stars	9-team league
2002-03	+ Superleague Playoff Ch'ship	Belfast Giants	London Knights	Won 5-3 at Nottingham
	+ Superleague	Sheffield Steelers	Belfast Giants	Only five teams in league
	+ Challenge Cup	Sheffield Steelers	Nottingham Panthers	Won 3-2 at Manchester
	British Nat'l Lge Ch'ship	Coventry Blaze	Cardiff Devils	Won 5-3 on agg. (3-2a,2-1h)
	British National League	Coventry Blaze	Dundee Stars	10-team league
	Findus Cup	Newcastle Vipers	Coventry Blaze	Won 3-0 at Newcastle
	Eng Nat'l Lge, Premier Div Ch'ship	Milton Keynes Lightning	Peterborough Phantoms	Won 16-4 on agg. (10-0h,6-4a)
	Eng Nat'l Lge, Premier Division	Peterborough Phantoms	Milton Keynes Lightning	12-team league
	Eng Nat'l Lge, Premier Cup	Peterborough Phantoms	Milton Keynes Lightning	Won 7-6 on agg. (2-4a,5-2h)
	Eng Nat'l Lge, Div. One Ch'ship	Basingstoke Buffalo	Altrincham Aces	Won 10-9 on agg. (4-5a,6-4h)
	Eng Nat'l Lge, Div One North	Sheffield Scimitars	Altrincham Aces	10-team league; Aces' last season
	Eng Nat'l Lge, Div One South	Basingstoke Buffalo	Bracknell Hornets	6-team league
2001-02	+ Superleague Playoff Ch'ship	Sheffield Steelers	Manchester Storm	Won 4-3 (ps) at Nottingham
	+*Sekonda* Superleague	Belfast Giants	Ayr Scottish Eagles	7-team lge; Giants' 2nd season
	+ Challenge Cup	Ayr Scottish Eagles	Belfast Giants	Won 5-0 at Belfast
	British Nat'l Lge Ch'ship	Dundee Stars	Coventry Blaze	Won 8-7 on agg. (7-4a, 1-3h)
	British National League	Dundee Stars	Coventry Blaze	12-team lge; Stars' first season
	Findus Cup	Fife Flyers	Coventry Blaze	Won 6-3 at Nottingham
	Eng Nat'l Lge, Premier Div Ch'ship	Invicta Dynamos	Isle of Wight Raiders	Won 6-3 on agg. (2-1a, 4-2h)
	Eng Nat'l Lge, Premier Division	Invicta Dynamos	Solihull Barons	8-team league
	Eng Nat'l Lge, Premier Cup	Romford Raiders	Invicta Dynamos	Won 9-7 on agg. ((5-3h, 4-4a)
	Eng Nat'l Lge, Div. One Ch'ship	Whitley Warriors	Basingstoke Buffalo	Won on agg. 12-7 (6-6a, 6-1h)
	Eng Nat'l Lge, Div. One North	Whitley Warriors	Altrincham Aces	10-team league
	Eng Nat'l Lge, Div. One South	Basingstoke Buffalo	Flintshire Freeze	10-team league

SEASON	COMPETITION	WINNER	RUNNER-UP	NOTES
2000-01	+= Superleague Playoff Ch'ship	Sheffield Steelers	London Knights	Won 2-1 at Nottingham
	+ *Sekonda* Superleague	Sheffield Steelers	Cardiff Devils	9-team lge; won by 19 points but censured for breaking wage cap.
	B&H Autumn Cup	Sheffield Steelers	Newcastle Jesters	Won 4-0 at Sheffield
	+Challenge Cup	Sheffield Steelers	Ayr Scottish Eagles	Won 4-2 at Belfast
	Findus British Nat'l Lge Ch'ship	Guildford Flames	Basingstoke Bison	Won 12-4 on agg. (7-2a, 5-2h)
	Findus British Nat'l Lge	Guildford Flames	Basingstoke Bison	10-team league
	Benson and Hedges Plate	Basingstoke Bison	Guildford Flames	Won 3-2 at Sheffield
	ntl Christmas Cup	Guildford Flames	Fife Flyers	Won 7-3 on agg. (4-1h,3-2a)
	Eng Nat'l Lge, Premier Div Ch'ship	Romford Raiders	Chelmsford Chieftains	Won 11-4 on agg. (7-2, 4-2)
	Eng Nat'l Lge, Premier Division	Swindon Phoenix	Chelmsford Chieftains	9-team league
	Eng Nat'l Lge, Premier Cup	Isle of Wight Raiders	Swindon Phoenix	Won 5-2 on agg. (3-2a, 2-0h)
	Eng Nat'l Lge, Div. One Ch'ship	Whitley Warriors	Billingham Eagles	Won 14-7 on agg. (4-6h,10-1a)
	Eng Nat'l Lge, Div. One North	Billingham Eagles	Whitley Warriors	9-team league
	Eng Nat'l Lge, Div. One South	Basingstoke Buffalo	Flintshire Freeze	10-team league
	Scottish Cup	Fife Flyers	Edinburgh Capitals	Won 7-4 at Kirkcaldy.
1999-00	+= Superleague Playoff Ch'ship	London Knights	Newcastle Riverkings	Won 7-3 at Manchester
	+ *Sekonda* Superleague	Bracknell Bees	Sheffield Steelers	8-team league
	B&H Autumn Cup	Manchester Storm	London Knights	Won 4-3 (ps) at Sheffield.
	+Challenge Cup	Sheffield Steelers	Nottingham Panthers	Won 2-1 at London Arena
	British National Lge Ch'ship	Fife Flyers	Basingstoke Bison	Won best-of-five series 3-0.
	British National Lge	Fife Flyers	Guildford Flames	10-team league
	Benson and Hedges Plate	Basingstoke Bison	Slough Jets	Won 5-1 at Sheffield
	ntl Christmas Cup	Fife Flyers	Basingstoke Bison	Won 6-5 on agg. (3-3,3-2)
	Eng. Lge, Premier Div. Ch'ship	Chelmsford Chieftains	Swindon Chill	Won 7-4 on agg. (5-2,2-2)
	English Lge, Premier Div.	Chelmsford Chieftains	Isle of Wight Raiders	5-team league
	Data Vision Millennium Cup	Chelmsford Chieftains	Swindon Chill	Won 10-7 at Swindon.
	English Lge, Div. One Ch'ship	Whitley Warriors	Billingham Eagles	Won 14-10 on agg. (7-4,7-6)
	English Lge, Div One North	Billingham Eagles	Whitley Warriors	10-team league
	English Lge, Div One South	Haringey Greyhounds	Basingstoke Buffalo	5-team league
	Scottish Cup	Fife Flyers	Paisley Pirates	Won 9-4 at Kirkcaldy
1998-99	+=Superleague Playoff Ch'ship	Cardiff Devils	Nottingham Panthers	Won 2-1 at Manchester
	+*Sekonda* Superleague	Manchester Storm	Cardiff Devils	8-team league
	B&H (Autumn) Cup	Nottingham Panthers	Ayr Scottish Eagles	Won 2-1 at Sheffield
	+Challenge Cup	Sheffield Steelers	Nottingham Panthers	Won 4-0 at Sheffield
	British National Lge Ch'ship	Fife Flyers	Slough Jets	Won 6-5 (ps) at Hull
	British National League	Slough Jets	Basingstoke Bison	9-team league
	Benson and Hedges Plate	Guildford Flames	Telford Tigers	Won 4-3 at Sheffield
	Vic Christmas Cup	Peterborough Pirates	Basingstoke Bison	Won 5-3 on agg. (2-1,3-2)
	Eng. Lge, Premier Div. Ch'ship	Solihull Blaze	Milton Keynes Kings	Won 5-3 on agg. (3-0,2-3)
	English Lge, Premier Div	Solihull Blaze	Milton Keynes Kings	9-team league
	English Cup	Milton Keynes Kings	Solihull Blaze	Won 13-9 on agg. (7-6,6-3)
	English Lge, Div. One Ch'ship	Whitley Warriors	Billingham Eagles	Won 14-10 on agg. (7-4,7-6)
	English Lge, Div One North	Billingham Eagles	Altrincham Aces	10-team league
	English Lge, Div One South	Cardiff Rage	Basingstoke Buffalo	9-team league
	Scottish Cup	Fife Flyers	Edinburgh Capitals	Won 6-4 at Kirkcaldy.
1997-98	+Superleague Playoff Ch'ship	Ayr Scottish Eagles	Cardiff Devils	Won 3-2ot at Manchester
	+Superleague	Ayr Scottish Eagles	Manchester Storm	8-team league
	B & H (Autumn) Cup	Ayr Scottish Eagles	Cardiff Devils	Won 2-1 at Sheffield
	+*The Express* Cup	Ayr Scottish Eagles	Bracknell Bees	Won 3-2 at Newcastle
	British National Lge Ch'ship	Guildford Flames	Kingston Hawks	Won 5-1 at Hull
	British National League	Guildford Flames	Telford Tigers	New 9-team league
	Southern Premier League	Guildford Flames	Slough Jets	4 BNL teams plus Cardiff Rage
	Northern Premier League	Fife Flyers	Paisley Pirates	Remaining 5 BNL teams
	Benson & Hedges Plate	Slough Jets	Telford Tigers	Won 4-3 at Sheffield
	Upper Deck Christmas Cup	Telford Tigers	Guildford Flames	Won 10-7 on agg. (5-5, 5-2)
	Eng. Lge, National Div Ch'ship.	Solihull Blaze	Chelmsford Chieftains	Won 18-6 on agg. (9-5,9-1)
	English Lge, National Div.	Solihull Blaze	Whitley Warriors	8-team league
	English Lge, Div One North	Solihull Blaze	Whitley Warriors	10-team league
	English Lge, Div One South	Invicta Dynamos	Chelmsford Chieftains	11-team league
	Scottish Cup	Fife Flyers	Paisley Pirates	Won 5-1 at Kirkcaldy

ROLL OF HONOUR

SEASON	COMPETITION	WINNER	RUNNER-UP	NOTES
1996-97	+Superleague Playoff Ch'ship	Sheffield Steelers	Nottingham Panthers	Won 3-1 at Manchester
	+Superleague	Cardiff Devils	Sheffield Steelers	New 8-team league
	B & H (Autumn) Cup	Nottingham Panthers	Ayr Scottish Eagles	Won 5-3 at Sheffield
	Premier League Playoffs	Swindon IceLords	Fife Flyers	Won 5-0 at Manchester
	(Southern) Premier League	Swindon IceLords	Solihull Blaze	New 8-team league
	Northern Premier League	Fife Flyers	Paisley Pirates	New 7-team league
	English League Championship	*Wightlink* Raiders	Chelmsford Chieftains	Won 10-6 on agg. (5-2,5-4)
	English League, North	Kingston Jets	Altrincham Aces	8-team league
	English League, South	Romford Raiders	Chelmsford Chietains	12-team league
	Scottish Cup	Paisley Pirates	Fife Flyers	Won 8-4 at Kirkcaldy
	British u16 Championship	Sunderland Arrows	Fife Flames	Won 3-2 at Manchester
1995-96	British Championship	Sheffield Steelers	Nottingham Panthers	Won on 2-1 PS (3-3ot) at Wembley.
	British League, Premier Div.	Sheffield Steelers	Cardiff Devils	10-team league
	British League, Div One	Manchester Storm	Blackburn Hawks	14-team league
	Promotion Playoffs	Manchester Storm	Milton Keynes Kings	Two playoff group winners
	B & H (Autumn) Cup	Sheffield Steelers	Nottingham Panthers	Won 5-2 at Sheffield
	English League Championship	*Wightlink* Raiders	Durham City Wasps	Won 15-8 on agg. (8-0,7-8)
	English League, North	Humberside Jets	Altrincham Aces	12-team league
	English League, South	Oxford City Stars	*Wightlink* Raiders	12-team league
	Autumn Trophy	Dumfries Border Vikings	Chelmsford Chieftains	Won 23-0, second leg not played.
	British u16 Championship	Guildford Firestars	Fife Flames	Won 3-2 at Wembley
1994-95	British Championship	Sheffield Steelers	Edinburgh Racers	Won 7-2 at Wembley
	British League, Premier Div.	Sheffield Steelers	Cardiff Devils	12-team league
	British League, Div One	Slough Jets	Telford Tigers	12-team league
	Promotion Playoffs	Slough Jets	Whitley Warriors	Two playoff group winners
	B & H (Autumn) Cup	Nottingham Panthers	Cardiff Devils	Won 7-2 at Sheffield
	English League Championship	*Wightlink* Raiders	Sunderland Chiefs	Won 11-5 on agg. (7-2,4-3)
	English League, North	Sunderland Chiefs	Nottingham Jaguars	11-team league
	English League, South	*Wightlink* Raiders	Peterborough Patriots	12-team league
	Autumn Trophy	Solihull Barons	Swindon Wildcats	Won 19-16 on agg. (7-6,12-10)
	Scottish Cup	Fife Flyers	Paisley Pirates	Won 11-2 at Kirkcaldy
	British u16 Championship	Fife Flames	Durham Mosquitoes	Won 5-1 at Wembley
1993-94	British Championship	Cardiff Devils	Sheffield Steelers	Won 12-1 at Wembley
	British League, Premier Div.	Cardiff Devils	Sheffield Steelers	Fife Flyers later placed 2nd
	British League, Div One	M Keynes Kings (N)	Slough Jets (S)	No playoff. Kings most points.
	Promotion Playoffs	Milton Keynes Kings	Peterborough Pirates	Two playoff group winners
	B & H (Autumn) Cup	Murrayfield Racers	Cardiff Devils	Won 6-2 at Sheffield
	English League Championship	*Wightlink* Raiders	Nottingham Jaguars	Won 17-7 on agg. (6-4,11-3)
	English League	*Wightlink* Raiders	Sunderland Chiefs	7-team league
	English Conference	Deeside Dragons	Grimsby Redwings	11-team league
	Autumn Trophy	Telford Tigers	Medway Bears	Won 11-7 on agg. (8-3,3-4)
	Scottish Cup	Fife Flyers	Murrayfield Racers	Won 6-5 at Kirkcaldy
	British u16 Championship	Fife Flames	Swindon Leopards	1-1ot at Wembley. Trophy shared.
1992-93	*British Championship	Cardiff Devils	Humberside Seahawks	Won 7-4 at Wembley
	*British League, Premier Div	Cardiff Devils	Murrayfield Racers	10-team league
	*British League, Div One	Basingstoke Beavers	Sheffield Steelers	9-team league
	*Promotion Playoffs	Basingstoke Beavers	Sheffield Steelers	Two group winners
	B & H (Autumn) Cup	Cardiff Devils	Whitley Warriors	Won 10-4 atSheffield
	English League Championship	Solihull Barons	Guildford Flames	Won 16-13 on agg. (6-7,10-6)
	English League, Conference A	Solihull Barons	Bristol Bulldogs	6-team league
	English League, Conference B	Guildford Flames	Chelmsford Chieftains	6-team league
	BL Entry Playoffs	Trafford Metros	Chelmsford Chieftains	Also EL PO. Two group winners
	Autumn Trophy	Milton Keynes Kings	Solihull Barons	Won 11-4 at Sheffield
	Scottish Cup	Murrayfield Racers	Whitley Warriors	Won 8-7 at Murrayfield
	British u16 Championship	Durham Mosquitoes	Fife Flames	Won 5-2 at Wembley

ROLL OF HONOUR

SEASON	COMPETITION	WINNER	RUNNER-UP	NOTES
1991-92	*British Championship	Durham Wasps	Nottingham Panthers	Won 7-6 at Wembley
	*British League, Premier Div.	Durham Wasps	Nottingham Panthers	10-team league
	*British League, Div One	Fife Flyers	Slough Jets	10-team league
	*Promotion Playoffs	Bracknell Bees	Fife Flyers	Two group winners
	Autumn Cup	Nottingham Panthers	Humberside Seahawks	Won 7-5 at Sheffield
	English League	Medway Bears	Sheffield Steelers	9-team lge; no champ'ship p/off.
	BL Entry Playoffs	Medway Bears	Sheffield Steelers	Also EL PO. Two group winners.
	Autumn Trophy	Swindon Wildcats	Milton Keynes Kings	Won 3-2 on PS (5-5ot) at Sheffield.
	Scottish Cup	Whitley Warriors	Ayr Raiders	Won 7-4 at Murrayfield
	British u16 Championship	Fife Flames	Durham Mosquitoes	Won 3-2 at Wembley
1990-91	*British Championship	Durham Wasps	Peterborough Pirates	Won 7-4 at Wembley
	*British League, Premier Div.	Durham Wasps	Cardiff Devils	10-team league
	*British League, Div One	Humberside Seahawks	Slough Jets	11-team league
	*Promotion Playoffs	Humberside Seahawks	Bracknell Bees	Two group winners
	Norwich Union (Autumn) Cup	Durham Wasps	Murrayfield Racers	Won 12-6 at Whitley
	English League	Oxford Stars	Milton Keynes Kings	First Division
	BL Entry Playoffs	Lee Valley Lions	Milton Keynes Kings	Also EL PO. Two group winners.
	Autumn Trophy	Chelmsford Chieftains	Oxford City Stars	League format.
	Scottish Cup	Murrayfield Racers	Ayr Raiders	Won 9-4 at Murrayfield
	British u16 Championship	Fife Flames	Romford Hornets	Won 5-0 at Wembley
1989-90	*British Championship	Cardiff Devils	Murrayfield Racers	Won 6-5 PS (6-6 ot) at Wembley.
	*British League, Premier Div.	Cardiff Devils	Murrayfield Racers	9-team league
	*British League, Div One	Slough Jets	Cleveland Bombers	9-team league
	*Promotion Playoffs	Cleveland Bombers	Slough Jets	Div One top four
	Norwich Union (Autumn) Cup	Murrayfield Racers	Durham Wasps	Won 10-4 at Basingstoke
	English League	Bracknell Bees	Romford Raiders	First Division
	BL Entry Playoffs	Basingstoke Beavers	Romford Raiders	Also EL playoffs
	Autumn Trophy	Humberside Seahawks	Bracknell Bees	Won 23-17 on agg. (15-9,8-8)
	Scottish Cup	Murrayfield Racers	Cardiff Devils	Won 13-4 at Murrayfield
	British Jnr Championship	Nottingham Cougars	Fife Flames	Won 3-1 at Wembley
1988-89	*British Championship	Nottingham Panthers	Ayr Bruins	Won 6-3 at Wembley
	*British League, Premier Div.	Durham Wasps	Murrayfield Racers	10-team league
	*British League, Div One	Cardiff Devils	Medway Bears	13-team league
	*Promotion Playoffs	Cardiff Devils	Streatham Redskins	Premier winner v last in Div One.
	Norwich Union (Autumn) Cup	Durham Wasps	Tayside Tigers	Won 7-5 at NEC, Birmingham
	English League	Humberside Seahawks	Bracknell Bees	First Division
	Autumn Trophy	Cardiff Devils	Medway Bears	Won 15-8 on agg. (9-4,6-4)
	Scottish Cup	Murrayfield Racers	Ayr Bruins	Won 9-5 at Murrayfield
	British Jnr Championship	Durham Mosquitoes	Dundee Bengals	Won pen shots at Wembley (5-5)
1987-88	*British Championship	Durham Wasps	Fife Flyers	Won 8-5 at Wembley
	*British League, Premier Div.	Murrayfield Racers	Whitley Warriors	
	*British League, Div One	Telford Tigers (S)	Cleveland Bombers (N)	Won 21-14 on agg. (12-10, 9-4)
	Promotion Playoffs	Peterborough Pirates	Telford Tigers	Premier winner v last in Div One
	British League, Div Two	Romford Raiders	Chelmsford Chieftains	
	Norwich Union (Autumn) Cup	Durham Wasps	Murrayfield Racers	Won 11-5 at Kirkcaldy
	Autumn Trophy	Cardiff Devils	Trafford Metros	Won 11-10 on agg. (7-5,4-5)
	Scottish Cup	Murrayfield Racers	Fife Flyers	Won 9-6 at Murrayfield
	British Jnr Championship	Nottingham Cougars	Fife Flames	Won 4-2 at Wembley
1986-87	*British Championship	Durham Wasps	Murrayfield Racers	Won 9-5 at Wembley
	*British League, Premier Div.	Murrayfield Racers	Dundee Rockets	
	*British League, Div One	Peterborough Pirates	Medway Bears	
	British League, Div Two	Aviemore Blackhawks	Cardiff Devils	Won playoff 10-9 at Cardiff
	Norwich Union (Autumn) Cup	Nottingham Panthers	Fife Flyers	Won 5-4ot at NEC, Birmingham
	Scottish Cup	Murrayfield Racers	Dundee Rockets	Won 7-6 at Kirkcaldy
	British Jnr Championship	Durham Mosquitoes	Murrayfield Ravens	Won 11-1 at Wembley

ROLL OF HONOUR

SEASON	COMPETITION	WINNER	RUNNER-UP	NOTES
1985-86	*British Championship	Murrayfield Racers	Dundee Rockets	Won 4-2 at Wembley
	*British League, Premier Div.	Durham Wasps	Murrayfield Racers	
	*British League, Div One	Solihull Barons	Lee Valley Lions	
	British League, Div Two	Medway Bears	Grimsby Buffaloes	Won playoff 26-4 at Medway
	Norwich Union (Autumn) Cup	Murrayfield Racers	Durham Wasps	Won 8-5 at Murrayfield
	Scottish Cup	Dundee Rockets	Murrayfield Racers	Won 7-3 at Dundee
	British Jnr Championship	Streatham Scorpions	Fife Flames	Won 7-0 at Wembley
1984-85	*British Championship	Fife Flyers	Murrayfield Racers	Won 9-4 at Wembley
	*British League, Premier Div.	Durham Wasps	Fife Flyers	
	*British League, Div One	Peterborough Pirates	Solihull Barons	
	British League, Div Two	Oxford Stars	Aviemore Blackhawks	Won playoff 6-1 at Oxford
	Bluecol Autumn Cup	Durham Wasps	Fife Flyers	Won 6-4 at Streatham
1983-84	*British Championship	Dundee Rockets	Murrayfield Racers	Won 5-4 at Wembley
	*British League, Premier Div.	Dundee Rockets	Durham Wasps	
	*British League, Div One	Southampton Vikings	Crowtree Chiefs	
	British League, Div Two	Whitley Braves	Streatham Bruins	Won playoff 14-9 on agg (6-7, 8-2)
	Autumn Cup	Dundee Rockets	Streatham Redskins	Won pen shots at Streatham (6-6)
1982-83	*British Championship	Dundee Rockets	Durham Wasps	Won 6-2 at Streatham
	British League Section A	Dundee Rockets	Murrayfield Racers	)
	Section B	Durham Wasps	Cleveland Bombers	)Div One - interlocking schedule
	Section C	Altrincham Aces	Blackpool Seagulls	)
	British League, Div Two	Solihull Barons	Grimsby Buffaloes	Won Play-off 8-5 at Solihull

= Sponsored by *Sekonda*   * Sponsored by *Heineken*   + All-professional competition

GOVERNING BODIES

ICE HOCKEY UK LTD

Chairman: Bob Wilkinson.
Address: 43 Parkhouse Gardens, Sherburn Village, Durham City DH6 1DU.
Tel/fax: 0191-372-1518.
e-mail: gb16bob@aol.com
The Board of Directors of the sport's national governing body are: **Stuart Robertson** (vice-chairman & Scottish IHA), **Bob Wilkinson** and **Neville Moralee** (EIHA), **John Lyttle** & **Andy Gibson** (N Ireland IHF), **Eamon Convery** and **Mike Cowley** (Elite Lge).
website: www.icehockeyuk.co.uk

ELITE ICE HOCKEY LEAGUE LTD

Chairman: Eamon Convery.
Director of Hockey: Andy French, Flat 1, 36 High Street, Soham, Ely, Cambs CB7 5HE.
Tel: 01353-722622. **Fax**: 01353-721332.
e-mail: andyhockey.french@btopenworld.com.
website: www.eliteleague.co.uk

ENGLISH ICE HOCKEY ASSOCIATION

Chairman: Ken Taggart.
English Premier League Secretary: Rob Laidler, 4 Victoria Street, Seaham, Co. Durham SR7 7ST.
Tel/fax: 0191-581-8159.
e-mail: Rob.Laidler@eiha.freeuk.com.
EIHA Executive Committee: **Ken Taggart** (chairman), **Tony Oliver** (deputy chairman), **Irene Jones** (secretary), **Neville Moralee** (treasurer), **Bob Wilkinson** and **Geoff Hemmerman**.
website: www.eiha.co.uk

SCOTTISH ICE HOCKEY ASSN.

Secretary: Mrs Pat Swiatek, 71 Prestwick Road, Ayr KA8 8LQ.
Tel/Fax: 01292-284053
website: www.siha.net
SCOTTISH NATIONAL LEAGUE
Chairman: David Beatson. **Tel**: 07768-236161
Secretary: Sandra Edgar, 5 St Anne's Road, Dumfries DG2 9HZ. **Tel**: 01387-264010.
e-mail: sandra@sharkshouse.wanadoo.co.uk

N IRELAND ICE HOCKEY FED.

Chairman: John Lyttle.
Secretary: Lorna Taylor, First Floor, 201 Upper Newtownards Road, Belfast BT4 3JD.
Tel: 02890-654040. **Fax**: 02890-651700.
e-mail: niihf@aol.com.

IRISH ICE HOCKEY ASSOCIATION

President: Cliff Saunders.
Address: 13 Raleigh Square, Crumlin, Dublin 12, Ireland.
Tel: (01) 455-0222, **fax**: (01) 473-4351
e-mail: info@iiha.org
website: www.iiha.org

BRITISH UNIVERSITIES IH ASSN

Communications to: Phil Andrews, Flat C, Fairfield Lodge, 1a Broomhall Road, Sheffield, S10 2DN. **Tel**: 07811 463077 (mobile).
e-mail: phil.andrews@buiha.org.uk.
website: www.buiha.org.uk

WOMEN'S ICE HOCKEY LEAGUE

Secretary: Sylvian Clifford, 14 Windrush Drive, Springfield, Chelmsford CM1 7QF.
Tel/Fax: 01245-259181.
e-mail: sylvian.clifford1@btopenworld.com
website: www.eiha.co.uk

ICE HOCKEY PLAYERS ASSN (GB)

Executive Director: Joanne Collins, 25 Caxton Ave, Addlestone, Weybridge, Surrey KT15 1LJ.
Tel: 01932-843660. **Fax**: 01932-844401.
e-mail: ihpa@virgin.net
website: www.ihpa.co.uk

BRITISH ICE HOCKEY WRITERS' ASSN

Chairman: Stewart Roberts.
Address: 50 Surrenden Lodge, Surrenden Road, Brighton BN1 6QB. **Tel/fax**: 01273-597889.
e-mail: stewice@aol.com
website: www.bihwa.co.uk

GB SUPPORTERS CLUB

Secretary: Annette Petrie, 65 Leas Drive, Iver, Bucks SL0 9RB. **Tel/Fax**: 01753-710778.
e-mail: gbsc@blueyonder.co.uk.
website: www.gbsc.co.uk

CLUB DIRECTORY 2005-06

ABERDEEN

Rink Address: Linx Ice Arena, Beach Leisure Centre, Beach Esplanade, Aberdeen AB2 1NR. **Tel**: 01224-655406/7. **Fax**: 01224-648693. **Ice Size**: 184 x 85 feet (56 x 26 metres). **Spectator Capacity**: 1,200. **Club Secretary**: Collette Cowie, 18 Woodhill Terrace, Bridge of Don AB15 5LE. **Tel**: 01224-312250. **e-mail**: collette.cowie@gpcp.co.uk *Juniors and recreational teams only 2005-06*

AYR

LIMEKILN ROAD RINK
Tel: 01292-262512. **Ice Size**: 160 x 85 feet (49 x 26 metres). **Spectator Capacity**: 700. **Team**: South Ayrshire. **Club Secretary**: Mark Bicker, 23 Moorpark, Prestwick. **Tel**: 01292-476234. **e-mail**: markbicker@aol.com *Juniors and recreational teams only 2005-06*

CENTRUM ARENA
Address: Ayr Road, Prestwick KA9 1TR. *Closed until further notice.*

BASINGSTOKE

Rink Address: Planet Ice Basingstoke Arena, Basingstoke Leisure Park, Worting Road, Basingstoke, Hants RG22 6PG. **Tel**: 01256-355266. **Fax**: 01256-357367. **Ice Size**: 197 x 98 feet (60 x 30 metres) **Spectator Capacity**: 1,600. **Senior Teams**: Bison (Elite League) and Buffalo (Eng Nat Lge South). **Bison's contact**: Mark Bernard at the rink. **Tel**: 01256-346159. **Fax**: 01256-357367. **Bison's Colours**: *home*: White, Red & Silver; *away*: Red & Silver. **website**: www.bstokebison.co.uk

BELFAST

ODYSSEY ARENA
Address: Queen's Quay, Belfast BT3. **Tel**: 02890-766000. **Fax**: 02890-766044. **Ice Size**: 197 x 98 feet (60 x 30 metres). **Spectator Capacity** (for ice hockey): 7,100. **Team**: Giants (Elite League). **Communications to**: John Elliott. **Club Address**: Belfast Giants Ltd, Unit 3, Ormeau Business Park, 8 Cromac Avenue, Belfast BT7 2JA. **Tel**: 028-9059-1111. **Fax**: 028-9059-1212. **e-mail**: office@belfastgiants.co.uk **Colours**: *home*: White, Red & Teal; *away*: Teal, White & Red. **website**: www.belfastgiants.co.uk

DUNDONALD INTERNATIONAL ICE BOWL
Address: 111 Old Dundonald Road, Dundonald, Co Down, N Ireland. **Tel**: 02890-482611. **Fax**: 02890-489604. **Ice Size**: 197 x 98 feet (60 x 30 metres). **Spectator Capacity**: 1,500. *Junior and recreational teams only 2005-06*

BILLINGHAM

Rink Address: Billingham Forum Leisure Centre, Town Centre, Billingham, Cleveland TS23 2OJ. **Tel/Fax**: 01642-551381. **Ice Size**: 180 x 80 feet (55 x 24 metres) **Spectator Capacity**: 1,200. **Senior Team**: Bombers (Eng Nat Lge North). **Club Secretary**: Brian McCabe, 7 Cranstock Close, Wolviston Court, Billingham, Cleveland TS22 5RS. **Tel/Fax**: 01642-534458. **e-mail**: bmccabe_1@hotmail.com **Colours**: *Home*: White, Red & Black; *away*: Black & Red. **website**: http://thebombers.co.uk/

BLACKBURN

Rink Address: Blackburn Arena, Lower Audley, Waterside, Blackburn, Lancs BB1 1BB. **Tel**: 01254-668686. **Fax**: 01254-691516. **Ice Size**: 197 x 98 feet (60 x 30 metres) **Spectator Capacity**: 3,200. **Senior Team**: Hawks (English Nat Lge North) **Club Secretary**: Mark Halliwell c/o the arena. **e-mail**: mark@blackburnicearena.co.uk **Colours**: Pacific Teal, Grey, Black & White. **website**: www.blackburnhawks.com

CLUB DIRECTORY

BRACKNELL

Rink Address: John Nike Leisuresport Complex, John Nike Way, Bracknell, Berks RG12 4TN.
Tel: 01344-789006, **Fax**: 01344-789201.
Ice Size: 197 x 98 feet (60 x 30 metres)
Spectator Capacity: 3,100.
Senior Teams: Bees (English Premier League) and Hornets (English Nat Lge South).
Communications to: David Taylor, 11B Woosehill Lane, Wokingham, Berks RG41 2TT
Tel: 0118-977-3338. **Fax**: 0118-977-3406
e-mail: david@davidtaylorestateagents.co.uk
Bees' colours: *home:* White, Gold & Black; *away:* Black, Gold & White.
website: www.bracknellbees.org

BRADFORD

Rink Address: Great Cause, Little Horton Lane, Bradford, Yorks BD5 0AE.
Tel: 01274-729091. **Fax**: 01274-778818.
Ice Size: 180 x 80 feet (55 x 24 metres)
Spectator Capacity: 700.
Juniors and recreational teams only 2005-06

BRISTOL

Rink Address: John Nike Leisuresport Bristol Ice Rink, Frogmore Street, Bristol BS1 5NA.
Tel: 0117-929-2148. **Fax**: 0117-925-9736.
Ice Size: 180 x 80 feet (55 x 24 metres).
Spectator Capacity: 650.
Club Secretary: Mary Faunt, c/o the rink.'
Juniors only 2005-06.

CAMBRIDGE UNIVERSITY

Home ice 2005-06: Planet Ice Peterborough Arena. (see Peterborough entry)
Communications to: Prof Bill Harris, Dept of Anatomy, Cambridge University, Downing St. Cambridge CB2 3DYUK.
Phone: 01223-333772. **Fax**: 01223-333786.
e-mail: harris@mole.bio.cam.ac.uk
Colours: Light Blue & White.
website: www.cam.ac.uk/societies/cuihc
Recreational.

CARDIFF

Rink Address: Wales National Ice Rink, Hayes Bridge Road, Cardiff CF1 2GH.
Tel: 02920-397198, **Fax**: 02920-397160.
Ice Size: 184 x 85 feet (56 x 26 metres).
Spectator Capacity: 2,500.
Senior Team: Devils (Elite League).
Communications to: Anne Hall at the rink.
Tel: 02920-396669. **Fax**: 02920-396668
e-mail: annehall35@yahoo.com
Colours: *home*: White, Red & Black; *away*: Red, Black & White.
website: www.thecardiffdevils.com

CHELMSFORD

Rink Address: Riverside Ice & Leisure Centre, Victoria Road, Chelmsford, Essex CM1 1FG.
Tel: 01245-615050. **Fax**: 01245-354919.
Ice Size: 184 x 85 feet (56 x 26 metres).
Spectator Capacity: 1,200.
Senior Team: Chieftains (Eng Premier Lge).
Club Secretary: Sue Green, 72 Stirrup Close, Springfield, Chelmsford, Essex CM1 6ST.
Tel/fax: 01245-461708.
e-mail: sue@braves.freeserve.co.uk
Colours: *home*: White, Blue & Red; *away*: Blue, White & Red.
website: www.chelmsfordchieftains.co.uk

COVENTRY

Rink Address: Planet Ice at Skydome Arena, Skydome Coventry, Croft Road, Coventry CV1 3AZ. **Tel**: 02476-630693. **Fax**: 02476-630674
Ice Size: 184 x 92 feet (56 x 28 metres)
Spectator Capacity (for ice hockey): 2,616.
Senior Team: Blaze (Elite League).
Communications to: Coventry Blaze IHC, The Hockey Locker, Co-op Extra Superstore, Queen Victoria Road, Coventry CV1 3LE.
Tel/fax: 02476-631352
e-mail: mikecowley@coventryblaze.co.uk
Colours: *Home:* White & Navy Blue; *away:* Navy Blue & White.
website: www.coventryblaze.co.uk

DEESIDE (QUEENSFERRY)

Rink Address: Deeside Ice Rink, Leisure Centre, Chester Road West, Queensferry, Clwyd CH5 5HA.
Tel: 01244-814725. **Fax:** 01244-836287.
Ice Size: 197 x 98 feet (60 x 30 metres).
Spectator Capacity: 1,200.
Senior Team: Flintshire Freeze (English National League North).
Club Secretary: Gary Shaw c/o the rink.
e-mail: flintshirefreeze@hotmail.com
Colours: *home:* White, Purple & Green; *away:* Green, Purple & White.
website: www.flintshirefreeze.btinternet.co.uk

DUMFRIES

Rink Address: The Ice Bowl, King Street, Dumfries DG2 9AN.
Tel: 01387-251300, **Fax:** 01387-251686.
Ice Size: 184 x 95 feet (56 x 29 metres).
Spectator Capacity: 1,000.
Senior Team: Solway Sharks (Scot. Nat. Lge).
Communications to: Sandra Edgar, 5 St Anne's Road, Dumfries DG2 9HZ. **Tel:** 01387-264010.
e-mail: sandra@sharkshouse.wanadoo.co.uk
Colours: Blue, White & Green.
website: www.solwaysharks.co.uk

DUNDEE

Rink Address: Camperdown Leisure Park, Kingsway West, Dundee.
Tel: 01382-608060. **Fax:** 01382-608070
Ice Size: 197 x 98 feet (60 x 30 metres).
Spectator Capacity: 2,400.
Senior Teams: Dundee Stars (Scottish National League).
Club Secretary: Steve/Marie Ward, Chamber of Commerce Buildings, Panmure Street, Dundee DD1 1ED.
Tel/fax: 01382-204700.
e-mail: dundeestars@btconnect.com
Colours: *home:* White, Red & Blue; *away:* Blue, Red & White.
website: www.dundeestars.com

EDINBURGH

Rink Address: Murrayfield Ice Rink, Riversdale Crescent, Murrayfield, Edinburgh EH12 5XN.
Tel: 0131-337-6933, **Fax:** 0131-346-2951.
Ice Size: 200 x 97 feet (61 x 29.5 metres).
Spectator Capacity: 3,800.
Senior Team: Capitals (Elite League and Scottish National League).
Communications to: Scott Neil at the rink.
Tel/fax: 0131-313-2977.
e-mail: edcapitals@aol.com
Colours: *Home:* White, Red & Blue; *away:* Red, White & Blue.
website: www.edinburgh-capitals.com

ELGIN

Rink Address: Moray Leisure Centre, Borough Briggs Road, Elgin, Moray IV30 1AP.
Tel: 01343-550033. **Fax:** 01343-551769
Ice Size: 147.5 x 82 feet (45 x 25 metres)
Spectator capacity: 200
Senior Team: Moray Tornadoes (Scot Nat Lge)
Club Secretary: Jim Feeley, 23 Covesea Rise, Elgin, Moray. **Tel:** 01343-551007.
e-mail: jimfeeley@tiscali.co.uk

FIFE

Rink Address: Fife Ice Arena, Rosslyn Street, Kirkcaldy, Fife KY1 3HS.
Tel: 01592-595100. **Fax:** 01592-595200.
Ice Size: 193.5 x 98 feet (59 x 30 metres).
Spectator Capacity: 3,280.
Senior Teams: Flyers (Scottish Nat. League).
Communications to: Tom Muir c/o the arena.
Tel: 01592-651076. **Fax:** 01592-651138.
e-mail: tom@flyershockey.co.uk
Colours: Flyers - *Home:* White, Gold & Blue; *away:* Blue, White & Gold.
Website: www.flyershockey.co.uk

GILLINGHAM

Rink Address: The Ice Bowl, Ambley Road, Gillingham Business Park, Gillingham, Kent ME8 0PP.
Tel: 01634-377244. **Fax:** 01634-374065.
Ice Size: 184 x 85 feet (56 x 26 metres).
Spectator Capacity: 1,500.
Senior Teams: Invicta Dynamos (English National League South)
Club Secretary: Jackie Mason, 17 Beckenham Drive, Maidstone, Kent ME16 0TG.
Tel: 01622-671065. **Fax:** 01622-754360.
e-mail: jackie.mason@invictadynamos.co.uk
Colours: *Home:* White, Red, Blue & Black; *Away:* Blue, White, Black & Red.
website: www.invictadynamos.co.uk

CLUB DIRECTORY

GOSPORT

Rink Address: Forest Way, Fareham Road, Gosport, Hants. PO13 0ZX.
Tel: 02392-511217. **Fax**: 02392-510445.
Ice Size: 145 x 73 feet (44 x 22 metres).
Spectator Capacity: 400.
Club Secretary: Peter Marshall, 15 Islands Close, Hayling Island, Hants PO11 0NA.
Tel: 02392-466809.
e-mail: peter.marshall@havant.gov.uk
website: www.solenticehockey.co.uk
Juniors and recreational teams only 2005-06

GRIMSBY

Rink Address: The Leisure Centre, Cromwell Road, Grimsby, South Humberside DN31 2BH.
Tel: 01472-323100. **Fax**: 01472-323102.
Ice Size: 120 x 60 feet (36.5 x 18 metres).
Spectator Capacity: 1,300.
Club Secretary: Allan Woodhead, Weelsby Park Riding School, Weelsby Road, Grimsby, South Humberside DN32 8PL.
Tel/Fax: 01472-346127.
Colours: *Home:* Red & White, *away*: Black, White & Red.
Juniors and recreational teams only 2005-06

GUILDFORD

Rink Address: Spectrum Ice Rink, Parkway, Guildford GU1 1UP.
Tel: 01483-444777. **Fax**: 01483-443311.
Ice Size: 197 x 98 feet (60 x 30 metres).
Spectator Capacity: 2,200.
Senior Team: Flames (English Premier League).
Communications to: Kirk Humphries at the rink.
Tel: 01483-452244, **Fax**: 01483-443373.
e-mail: kirk@guildfordflames.com
Colours: *Home*: Gold, Red & Black;
        away: Black, Red & Gold.
website: www.guildfordflames.com

HARINGEY (LONDON)

Rink Address: The Ice Rink, Alexandra Palace, Wood Green, London N22 4AY.
Tel: 0208-365-2121. **Fax**: 0208-444-3439.
Ice Size: 184 x 85 feet (56 x 26 metres).
Spectator Capacity: 1,750.
Senior Team: Greyhounds (English Lge South).
Club Secretary: Jan Bestic, 71 Osier Crescent, Muswell Hill, London N10 1QT.
Tel/fax: 0208-444-1843.
e-mail: jan.bestic@btconnect.com
Colours: Blue, Gold, White & Silver.
website: www.haringeygreyhounds.co.uk

HULL

Rink Address: The Hull Arena, Kingston Park, Hull HU1 2DZ.
Tel: 01482-325252. **Fax**: 01482-216066.
Ice Size: 197 x 98 feet (60 x 30 metres).
Spectator Capacity: 2,000.
Senior Teams: Stingrays (English Premier Lge) and Kingston Jets (English Nat Lge North).
Stingrays' communications to: Mike/Sue Pack.
Tel/fax: 01908-317029 .
e-mail: info@hullstingrays.co.uk
Stingrays' colours: *Home*: White, Purple & Black, *away:* Purple, Black & Silver.
Website: www.hullstingrays.co.uk

IRVINE

Rink Address: Magnum Leisure Centre, Harbour Street, Irvine, Strathclyde KA12 8PD.
Tel: 01294-278381. **Fax**: 01294-311228.
Ice Size: 150 x 95 feet (45.5 x 29 metres).
Spectator Capacity: 750.
Senior Team: North Ayr Bruins (Scot Nat Lge)
Club Secretary: Bobby Peters, 2 Somerville Park, Lawthorn, Irvine KA11 2EL.
Tel/Fax: 01294-213755.
e-mail: audrey.peters@virgin.net

ISLE OF WIGHT (RYDE)

Rink Address: Planet Ice Ryde Arena, Quay Road, Esplanade, Ryde, I of Wight PO33 2HH.
Tel: 01983-615155. **Fax**: 01983-567460.
Ice Size: 165 x 80 feet (50 x 24 metres)
Spectator Capacity: 1,000.
Senior Team: *Wightlink* Raiders (English Premier League).
Club Secretary: Mavis Siddons, 6 Port Helens, Embankment Road, St Helens, Isle of Wight PO33 1XG. **Tel**: 01983-873094.
e-mail: hockey@twin2.plus.com
Colours: *Home*: White, Red & Black;
        away: Red, Black & White.
website: www.wightlinkraiders.com

KILMARNOCK

Rink Address: Galleon Leisure Centre, 99 Titchfield Street, Kilmarnock, Ayr KA1 1QY.
Tel: 01563-524014. **Fax**: 01563-572395.
Ice Size: 146 x 75 feet (44.6 x 23 metres)
Spectator Capacity: 200
Club Secretary: Anne Davidson, 23 Rawson Crescent, Mauchline KA5 5AT.
Tel/fax: 0141-577-6946.
e-mail: anne@rawsonc.freeserve.co.uk
Junior and recreational teams only 2005-06.

CLUB DIRECTORY

LEE VALLEY (LONDON)

Rink Address: Lee Valley Ice Centre, Lea Bridge Road, Leyton, London E10 7QL.
Tel: 0208-533-3156. **Fax No**: 0208-446-8068.
Ice Size: 184 x 85 feet (56 x 26 metres).
Spectator Capacity: 1,000.
Senior Team: London Racers (Elite League)
Communications to: Roger Black, 13 New North Street, London WC1N 3PJ.
Tel:0207-420-5955.
e-mail: roger@racershockey.com
Colours: *Home*: Red & White;
away: White & Red.
website: www.londonracers.co.uk

MILTON KEYNES

Rink Address: Planet Ice Milton Keynes Arena, The Leisure Plaza, 1 South Row, (off Childs Way H6), Central Milton Keynes, Bucks MK9 1BL.
Tel: 01908-696696. **Fax**: 01908-690890.
Ice Size: 197 x 98 feet (60 x 30 metres)
Spectator Capacity: 2,200.
Senior Teams: Lightning (English Premier Lge) and Thunder (Eng Nat Lge South).
Communications to: Harry Howton, Oldbrook House, Boycott Avenue, Oldbrook, Milton Keynes.
Tel: 01908-696993. **Fax**: 01908-696995.
e-mail: howtons.ltd@btinternet.com
Lightning's Colours: *Home:* White, Gold & Black; *away*: Black, White & Gold.
website: http://lightning.miltonkeynes.com

NEWCASTLE

Arena Address: *Metro Radio* Arena, Arena Way, Newcastle-on-Tyne NE4 7NA.
Tel: 0191-260-5000. **Fax**: 0191-260-2200.
Ice Size: 197 x 98 feet (60 x 30 metres).
Spectator Capacity (for ice hockey): 5,500
Senior Team: Vipers (Elite League and English National League North).
Communications to: Liz Pullan at the rink.
Tel: 0191-242-2420. **Fax**: 0191-260-2328
e-mail: liz.pullan@newcastlevipers.com
Colours: *Home*: White, Gold & Black; *away*: Black, Gold & White.
website: www.newcastlevipers.com

NOTTINGHAM

Rink Address: National Ice Centre, Lower Parliament Street, Nottingham NG1 1LA.
Tel: 0115-853-3000. **Fax**: 0115-853-3034.
Ice Size: 197 x 98 feet (60 x 30 metres).
Spectator Capacity (for ice hockey): 6,500.
Senior Teams: Panthers (Elite League) and Lions (English Nat League North).
Panthers' office: Gary Moran, 2 Broadway, The Lace Market, Nottingham NG1 1PS.
Tel: 0115-941-3103. **Fax**: 0115-941-8754. .
e-mail: info@panthers.co.uk
Panthers' colours: *Home*: White, Gold & Red; *away*: Black, Gold & Red.
Website: www.panthers.co.uk

OXFORD

Rink Address: The Ice Rink, Oxpens Road, Oxford OX1 1RX.
Tel: 01865-467002. **Fax**: 01865-467001.
Ice Size: 184 x 85 feet (56 x 26 metres).
Spectator Capacity: 1,025.
Senior Team: City Stars (Eng Nat Lge South)
Communications to: Gary Dent, 42 Westfield Way, Wantage, Oxon OX12 7EW.
Tel/fax: 01235-763264.
e-mail: garyndent@aol.com.
Colours: *Home*: Red & White, *away*: amarillo.
website: www.oxfordstars.com

OXFORD UNIVERSITY

Home Ice: The Ice Rink, Oxpens Road, Oxford OX1 1RX (details above).
Communications to: Sam Salisbury, Wolfson College, Oxford, OX2 6UD.
Tel: 01865 284357, mob: 07906 318360
e-mail: Samuel.Salisbury@eng.ox.ac.uk
Colours: Dark Blue and White.
website: www.ouihc.org/home.asp
Recreational.

PAISLEY

Rink Address: Lagoon Leisure Complex, Mill Street, Paisley PA1 1LZ.
Tel: 0141-889-4000. **Fax**: 0141-848-0078.
Ice Size: 184 x 85 feet (56 x 26 metres).
Spectator Capacity: 1,000.
Senior Team: Pirates (Scottish Nat League).
Club Secretary: Jacquie Campbell, 5 Baron St, Renfrew PA4 0JU. **Tel**: 0141-561-3060.
e-mail: i.campbell4@ntlworld.com
Colours: Black & White
website: www.paisleypirates.net

CLUB DIRECTORY

PETERBOROUGH

Rink Address: Planet Ice Peterborough Arena, 1 Mallard Road, Bretton, Peterborough, Cambs PE3 8YN.
Tel: 01733-260222. **Fax**: 01733-261021.
Ice Size: 184 x 85 feet (56 x 26 metres).
Spectator Capacity: 1,500.
Senior Teams: Phantoms (English Premier League) and Islanders (Eng Nat Lge South).
Communications to: Phil Wing, Manor Farm, Great North Road, Stibbington, Peterborough.
Tel/fax: 01780-783963
e-mail: phil.wing@peterborough-phantoms.com
Phantoms' colours: *Home*: White, Black, Silver & Red; *away*: Black, Silver, White & Red.
website: www.peterborough-phantoms.com

ROMFORD

Rink Address: Rom Valley Way, Romford, Essex RM7 0AE.
Tel: 01708-724731. **Fax:** 01708-733609.
Ice Size: 184 x 85 feet (56 x 26 metres).
Spectator Capacity: 1,500.
Senior Team: Raiders (English Premier Lge).
Communications to: Ollie Oliver, Kings Ridden, Chelmsford Road, High Ongar, Essex CM5 9NX.
Tel/Fax: 01277-822688.
Colours: *Home*: White, Gold & Blue;
          away: Blue, Gold & White.
website:
http://romfordraiders.wdc-webdesign.co.uk

SHEFFIELD

Hallam FM ARENA
Address: Broughton Lane, Sheffield S9 2DF.
Tel: 0114-256-5656. **Fax**: 0114-256-5520.
Ice Size: 197 x 98 feet (60 x 30 metres).
Spectator Capacity (for ice hockey): 10,000.
Senior Team: Steelers (Elite League).
Communications to: Betty Waring at Arena.
Tel: 0114-242-3535. **Fax**: 0114-242-3344.
e-mail: offce@sheffieldsteelers.co.uk
Colours: *Home*: White, Blue, Orange & Teal; *away*: Black, Blue, Orange & Teal.
website: www.sheffieldsteelers.co.uk

iceSHEFFIELD
Address: Coleridge Road, Sheffield S9 5DA.
Tel: 0114-223-3900. **Fax**: 0114-223-3901.
e-mail: info@icesheffield.com
Spectator Capacity: 1,500 (main rink).
Senior Team: Scimitars (English Premier Lge).
Communications to: Martin Birch, 39 Stanley Street, Sheffield S3 8HH.
Tel: 0114-272-5527. **Fax**: 0114-272-7533
e-mail: bakerblower@aol.com
Colours: *Home*: White, Black & Blue; *away*: Black, White & Blue.
website: www.sheffice.co.uk

SLOUGH

Rink Address: The Ice Arena, Montem Lane, Slough, Berks SL1 2QG.
Tel: 01753-821555. **Fax**: 01753-824977.
Ice Size: 184 x 85 feet (56 x 26 metres).
Spectator Capacity: 1,500.
Senior Team: Jets (English Premier League).
Communications to: Joe Ciccarello c/o the rink.
Tel: 01753-821171.
Colours: *Home*: White, Blue & Red;
          away: Blue, White & Red.
website: www.sloughjets.co.uk

SOLIHULL

Rink Address: Hobs Moat Road, Solihull, West Midlands B92 8JN.
Tel: 0121-742-5561. **Fax**: 0121-742-4315.
Ice Size: 185 x 90 feet (56 x 27 metres).
Spectator Capacity: 1,500.
Senior Team: Barons (English Premier Lge).
Club Secretary: Charlotte Witteridge, Solihull Barons IHC, PO Box 299, Bicester OX26 9AU.
Tel: 01869-277660.
e-mail: secretary@solihullbarons.co.uk
Colours: *Home*: White & Red; *away*: Black & Red.
website: www.solihullbarons.co.uk

STREATHAM (LONDON)

Rink Address: 386 Streatham High Road, London SW16 6HT.
Tel: 0208-769-7771. **Fax**: 0208-769-9979.
Ice Size: 197 x 85 feet (60 x 26 metres).
Club Secretary: Judith Koral, 78 Tankerville Road, Streatham, London SW16 5LP.
Tel: 0208-480-8641
e-mail: judith@streathamicehockey.com
Senior Team: Redskins (English Nat Lge South).
Colours: *Home:* White & Red;
          away: Black & Red.
website: www.streathamicehockey.com

SWINDON

Rink Address: Link Centre, White Hill Way, Westlea, Swindon, Wilts SN5 7DL.
Tel: 01793-445566. **Fax**: 01793-445569.
Ice Size: 184 x 85 feet (56 x 26 metres).
Spectator Capacity: 1,650.
Senior Team: Wildcats (English Premier Lge).
Communications to: Mark Thompson, 21 Senlac Road, Romsey, Hants SO51 5RE.
Tel: 07906-024042 (mobile).
e-mail: mark.thompson@swindonwildcats.com
Colours: *Home*: White, Blue, Silver & Gold;
         away: Blue, White, Silver & Gold.
website: www.swindonwildcats.com/

TELFORD

Rink Address: The Ice Rink, St Quentins Gate, Town Centre, Telford, Salop TF3 4JQ.
Tel: 01952-291511. **Fax**: 01952-291543.
Ice Size: 184 x 85 metres (56 x 26 metres).
Spectator Capacity: 2,250.
Senior Team: Tigers (English Premier League).
Club Secretary: Mrs Jen Roden, 12 Dee Close, Wellington, Telford TF1 3HJ.
Tel/fax: 01952-405505.
e-mail: jenrod@tiscali.co.uk
Colours: *Home*: White, Orange & Black; *away*: Orange, Black & White.
website: www.telfordtigers.co.uk

WHITLEY BAY

Rink Address: The Ice Rink, Hillheads Road, Whitley Bay, Tyne & Wear NE25 8HP.
Tel: 0191-291-1000. **Fax**: 0191-291-1001.
Ice Size: 186 x 81 feet (56.5 x 24.5 metres).
Spectator Capacity: 3,200.
Senior Team: Warriors (Eng Nat Lge North).
Club Secretary: Stuart Graham, 12 Wark Street, Chester-le-Street, Co Durham DH3 3JP
Tel/Fax: 0191-388-0940.
e-mail: stu_warriors@hotmail.com
Colours: *Home*: White, Gold & Maroon; *away*: Maroon, White & Gold.
website: www.whitleywarriors.net

LEGEND

The abbreviations used in the *Annual* are -

LEAGUES

EIHL/EL	Elite Ice Hockey League
EPL	English Premier League
ENL	English National League

SCORERS

GP	-	Games Played
G	-	Goals
A	-	Assists
Pts	-	total Points
Pim(s)	-	Penalties in minutes
N	-	Netminder
Ave		Points per Games Played

NETMINDERS

GPI	-	Games Played In
Mins	-	Minutes played
SoG	-	Shots on Goal
GA		Goals Against
SO	-	Shutouts
Sv%	-	*Save percentage

TEAMS

S	-	Seasons
W	-	Win
RW		Win in regulation time (60 Mins)
OW	-	Win in overtime
RL		Loss in regulation time
OL		Loss in overtime
D	-	Draw
GF	-	Goals For
GA	-	Goals Against
Pct	-	Points gained as a percentage of total games played.

PLAYERS

(l)	'Limited' ITC holder (see *League Organisation*)
(N)	Netminder

TIE BREAKERS

The method using for deciding the places of teams tied on points is as follows -

Elite League/Challenge Cup
- games won, *if still tied*
- goal difference, *if still tied*
- goals scored, *if still tied*
- results of games between tied teams

English Premier and National Leagues
- results of games between tied teams, then as per IIHF Rule Book.

---

*SAVE PERCENTAGE - CALCULATION METHOD
Shots on goal less goals against, divided by shots on goal, multiplied by 100.
Example: 100 shots less 10 goals scored, equals 90, divided by 100, equals 90 per cent.